Get the eBook FREE!

(PDF, ePub, Kindle, and liveBook all included)

We believe that once you buy a book from us, you should be able to read it in any format we have available. To get electronic versions of this book at no additional cost to you, purchase and then register this book at the Manning website.

Go to https://www.manning.com/freebook and follow the instructions to complete your pBook registration.

That's it!
Thanks from Manning!

Street Coder

THE RULES TO BREAK AND HOW TO BREAK THEM

SEDAT KAPANOĞLU

MANNING
SHELTER ISLAND

For online information and ordering of this and other Manning books, please visit
www.manning.com. The publisher offers discounts on this book when ordered in quantity.
For more information, please contact

> Special Sales Department
> Manning Publications Co.
> 20 Baldwin Road
> PO Box 761
> Shelter Island, NY 11964
> Email: orders@manning.com

Manning Publications Co.
20 Baldwin Road
PO Box 761
Shelter Island, NY 11964

Development editors:	Toni Arritola and Becky Whitney
Technical development editor:	Frances Buontempo
Review editor:	Aleksandar Dragosavljević
Production editor:	Keri Hales
Copy editor:	Suzanne G. Fox
Proofreader:	Katie Tennant
Technical proofreader:	Orlando Méndez Morales
Typesetter:	Gordan Salinovic
Cover designer:	Marija Tudor

ISBN 9781617298370
Printed in the United States of America

To my brother Muzaffer,
who introduced me to the fantastic world of computers

brief contents

contents

9 Living with bugs 222

preface

I've experienced many distinct aspects of becoming proficient in software development as a self-taught programmer (other than reading books), ranging from trying to learn machine language by putting random numbers in memory and observing whether the results were anything other than a simple halt, to spending nights in smoke-filled offices, to sneaking off the university campus in the middle of the night after working clandestinely in the lab as a high schooler, to reading the contents of binary files and just hoping that getting exposed to some bytes would make me magically understand how the code works, to memorizing opcodes, and to trying every combination of the order of arguments to figure out the correct one in a function due to lack of documentation.

Back in 2013, my friend Aziz Kedi, who used to own a bookstore in Istanbul, asked me to write a book about software development based on my experiences. That was the first time I considered writing a book about my profession. I had to shelve the idea soon thereafter because Aziz closed his bookstore and moved to London.

I kept entertaining the idea of having a book I could hand out to new team members who were at the start of their career so they could close the experience gap while widening their perspective. The pre-career understanding of software development is heavily shaped by curricula, preconceptions, and best practices. A newly minted programmer naturally thinks of their accumulated knowledge as a core investment and doesn't want to wander far from it.

At some point, I decided to write such a book—very slowly. I called the fictional book *Street Coder* and started making notes of random ideas that could make the lives of new developers easier. They didn't have to be best practices, either—they could even be bad practices, if you will, as long as they made developers better thinkers about the problems they faced. The document had grown, and at a certain point, I forgot about it, until the day I got a call from London.

It wasn't Aziz Kedi this time. He was probably busy writing screenplays back then, and I'm sure he's working on another one as I'm writing this. This time, it was Andy Waldron from Manning Publications. He asked me, "What idea do you have for a book?" I couldn't think of anything at first, and I was preparing—just to gain some time—to counter his question with this question: "Well, what did you have in mind?" I pretty much mumbled a bit, and then it suddenly struck me. I remembered the notes I'd been taking and the title I had given it: *Street Coder*.

The title comes from what I learned in the streets, the professional software development world, by many trials and errors, which gave me a pragmatic, down-to-earth perspective about approaching software development as a craft. This book conveys the changes in perspective I've experienced so you'll have a head start in your career.

acknowledgments

This book wouldn't have been possible without my wife, Günyüz. She's carried everything on her shoulders while I've been busy writing. Thank you, babe. I love you.

Thanks go to Andrew Waldron, who kick-started my passion for authoring this book. This has been a phenomenal experience. Andy has always been tolerant and understanding, even when I accused him of secretly sneaking into my home and changing the book's text. I owe you a drink, Andy.

Thanks go to my development editors, Toni Arritola, who taught me everything I know about writing programming books, and Becky Whitney, who's been patient and good natured about all the badly written parts I originally turned in—which were Andy's doing, really.

Thanks go to the technical reviewer, Frances Buontempo, who's been extremely constructive and on-point for the technical feedback. Thanks also go to Orlando Méndez Morales for making sure that the code I share in the book actually makes sense.

Thanks go to my friends Murat Girgin and Volkan Sevim, who reviewed the earliest drafts and assured me that my jokes would've been funny if the reader knew me.

I thank Donald Knuth for letting me quote him. I find myself lucky to have gotten a personal response from him, even if it was only "OK." I also thank Fred Brooks for reminding me that there's a fair use clause in the copyright law, so I don't need to call him every day to ask for his permission, and also not to trespass in his home at 3 a.m. There was really no need to involve the cops, Fred—I was just leaving! Thanks also go to Leon Bambrick for letting me quote him peacefully.

Thanks go to MEAP readers, especially Cihat İmamoğlu, whom I don't know personally, but who wrote a crazy amount of in-depth feedback. I thank all the Manning reviewers: Adail Retamal, Alain Couniot, Andreas Schabus, Brent Honadel, Cameron Presley, Deniz Vehbi, Gavin Baumanis, Geert Van Laethem, Ilya Sakayev, Janek López Romaniv, Jeremy Chen, Jonny Nisbet, Joseph Perenia, Karthikeyarajan Rajendran, Kumar Unnikrishnan, Marcin Sęk, Max Sadrieh, Michael Rybintsev, Oliver Korten, Onofrei George, Orlando Méndez Morales, Robert Wilk, Samuel Bosch, Sebastian Felling, Tiklu Ganguly, Vincent Delcoigne, and Xu Yang—your suggestions helped make this a better book.

And finally, I thank my dad for teaching me that I can make my own toys.

about this book

Street Coder fills in the gaps of the professional experience of a software developer by tackling well-known paradigms, showing anti-patterns, and seemingly bad or less-known practices that can be useful in the streets—the professional world. The goal of the book is to equip you with a questioning and practical mindset and to help you understand that the cost of creating software is more than just Googling and typing. It also shows that some mundane work can help you save more time than it takes. In general, the book aims to be a perspective changer.

Who should read this book

This book is for beginning- and medium-level programmers who have managed to learn programming by means other than traditional schooling, but who still need an expanded perspective on paradigms and best practices of software development. The examples are in C# and .NET, so familiarity with those languages can help as you read, but the book strives to be, as much as possible, language and framework agnostic.

How this book is organized: A road map

- Chapter 1 introduces the concept of a street coder—a developer who has been molded by professional experience—and describes the qualities that can help you become that person.
- Chapter 2 discusses how theory matters in practical software development and why you should care about data structures and algorithms.

- Chapter 3 explains how certain anti-patterns or bad practices can actually be useful or even be preferable in many situations.
- Chapter 4 tackles the mysterious world of unit testing and how it can help you write less code and do less work, even though it may seem to be more work initially.
- Chapter 5 discusses techniques for refactoring, how to do it easily and safely, and when to avoid it.
- Chapter 6 introduces some basic security concepts and techniques and shows defenses against most common attacks.
- Chapter 7 shows some hard-core optimization techniques, shamelessly recommends premature optimization, and describes a methodical approach to fixing performance problems.
- Chapter 8 describes techniques to make your code more scalable and tackles parallelization mechanics and their impact on performance and responsiveness.
- Chapter 9 goes over best practices for handling bugs and errors. Specifically, it encourages not handling errors and describes techniques for writing fault-resilient code.

About the code

Most of the code is included to support concepts and may be missing implementation details to focus on the actual topic. Fully functioning code has been provided for several projects in the online GitHub repository (https://github.com/ssg/streetcoder) and on the Manning website (https://www.manning.com/books/street-coder), so you can run them and experiment on them locally. One example specifically focuses on a migration scenario from .NET Framework, which means that specific project may not build on non-Windows machines. An alternate solution file for the book is provided in the repository for those platforms so you can build without any issues.

This book contains many examples of source code both in numbered listings and in line with normal text. In both cases, source code is formatted in a `fixed-width font like this` to separate it from ordinary text. Sometimes code is also **in bold** to highlight code that has changed from previous steps in the chapter, such as when a new feature adds to an existing line of code.

In many cases, the original source code has been reformatted; we've added line breaks and reworked indentation to accommodate the available page space in the book. In rare cases, even this was not enough, and listings include line-continuation markers (➥). Additionally, comments in the source code have often been removed from the listings when the code is described in the text. Code annotations accompany many of the listings, highlighting important concepts.

liveBook discussion forum

Purchase of *Street Coder* includes free access to liveBook, Manning's online reading platform. Using liveBook's exclusive discussion features, you can attach comments to the book globally or to specific sections or paragraphs. It's a snap to make notes for yourself, ask and answer technical questions, and receive help from the author and other users. To access the forum, go to https://livebook.manning.com/#!/book/street-coder/discussion. You can also learn more about Manning's forums and the rules of conduct at https://livebook.manning.com/#!/discussion.

Manning is committed to providing our readers with a venue where a meaningful dialogue between individual readers and between readers and the author can take place. It is not a commitment to any specific amount of participation on the part of the author, whose contribution to the forum remains voluntary (and unpaid). We suggest you try asking him some challenging questions, lest his attention stray! The forum and the archives of previous discussions will be accessible from the publisher's website as long as the book is in print.

about the author

SEDAT KAPANOĞLU is a self-taught software developer from Eskişehir, Turkey, who later worked as an engineer at Microsoft Corporation in Seattle, Washington, in the Windows Core Operating System division. His professional software development career spans three decades.

Sedat is the youngest of five children born to Bosnian parents who emigrated from the former Yugoslavia to Turkey. He founded the most popular Turkish social platform in the world, Ekşi Sözlük (https://eksisozluk.com), which means "sour dictionary." In the 1990s, he was active in the Turkish demoscene, which is an international digital art community for creating code-generated graphical and musical presentations.

Find him on Twitter @esesci or on his programming blog at https://ssg.dev.

about the cover illustration

The figure on the cover of *Street Coder* is captioned "Lépero," meaning "vagabond." The illustration is taken from *Trajes civiles, militares y religiosos de México* by Claudio Linati (1708–1832), published in 1828. Linati was an Italian painter and lithographer who established the first lithographic press in Mexico. The book depicts civil, military, and religious costumes of Mexican society and was one of the first color-plate books about Mexico to be printed, as well as the first book about Mexican people written by a foreigner. The volume includes 48 hand-colored lithographs, with brief descriptions of each one. The rich variety of drawings in the collection reminds us vividly of how culturally separated the world's regions, towns, villages, and neighborhoods were just 200 years ago. Isolated from each other, people spoke different dialects and languages. In the streets or in the countryside, it was easy to identify where they lived and what their trade or station in life was just by their dress.

Dress codes have changed since then, and diversity by region, so rich at the time, has faded. It is now hard to tell the inhabitants of different continents apart, let alone those of different towns or regions. Perhaps we have traded cultural diversity for a more varied personal life—certainly for a more varied and fast-paced technological life.

At a time when it is hard to tell one computer book from another, Manning celebrates the inventiveness and initiative of the computer business with book covers based on the rich diversity of regional life two centuries ago, brought back to life by images from collections such as this one.

To the streets *1*

I am lucky. I wrote my first program in the 1980s. It only required me to turn on the computer, which took less than a second, write 2 lines of code, type RUN, and voila! The screen was suddenly filled with my name. I was immediately awestruck by the possibilities. If I could do this with 2 lines, imagine what I could do with 6 lines, or even 20 lines! My nine-year-old brain was flooded with so much dopamine that I was addicted to programming at that instant.

Today, software development is immensely more complex. It's nowhere close to the simplicity of the 1980s, when user interactions only consisted of "press any key to continue," although users occasionally struggled to find an "any" key on their keyboard. There were no windows, no mice, no web pages, no UI elements, no libraries, no frameworks, no runtimes, no mobile devices. All you had was a set of commands and a static hardware configuration.

1

There is a reason for every level of abstraction we now have, and it's not that we are masochists, with the exception of Haskell[1] programmers. Those abstractions are in place because they're the only way to catch up with current software standards. Programming isn't about filling the screen with your name anymore. Your name must be in the correct font, and it must be in a window so you can drag it around and resize it. Your program must look good. It should support copy and paste. It must support different names for configurability as well. Perhaps it should store the names in a database, even in the cloud. Filling the screen with your name isn't so much fun anymore.

Fortunately, we have resources to contend with the complexity: universities, hackathons, boot camps, online courses, and *rubber ducks*.

> **TIP**   Rubber duck debugging is an esoteric method for finding solutions to programming problems. It involves talking to a yellow plastic bird. I'll tell you more about it in the debugging chapter.

We should be well equipped with all the resources we have, but the foundation we build for ourselves may not always be sufficient in a high-competition, high-demanding career of software development, *the streets*.

1.1   *What matters in the streets*

The world of professional software development is quite mysterious. Some customers swear that they will pay you in a couple of days every time you call them for months on end. Some employers don't pay you any salary at all, but they insist they will pay you "once they make money." The chaotic randomness of the universe decides who gets the window office. Some bugs disappear when you use a debugger. Some teams don't use any source control at all. Yes, it's frightening. But you must face the realities.

One thing is clear in the streets: your throughput is what matters most. Nobody cares about your elegant design, your knowledge of algorithms, or your high-quality code. All they care about is how much you can deliver in a given time. Counterintuitively, good design, good use of algorithms, and good quality code can impact your throughput significantly, and that's what many programmers miss. Such matters are usually thought of as hindrances, frictions between a programmer and the deadline. That kind of thinking can turn you into a zombie with a ball and chain attached to your foot.

In fact, some people do care about the quality of your code: your colleagues. They don't want to babysit your code. They want your code to work and be easily understandable and maintainable. This is something you owe them because once you commit your code to the repository, it's everybody's code. In a team, the team's throughput is more important than that of each member. If you are writing bad code, you are slowing your colleagues down. Your code's lack of quality hurts the team, and a slowed-down team hurts the product, and an unreleased product hurts your career.

---

[1] Haskell is an esoteric language that was created as a challenge to fit as many academic papers as possible into a single programming language.

The easiest thing you can write from scratch is the idea, and the next easiest thing is the design. That's why good design matters. Good design isn't something that looks good on paper. You can have a design in your mind that works. You will encounter people who don't believe in designing and just improvise the code. Those people don't value their time.

Similarly, a good design pattern or a good algorithm can increase your throughput. If it doesn't help your throughput, it's not useful. Because almost everything can be given a monetary value, everything you do can be measured in terms of throughput.

You can have high throughput with bad code too, but only in the first iteration. The moment the customer requests a change, you are stuck with maintaining terrible code. Throughout this book, I'll be talking about cases in which you can realize that you are digging yourself into a hole and get yourself out of it before you lose your mind.

1.2 Who's a street coder?

Microsoft considers two distinct categories of candidates when hiring: new graduates of a computer science department and industry experts who have substantial experience in software development.

Be it a self-taught programmer or someone who studied computer science, they are missing a common piece at the beginning of their career: *street lore*, which is the expertise to know what matters most. A self-taught programmer has many trials and errors under their belt but can lack knowledge of formal theory and how it applies to everyday programming. A university graduate, on the other hand, knows a lot about theory but lacks practicality and, sometimes, a questioning attitude toward what they learned. See figure 1.1.

The corpus you learn at school doesn't have priority associated with it. You learn in the order of the learning path, not in the order of importance. You have no idea how useful certain subjects might be in the streets, where competition is relentless. Timelines are unrealistic. Coffee is cold. The best framework in the world has that single

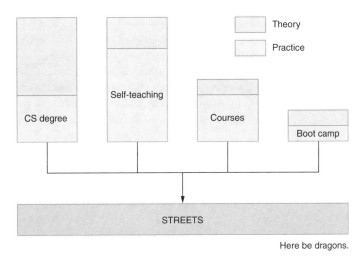

Figure 1.1 Starting a career through different paths

bug that renders a week of your work worthless. Your perfectly designed abstraction crumbles under pressure from the customer who constantly changes their requirements. You manage to quickly refactor your code with some copy-paste, but now you must edit 15 separate places just to change one configuration value.

Over the years, you develop new skills to tackle ambiguity and complexity. Self-taught programmers learn some algorithms that help them, and university graduates eventually understand that the best theory isn't always the most practical.

A street coder is anyone with software development experience in the industry who has had their beliefs and theories shaped by the realities of an unreasonable boss who wanted a week's worth of work done in the morning. They have learned to back up everything on multiple media after they lose thousands of lines of code and have to rewrite it all from scratch. They have seen C-beams glitter in the server room from burning hard drives and have fought with the systems administrator at the doors of the server room just to get access to production because someone has just deployed an untested piece of code. They have tested their software-compression code on its own source code, only to discover that it's compressed everything into one byte and the value of that byte is 255. The decompression algorithm is yet to be invented.

You've just graduated and are looking for a job, or you've been fascinated by programming but have no idea what awaits you. You've gotten out that boot camp and are looking for job opportunities, but you're not sure about the knowledge gap you have. You've taught yourself a programming language, but you're not sure what is missing from your skills tool belt. Welcome to the streets.

1.3   *Great street coders*

In addition to street cred, honor, and loyalty, a street coder ideally possesses these qualities:

- Questioning
- Results-driven (aka, "results-oriented" in HR-speak)
- High-throughput
- Embracing complexity and ambiguity

Great software developers are not just great coders

Being a great work colleague involves many more skills than just putting bits and bytes into a computer. You need to be good at communication, provide constructive feedback, and accept criticism like a champion. Even Linus Torvalds[a] admitted that he needed to work on his communication skills. However, such skills are outside the scope of this book. You will have to make friends.

---

[a] Linus Torvalds created the Linux operating system and Git source control software and endorsed the belief that swearing at your project's volunteers is okay if they are technically wrong.

1.3.1 Questioning

Someone talking to themselves is considered unusual at best, especially if they don't have answers to the questions they are asking themselves. However, being a questioning person, asking questions of yourself, asking questions about the most accepted notions, and deconstructing them can clarify your vision.

Many books, software experts, and Slavoj Žižek[2] emphasize the importance of being critical and inquisitive, but few of them give you something to work with. In this book, you'll find examples of very well-known techniques and best practices and how they can be less efficient than they claim to be.

A critique of a technique doesn't mean it's useless. However, it will expand your horizon so you can identify some use cases in which an alternative technique might actually be better.

The goal of this book isn't to cover every programming technique from end to end, but to give you a perspective on how to treat best practices, how to prioritize them based on merit, and how you can weigh the pros and cons of alternative approaches.

1.3.2 Results-driven

You can be the best programmer in the world with the best understanding of the intricacies of software development and can come up with the best design for your own code, but those will mean nothing if you are not shipping, if you are not getting the product out.

According to Zeno's paradox,[3] to reach an end goal, you must first reach the halfway-through point. It's a paradox because to reach the halfway-through point, you have to reach the quarter-way-through point, and so on, which makes you unable to reach anywhere. Zeno had a point: having an end product requires you to meet deadlines and the milestones in between, too. Otherwise, it's impossible to reach your end goal. Being results-driven also means being milestones-driven, being progress-driven.

> *"How does a project get to be a year late? … One day at a time."*
> —Fred Brooks, *The Mythical Man Month*

Getting results can mean sacrificing code quality, elegance, and technical excellence. It's important to have that perspective and keep yourself in check for what you're doing and for whose sake.

Sacrificing code quality doesn't mean sacrificing product quality. If you have good tests in place, if there is a good set of written requirements, you can even go ahead and write everything in PHP.[4] It could mean, however, you will have to bear

---

[2] Slavoj Žižek is a modern philosopher who suffers from a condition that forces him to criticize everything in the world, without exceptions.

[3] Zeno was a Greek guy who lived thousands of years ago and who couldn't stop asking frustrating questions. Naturally, none of his written works survived.

[4] PHP was once a programming language that exemplified how not to design a programming language. From what I've heard, PHP has come a long way since it was the butt of programming jokes and is a fantastic programming language now. However, it still has some brand image issues to address.

some pain in the future because bad-quality code will eventually bite you. It's called code karma.

Some of the techniques you'll learn in the book will help you make decisions to get results.

1.3.3   *High-throughput*

The greatest factors affecting the speed of your development are experience, good and clear specifications, and mechanical keyboards. Just kidding—contrary to popular belief, mechanical keyboards don't help your speed at all. They just look cool and are great at annoying your significant other. In fact, I don't think typing speed helps development speed at all. Your confidence in your typing speed might even encourage you to write more elaborate code than is necessary.

Some expertise can be gained by learning from others' mistakes and despair. In this book, you'll find examples of such cases. The techniques and knowledge you gained will make you write less code and make decisions faster and will allow you to have as little technical debt as possible so you won't be spending days untangling code you wrote only six months ago.

1.3.4   *Embracing complexity and ambiguity*

Complexity is scary, and ambiguity more so, because you don't even know how much you should be scared and that scares you even more.

Dealing with ambiguity is one of the core skills Microsoft recruiters ask questions about in interviews. That usually entails hypothetical questions like "How many violin repair shops are there in New York?," "How many gas stations are there in Los Angeles?," or "How many Secret Service agents does the president have, and what's their shift schedule? List their names, and preferably show their walking paths on this blueprint of the White House."

The trick to solving these questions comes down to clarifying everything you know about the problem and arriving at an approximation based on those facts. For example, you can start with New York's population and how many people might be playing violin in the population. That would give you an idea about the size of the market and how much competition the market can support.

Similarly, when faced with a problem with some unknown parameters, such as estimating the time it would take to develop a feature, you can always narrow the window of approximation based on what you know. You can use what you know to your advantage and leverage it as much as possible, which can reduce the ambiguous part to minuscule.

Interestingly, dealing with complexity is similar. Something that looks extremely complex can be divided into parts that are much more manageable, less complex, and, in the end, simpler.

The more you clarify, the more you can tackle the unknown. The techniques you'll learn in this book will clarify some of these things and will make you more confident in tackling ambiguity and complexity.

1.4   *The problems of modern software development*

Besides increased complexity, countless layers of abstractions, and Stack Overflow moderation, modern software development has other issues:

- There are too many technologies: too many programming languages, too many frameworks, and certainly too many libraries, considering that npm (the package manager for Node.js framework) had a library called "left-pad" solely to add space characters to the end of a string.
- It's paradigm-driven, and hence, conservative. Many programmers consider programming languages, best practices, design patterns, algorithms, and data structures relics of an ancient alien race and have no idea how they work.
- Technology is becoming more opaque, like cars. People used to be able to repair their own cars. Now as the engines become increasingly advanced, all we see under the hood is a metal cover, like the one on a pharaoh's tomb that will release cursed spirits onto whoever opens it. Software development technologies are no different. Although almost everything is now open source, I think new technologies are more obscure than reverse-engineered code from a binary from the 1990s because of the immensely increased complexity of software.
- People don't care about the overhead of their code because we have orders of magnitude of more resources at our disposal. Did you write a new simple chat application? Why not bundle it with an entire package of a full-blown web browser because you know it just saves you time and nobody bats an eye when you use gigabytes of memory anyway?
- Programmers are focused on their stack and disregard how the rest works, and rightfully so: they need to bring food to the table, and there is no time to learn. I call this "The Dining Developers Problem." Many things that influence the quality of their product go unnoticed because of the constraints they have. A web developer usually has no idea how the networking protocols underneath the web work. They accept the delay when loading a page as is and learn to live with it because they don't know that a minor technical detail like an unnecessarily long certificate chain can slow down a web page's loading speed.
- Thanks to the paradigms that have been taught, there is a stigma against menial work, like repeating yourself or copy and paste. You are expected to find a DRY[5] solution. That kind of culture makes you doubt yourself and your abilities and therefore hurts your productivity.

---

[5] DRY. Don't Repeat Yourself. A superstition that if someone repeats a line of code instead of wrapping it in a function, they will instantly be transformed into a frog.

The story of npm and left-pad

npm became the de facto JavaScript library package ecosystem in the last decade. People could contribute their own packages to the ecosystem, and other packages could use them, making it easier to develop large projects. Azer Koçulu was one of those developers. Left-pad was only one of the packages out of the 250 he contributed to the npm ecosystem. It had only one function: to append spaces to a string to make sure that it's always a fixed size, which is quite trivial.

One day, he received an email from npm saying that they had removed one of his packages called "Kik," because a company with the same name complained. npm decided to remove Azer's package and give the name to the other company. That made Azer so angry that he removed all the packages that he contributed, including left-pad. The thing is, you see, there were hundreds of large-scale projects in the world directly or indirectly using the package. His actions caused all those projects to stop in their tracks. It was quite a catastrophe and a good lesson about the trust we have on the platforms.

The moral of the story is that life in the streets is full of unwelcome surprises.

In this book, I propose some solutions to these problems, including going over some core concepts that you might have found boring, prioritizing practicality, simplicity, rejecting some long-held unquestionable beliefs, and, most importantly, questioning everything we do. There is value in asking questions first.

1.4.1   *Too many technologies*

Our constant search for the best technology usually arises from the fallacy of a silver bullet. We think that there is a technology out there that can increase our productivity by orders of magnitude. There isn't. For example, Python[6] is an interpreted language. You don't need to compile Python code—it just runs right away. Even better, you don't need to specify types for the variables you declare, which makes you even faster, so Python must be a better technology than C#, right? Not necessarily.

Because you don't spend time annotating your code with types and compiling it, you miss the mistakes you make. That means you can only discover them during testing or in production, which are much more expensive than simply compiling code. Most technologies are tradeoffs rather than productivity boosters. What boosts your productivity is how adept you are with that technology and your techniques, rather than which technologies you're using. Yes, there are better technologies, but they rarely make an order of magnitude difference.

When I wanted to develop my first interactive website back in 1999, I had absolutely no idea how to go about writing a web application. Had I tried to search for the best technology first, it would have meant teaching myself VBScript or Perl. Instead, I used what I knew best then: Pascal.[7] It was one of the least suitable languages for that

---

[6] Python is a collective effort to promote whitespace, disguised as a practical programming language.
[7] Ekşi Sözlük's early source code is available on GitHub: https://github.com/ssg/sozluk-cgi.

purpose, but it worked. Of course, there were problems with it. Whenever it hung up, the process stayed active in the memory in a random server in Canada, and the user had to call the service provider every time and ask them to restart the physical server. Yet, Pascal let me reach a prototype quickly because I was comfortable with it. Instead of launching the website I imagined after months of development and learning, I wrote and released the code in three hours.

I'm looking forward to showing you ways that you can be more efficient in using the existing tool set you have on your belt.

1.4.2 Paragliding on paradigms

The earliest *programming paradigm* I encountered was structured programming back in the 1980s. Structured programming is basically writing your code in structured blocks like functions and loops instead of line numbers, GOTO statements, blood, sweat, and tears. It made your code easier to read and to maintain without sacrificing performance. Structured programming sparked my interest in programming languages like Pascal and C.

The next paradigm I encountered came at least half a decade after I learned about structured programming: object-oriented programming, or OOP. I remember that at the time, computer magazines couldn't get enough of it. It was the next big thing that would allow us to write even better programs than we did with structured programming.

After OOP, I thought I would encounter a new paradigm every five years or so. However, they started to appear more frequently. The 1990s introduced us to JIT-compiled[8] managed programming languages with the advent of Java, web scripting with JavaScript, and functional programming that slowly crept into the mainstream toward the end of the 1990s.

Then came the 2000s. In the next decades, we saw increased use of the term *N-tier applications*. Fat clients. Thin clients. Generics. MVC, MVVM, and MVP. Asynchronous programming started to proliferate with promises, futures, and finally, reactive programming. Microservices. More functional programming concepts like LINQ, pattern matching and immutability have made it into the mainstream languages. It's a tornado of buzzwords.

I haven't even addressed design patterns or best practices. We have countless best practices, tips, and tricks about almost every subject. There are *manifestos* written about whether we should use tabs or space characters for indenting the source code, despite the fact that the obvious answer is spaces.[9]

We assume our problems can be solved by employing a paradigm, a pattern, a framework, or a library. Considering the complexity of the problems we now face, that

---

[8] JIT, just-in-time compilation. A myth created by Sun Microsystems, creator of Java, that if you compile some code while it's running, it will become faster because the optimizer will have collected more data during runtime. It's still a myth.

[9] I have written about the tabs versus spaces debate from a pragmatic point of view: https://medium.com/@ssg/tabs-vs-spaces-towards-a-better-bike-shed-686e111a5cce.

is not unfounded. However, the blind adoption of those tools can cause more problems in the future: they can slow you down more by introducing new domain knowledge to learn and their own sets of bugs. They can even force you to change your design. This book will give you more confidence that you're using patterns correctly, approaching them more inquisitively, and accumulating good comebacks to use during code reviews.

1.4.3   *The black boxes of technology*

A framework or a library is a package. Software developers install it, read its documentation, and use it. But they usually don't know how it works. They approach algorithms and data structures the same way. They use a dictionary datatype because it's handy to keep keys and values. They don't know the consequences.

Unconditional trust in package ecosystems and frameworks is prone to significant mistakes. It can cost us days of debugging because we just didn't know that adding items to a dictionary with the same key would be no different than a list in lookup performance. We use C# generators when a simple array would suffice, and we suffer significant degradation in performance without knowing why.

One day in 1993, a friend handed me a sound card and asked me to install it on my PC. Yes, we used to need add-on cards to get decent sound from a PC, because otherwise all we heard was just a beep. Anyway, I had never opened my PC case before, and I was afraid to damage it. I told him, "Can't you do this for me?" My friend told me, "You have to open it to see how it works."

That resonated with me, because I understood that my anxiety was caused by my ignorance rather than my incapability. Opening the case and seeing the insides of my own PC calmed me down. It held only a couple of boards. The sound card went into one of the slots. It wasn't a mystery box to me anymore. I later used the same technique when teaching art school students the basics of computers. I opened a mouse and showed them its ball. Mice had balls back then. Welp, this was unfortunately ambiguous. I opened the PC case. "You see, it's not scary, it's a board and some slots."

That later became my motto in dealing with anything new and complex. I stopped being afraid to open the box and usually did it first thing so I could face the whole extent of the complexity, which was always less than I feared it to be.

Similarly, the details of how a library, a framework, or a computer works can have a tremendous effect on your understanding of what's built on top of it. Opening the box and looking at the parts can help you use the box correctly. You don't really have to read its code from scratch or go through a thousand-page theory book, but you should at least be able to see which part goes where and how it can affect your use cases.

That's why some of the topics I'll be talking about are fundamental or low-level subjects. It's about opening the box and seeing how things work, so we can make better decisions for high-level programming.

1.4.4 *Underestimating overhead*

I'm glad that we are seeing more cloud-based apps every day. Not only are they cost effective, but they are also a reality check for understanding the actual cost of our code. When you start paying an extra cent for every wrong decision you make in your code, overhead suddenly becomes a concern.

Frameworks and libraries usually help us avoid overhead, which makes them useful abstractions. However, we can't delegate all our decision-making process to frameworks. Sometimes, we have to make decisions for ourselves, and we have to take overhead into account. At-scale applications make overhead even more crucial. Every millisecond you save can help you recover precious resources.

A software developer's priority shouldn't be eliminating overhead. However, knowing how overhead can be avoided in certain situations and having that perspective as a tool in your tool belt will help you save time, both for yourself and for the user who is waiting on that spinner[10] on your web page.

Throughout the book, you'll find scenarios and examples of how overhead can be avoided easily without making it your utmost priority.

1.4.5 *Not my job*

One way to deal with complexity is to focus solely on our responsibilities: the component we own, the code we write, the bugs we have caused, and occasionally the exploded lasagna in the office kitchen microwave. It may sound like the most time-efficient way to do our work, but like all beings, all code is also interconnected.

Learning how a specific technology ticks, how a library does its job, and how dependencies work and are connected can allow us to make better decisions when we write code. The examples in this book will provide you a perspective to focus on not only your area, but also its dependencies and issues that are outside your comfort zone because you'll discover that they predict the fate of your code.

1.4.6 *Menial is genial*

All the principles taught about software development come down to a single admonition: spend less time doing your work. Avoid repetitive, brainless tasks like copying and pasting and writing the same code with minor changes from scratch. First of all, they take longer, and second, it's extremely hard to maintain them.

Not all menial tasks are bad. Not even all copy and paste is bad. There is a strong stigma against them, but there are ways to make them more efficient than some of the best practices you've been taught.

Furthermore, not all the code you write works as code for the actual product. Some of the code you write will be used to develop a prototype, some will be for tests,

---

[10] Spinners are the modern hourglasses of computing. In ancient times, computers used hourglasses to make you wait for an indefinite time. A spinner is the modern equivalent of that animation. It's usually a circular arc that rotates indefinitely. It's just a distraction to keep the user's frustration in check.

and some will be for warming you up for the actual task at hand. I'll be discussing some of those scenarios and how you can use those tasks to your advantage.

1.5   *What this book isn't*

This book is not a comprehensive guide on programming, algorithms, or any subject matter whatsoever. I do not consider myself expert on specific topics, but I possess enough expertise in software development. The book mostly consists of pieces of information that are not apparent from the well-known, popular, and great books out there. It's definitely not a guide to learning programming.

Experienced programmers might find little benefit from this book because they have already acquired sufficient knowledge and have already become street coders. That said, they might still be surprised by some of its insights.

This book is also an experiment in how programming books can be fun to read. I'd like to introduce programming primarily as a fun practice. The book doesn't take itself seriously, so you shouldn't either. If you feel like a better developer after reading the book and have fun reading it, I will consider myself successful.

1.6   *Themes*

Certain themes will be repeated throughout the book:

- Minimal foundational knowledge that is enough for you to get by in the streets. Those subjects will not be exhaustive, but they might spark your interest if you previously thought them boring. They are usually core knowledge that helps you make decisions.
- Well-known or well-accepted best practices or techniques that I propose as an anti-patterns that could be more effective in certain cases. The more you read about these, the more amplified will be your sixth sense for critical thinking about programming practices.
- Some seemingly irrelevant programming techniques, such as some CPU-level optimization tricks, which might influence your decision making and code writing at the higher level. There is immense value in knowing the internals, "opening the box," even if you don't use that piece of information directly.
- Some techniques that I find useful in my day-to-day programming activities that might help you increase your productivity, including biting your nails and being invisible to your boss.

These themes will emphasize a new perspective when you are looking at programming topics, will change your understanding of certain "boring" subjects, and perhaps will change your attitude toward certain dogmas. They will make you enjoy your work more.

Summary

- The harsh reality of "the streets," the world of professional software development, requires a set of skills that are not taught or prioritized in formal education or sometimes are completely missed in self-teaching.
- New software developers tend to either care about theory or to completely ignore it. You'll find a middle point eventually, but achieving that can be accelerated with a certain perspective.
- Modern software development is vastly more complex than it was a couple of decades ago. It requires tremendous knowledge on many levels just to develop a simple running application.
- Programmers face a dilemma between creating software and learning. This can be overcome by reframing topics in a more pragmatic way.
- Lack of clarity about what you work on makes programming a mundane and boring task and thus reduces your actual productivity. A better understanding about what you do will bring you more joy.

Practical theory

2

This chapter covers

- Why computer science theory is relevant to your survival
- Making types work for you
- Understanding the characteristics of algorithms
- Data structures and their weird qualities that your parents didn't tell you about

Contrary to widely held belief, programmers are human. They have the same cognitive biases other humans have about the practice of software development. They widely overestimate the benefits of not having to use types, not caring about correct data structures, or assuming that algorithms are only important for library authors.

You're no exception. You're expected to deliver a product on time, with good quality, and with a smile on your face. As the saying goes, a programmer is effectively an organism that receives coffee as input and creates software as output. You might as well write everything the worst way possible, use copy and paste, use the code you found on Stack Overflow, use plain text files for data storage, or make a deal with a demon if your soul isn't already under NDA.[1] Only your peers really care about how you do things—everybody else wants a good, working product.

---

[1] Non-disclosure agreement, an agreement that prevents employees from talking about their work unless they start the conversation with "You didn't hear this from me, but…"

Theory can be overwhelming and unrelatable. Algorithms, data structures, type theory, Big-O notation, and polynomial complexity can look complicated and irrelevant to software development. Existing libraries and frameworks already handle this stuff in an optimized and a well-tested way. You're encouraged to never implement an algorithm from scratch anyway, especially in the context of information security or tight deadlines.

Then why should you care about theory? Because not only does knowledge of computer science theory let you develop algorithms and data structures from scratch, but it also lets you correctly determine when you need to use one. It helps you understand the costs of tradeoff decisions. It helps you understand the scalability characteristics of the code you're writing. It makes you see ahead. You will probably never implement a data structure or an algorithm from scratch, but knowing how one works will make you an efficient developer. It will improve your chances of survival in the streets.

This book will only go over certain critical parts about theory that you might have missed when you were studying them—some less-known aspects of data types, understanding the complexities of algorithms, and how certain data structures work internally. If you haven't learned about types, algorithms, or data structures before, this chapter will give you cues to get you interested in the subject.

2.1   *A crash course on algorithms*

An algorithm is a set of rules and steps to solve a problem. Thank you for attending my TED talk. You were expecting a more complicated definition, weren't you? For example, going over the elements of an array to find out if it contains a number is an algorithm, a simple one at that:

```
public static bool Contains(int[] array, int lookFor) {
    for (int n = 0; n < array.Length; n++) {
        if (array[n] == lookFor) {
            return true;
        }
    }
    return false;
}
```

We could have called this *Sedat's Algorithm* if I were the person who invented it, but it was probably one of the first algorithms that ever emerged. It's not clever in any way, but it works, and it makes sense. That's one of the important points about algorithms: they only need to work for your needs. They don't necessarily have to perform miracles. When you put dishes in the dishwasher and run it, you follow an algorithm. The existence of an algorithm doesn't mean it's clever.

That said, there can be smarter algorithms, depending on your needs. In the previous code example, if you know that the list only contains positive integers, you can add special handling for non-positive numbers:

```
public static bool Contains(int[] array, int lookFor) {
    if (lookFor < 1) {
        return false;
    }
    for (int n = 0; n < array.Length; n++) {
        if (array[n] == lookFor) {
            return true;
        }
    }
    return false;
}
```

This could make your algorithm much faster depending on how many times you call it with a negative number. At best, your function would always be called with negative numbers or zeros, and it would return immediately, even if the array had billions of integers. In the worst case, your function would always be called with positive numbers, and you'd be incurring just an extra unnecessary check. Types can help you here because there are unsigned versions of integers called uint in C#. Thus, you can always receive positive numbers, and the compiler will check for it if you violate that rule, incurring zero performance issues:

```
public static bool Contains(uint[] array, uint lookFor) {
    for (int n = 0; n < array.Length; n++) {
        if (array[n] == lookFor) {
            return true;
        }
    }
    return false;
}
```

We fixed the positive number requirement with type restrictions rather than changing our algorithm, but it can still be faster based on the shape of the data. Do we have more information about the data? Is the array sorted? If it is, we can make more assumptions about where our number might be. If we compare our number with any item in the array, we can eliminate a huge number of items easily (see figure 2.1).

Sort order (ascending) ────────▶

Every item is ≤ here   5   Every item is ≥ 5 here

Figure 2.1 We can eliminate one side of the element with one comparison on a sorted list.

If our number is, say, 3, and if we compare it with 5, we can make sure that our number won't be anywhere right of 5. That means we can eliminate all the elements right of the list immediately.

Thus, if we pick the element from the middle of the list, it is guaranteed that we can eliminate at least half of the list after the comparison. We can apply the same logic to the remaining half, pick a middle point there, and go on. That means we only need to make 3 comparisons at most for a sorted array with 8 items to determine if an item exists in it. More importantly, it will only take about 10 lookups at most to determine if an item exists in an array with 1,000 items. That's the power you get by going over in halves. Your implementation could look like listing 2.1. We basically continuously find a middle spot and eliminate the remaining half depending on how the value we're looking for would fall into it. We write the formula in a longer, more elaborate form even though it corresponds to $(start + end) v/2$. That's because $start + end$ can overflow for large values of $start$ and end and would find an incorrect middle spot. If you write the expression as in the following listing, you will avoid that overflow case.

> **Listing 2.1 Searching a sorted array with binary search**

```
public static bool Contains(uint[] array, uint lookFor) {
  int start = 0;
  int end = array.Length - 1;
  while (start <= end) {
    int middle = start + ((end - start) / 2);    ← Find the middle spot
    uint value = array[middle];                      and avoid overflows.
    if (lookFor == value) {
      return true;
    }
    if (lookFor > value) {          Eliminate the left
      start = middle + 1;       ←   half of the range.
    } else {
      end = middle - 1;   ←   Eliminate the right
    }                           half of the range.
  }
  return false;
}
```

Here, we implemented a binary search, a much faster algorithm than *Sedat's Algorithm*. Since we can now imagine how a binary search can be faster than a plain iteration, we can start thinking about the revered Big-O notation.

2.1.1 Big-O better be good

Understanding growth is a great skill for a developer to possess. Be it in size or numbers, when you know how fast something grows, you can see the future and therefore what kind of trouble you're getting into before you spend too much time on it. It's especially useful when the light at the end of the tunnel is growing even though you're not moving.

Big-O notation, as the name suggests, is just a notation to explain growth, and it's also subject to misconceptions. When I first saw $O(N)$, I thought it was a regular function that is supposed to return a number. It isn't. It's a way mathematicians explain growth. It gives us a basic idea about how scalable an algorithm is. Going over every element sequentially (aka *Sedat's Algorithm*) has a number of operations that is linearly proportional to the number of elements in the array. We denote that by writing $O(N)$, with N denoting the number of elements. We still can't know how many steps the algorithm will take just by looking at O(N), but we know that it grows linearly. That allows us to make assumptions about the performance characteristics of an algorithm depending on the data size. We can foresee at which point it can turn bad by looking at it.

The binary search we implemented has a complexity of $O(log2^n)$. If you're not familiar with logarithms, it's the opposite of exponential, so a logarithmic complexity is actually a wonderful thing unless money's involved. In this example, if our sorting algorithm magically had logarithmic complexity, it would take only 18 comparisons to sort an array with 500,000 items. This makes our binary search implementation great.

Big-O notation isn't only used for measuring increase in computational steps, aka *time complexity*, but it's also used for measuring the increase in memory usage, which is called *space complexity*. An algorithm might be fast, but it could have polynomial growth in memory, like our sorting example. We should understand the distinction.

> **TIP** Contrary to popular belief, $O(N^x)$ doesn't mean exponential complexity. It denotes polynomial complexity, which, although quite bad, is not as terrible as exponential complexity, which is denoted by $O(x^n)$ instead. With a mere 100 items, $O(N^2)$ would iterate 10,000 times, while $O(2^n)$ would iterate some mind-boggling number of times with 30 digits—I can't even pronounce it. There is also factorial complexity, which is even worse than exponential, but I haven't seen any algorithms apart from calculating permutations or combinations using it, probably because nobody has been able to finish inventing it.

Since Big-O is about growth, the largest growth function in the notation is the most important part. So, practically speaking, O(N) and O(4N) are equivalent as far as Big-O cares. O(N.M), on the other hand, the dot being the multiplication operator, may not be so when both N and M are growing. It can even effectively be $O(N^2)$. O(N.logN) is slightly worse than O(N), but not as bad as $O(N^2)$.

O(1), on the other hand, is amazing. It means that the performance characteristics aren't related to the number of elements in the given data structure for an algorithm, also known as *constant time.*

Imagine that you implemented a search feature that finds a record in the database by iterating over all of them. That means your algorithm would grow linearly proportional to the number of items in the database. Assume that accessing every record takes a second because I guess we're using an abacus for data storage now. This means searching for an item in a database of 60 items would take up to a minute. That's O(N) complexity. Other developers in your team can come up with different algorithms, as table 2.1 shows.

You need to be familiar with how Big-O notation explains the growth in an algorithm's execution speed and memory usage so you can make informed decisions when choosing which data structure and algorithm to use. Be familiar with Big-O, even though you may not need to implement an algorithm. Beware of complexity.

Table 2.1   Impact of complexity on performance

Search algorithm	Complexity	Time to find a record among 60 rows
The DIY quantum computer Lisa's uncle has in his garage	$O(1)$	1 second
Binary search	$O(\log N)$	6 seconds
Linear search (because your boss asked you to do it an hour before the presentation)	$O(N)$	60 seconds
The intern accidentally put 2 for loops nested.	$O(N^2)$	1 hour
Some randomly pasted code from Stack Overflow that also finds a solution to some chess problem while searching, but the developer didn't bother to remove that part	$O(2^N)$	36.5 billion years
Instead of finding the actual record, the algorithm tries to find the arrangement of records that spell out the record you're looking for when sorted in a certain way. The good news is that the developer doesn't work here anymore.	$O(N!)$	The end of the universe, but still before those monkeys finish their so-called Shakespeare

2.2   *Inside data structures*

In the beginning, there was void. When the first electrical signals hit the first bit in the memory, there became data. Data was only free-floating bytes. Those bytes got together and created structure.

—Init 0:1

Data structures are about how data is laid out. People discovered that when data is laid out in a certain way, it can become more useful. A shopping list on a piece of paper is easier to read if every item is on a separate line. A multiplication table is more useful if it's arranged in a grid. Understanding how a certain data structure works is essential for you to become a better programmer. That understanding begins with popping the hood and looking at how it works.

Let's look at arrays, for example. An array in programming is one of the simplest data structures, and it's laid out like contiguous elements in memory. Let's say you have this array:

```
var values = new int[] { 1, 2, 3, 4, 5, 6, 7, 8 };
```

You can imagine what it'd look like in memory, as in figure 2.2.

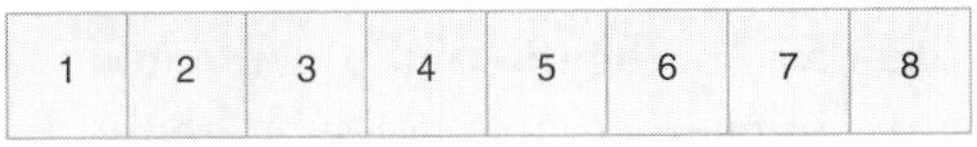

| 1 | 2 | 3 | 4 | 5 | 6 | 7 | 8 |

Figure 2.2   A symbolic representation of an array

Actually, it wouldn't look like that in memory because every object in .NET has a certain header, a pointer to the virtual method table pointer, and length information contained within as in figure 2.3.

Array
reference
address –8

Array
reference
address

**Figure 2.3   Actual layout
of an array in memory**

It becomes even more realistic if you look at it how it's placed in RAM, because RAM isn't built in integers, as figure 2.4 shows. I'm sharing these because I want you to be unafraid of these low-level concepts. Understanding them will help you at all levels of programming.

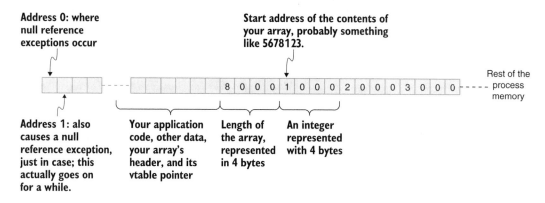

Figure 2.4   Memory space of a process and an array

This isn't how your actual RAM looks because every process has its own slice of memory dedicated to it, related to how modern operating systems work. But this is the layout that you'll always be dealing with unless you start developing your own operating system or your own device drivers.

All in all, how data is laid out can make things faster or more efficient, or the opposite. It's crucial to know some basic data structures and how they work internally.

2.2.1   String

Strings could be the most humane data type in the world of programming. They represent text and can usually be read by humans. You're not supposed to use strings when a different type is better suited, but they are inevitable and convenient. When you use strings, you have to know some basic facts about them that are not apparent from the get-go.

Although they resemble arrays in usage and structure, strings in .NET are *immutable. Immutability* means that the contents of a data structure cannot be changed after it's initialized. Assume that we'd like to join people's names to produce a single, comma-separated string and that we have traveled two decades back in time so there is no better way of doing this:

```
public static string JoinNames(string[] names) {
    string result = String.Empty;
    int lastIndex = names.Length - 1;
    for (int i = 0; i < lastIndex; i++) {
        result += names[i] + ", ";
    }
    result += names[lastIndex];
    return result;
}
```

If we didn't initialize the string, it would have a default value of null, which would have been caught by nullability checks if you had used them.

Index of the last element

This way, we avoid finishing the string with a comma.

At first glance, it might seem like we have a string called `result` and we are modifying the same string over the course of execution, but that's not the case. Every time we assign `result` a new value, we are creating a new string in memory. .NET needs to determine the length of the new string, allocate new memory for it, copy the contents of other strings into the newly built memory, and return it to you. That is quite an expensive operation, and the cost increases as the string and the trail of garbage to collect get longer.

There are tools in the framework to avoid this problem. Even if you don't care about performance, these tools are free, so you don't really need to change your logic or jump through hoops to get better performance. One of those is `StringBuilder`, with which you can work to build your final string and retrieve it with a `ToString` call in one shot:

```
public static string JoinNames(string[] names) {
    var builder = new StringBuilder();
    int lastIndex = names.Length - 1;
    for (int i = 0; i < lastIndex; i++) {
        builder.Append(names[i]);
        builder.Append(", ");
    }
    builder.Append(names[lastIndex]);
    return builder.ToString();
}
```

`StringBuilder` uses consecutive memory blocks internally instead of reallocating and copying every time it needs to grow the string. Therefore, it's usually more efficient than building a string from scratch.

Obviously, an idiomatic and a much shorter solution has been available for a long time, but your use cases may not always overlap with these:

```
String.Join(", ", names);
```

Concatenating a string is usually okay when initializing the string because that involves only a single buffer allocation after calculating the total length required. For example, if you have a function that joins first name and last name with a space in between using the addition operator, you're only creating a single new string in one shot, not multiple steps:

```
public string ConcatName(string firstName, string middleName,
   string lastName) {
   return firstName + " " + middleName + " " + lastName;
}
```

This might seem like a no-no if we assume that `firstName + " "` would create a new string first and then create a new string with `middleName` and so on, but the compiler actually turns it into a single call to a `String.Concat()` function, which allocates a new buffer with the length of the sum of the lengths of all strings and returns it in one shot. Therefore, it's still fast. But when you concatenate strings in multiple shots with `if` clauses in between, or loops, the compiler can't optimize that. You need to know when it's okay to concatenate strings and when it's not.

That said, immutability isn't a holy seal that cannot be broken. There are ways around modifying strings in place, or other immutable structures, for that matter, which mostly involve unsafe code and astral beings, but they're not usually recommended because strings are deduplicated by the .NET runtime and some of their properties, such as hash codes, are cached. The internal implementation relies heavily on the immutability characteristic.

String functions work with the current *culture* by default, and that might be painful to experience when your app stops working in another country.

> **NOTE** A culture, also known as locale in some programming languages, is a set of rules for performing region-specific operations like sorting strings, displaying date/time in the correct format, placing utensils on the table, and so forth. Current culture is usually what the operating system thinks it's using.

Understanding cultures can make your string operations safer and faster. For instance, consider a code whereby we detect if the given file name has a .gif extension:

```
public bool isGif(string fileName) {
    return fileName.ToLower().EndsWith(".gif");
}
```

We are smart, you see: we turn the string to lowercase so we handle the case where the extension could be .GIF or .Gif or any other combination of cases. The thing is, not all languages have the same lowercase semantics. In the Turkish language, for instance, the lowercase of "I" is not "i," but "ı," also known as the dotless-I. The code in this example would fail in Turkey, and maybe in some other countries like Azerbaijan as well. By lowercasing the string, we are in fact creating a new string, which, as we've learned, is inefficient.

.NET supplies culture-invariant versions of some string methods, like `ToLower-Invariant`. It also provides some overloads of the same method that receive a `String-Comparison` value that has invariant and ordinal alternatives. Therefore, you can write the same method in a safer and faster way:

```
public bool isGif(string fileName) {
    return fileName.EndsWith(".gif",
        StringComparison.OrdinalIgnoreCase);
}
```

By using this method, we avoid creating a new string, and we're using a culture-safe and faster string comparison method that doesn't involve our current culture and its intricate rules. We could have used `StringComparison.InvariantCultureIgnore-Case`, but unlike ordinal comparison, it adds a couple more translation rules such as treating German umlauts or graphemes with their Latin counterparts (ß versus ss) that might cause problems with filenames or other resource identifiers. Ordinal comparison compares character values directly without involving any translation.

2.2.2 *Array*

We have looked at what an array looks like in memory. Arrays are practical for keeping several items that have numbers that won't be growing beyond the array's size. They are static structures. They cannot grow or change size. If you want a larger array, you have to create a new one and copy the contents of the old one over. There are a couple of things you need to know about arrays.

Arrays, unlike strings, are mutable. That's what they are about. You can freely play with their contents. Actually, it's really hard to make them immutable, which makes them poor candidates for interfaces. Consider this property:

```
public string[] Usernames { get; }
```

Even though the property has no setter, the type is still an array, which makes it mutable. There is nothing that prevents you from doing

```
Usernames[0] = "root";
```

which can complicate things, even when it's only you who's using the class. You shouldn't allow yourself to make changes to the state unless it's absolutely needed. State is the root of all evil, not null. The fewer states your app has, the fewer problems you'll have.

Try to stick to the type that has the smallest functionality for your purpose. If you only need to go over the items sequentially, stick to `IEnumerable<T>`. If you also need a repetitively accessible count, use `ICollection<T>`. Note that the LINQ extension method `.Count()` has special handling code for types that support `IReadOnlyCollection<T>`, so even if you use it on an `IEnumerable`, there is a chance that it might return a cached value instead.

Arrays are best suited for use inside the local scope of a function. For any other purpose, there is a better-suited type or interface to expose in addition to IEnumerable<T>, like IReadOnlyCollection<T>, IReadOnlyList<T>, or ISet<T>.

2.2.3   *List*

A list behaves like an array that can grow slightly, similarly to how StringBuilder works. It's possible to use lists over arrays almost everywhere, but that will incur an unnecessary performance penalty because indexed accesses are *virtual calls* in a list, while an array uses direct access.

You see, object-oriented programming comes with a nice feature called *polymorphism*, which means an object can behave according to the underlying implementation without its interface changing. If you have, say, a variable a with a type of IOpenable interface, a.Open() might open a file or a network connection, depending on the type of the object assigned to it. This is achieved by keeping a reference to a table that maps virtual functions to be called to the type at the beginning of the object, called the *virtual method table*, or *vtable* for short. This way, although Open maps to the same entry in the table in every object with the same type, you wouldn't know where it's going to lead until you look up the actual value in the table.

Because we don't know what exactly we're calling them, they are named *virtual calls*. A virtual call involves an extra lookup from the virtual method table, so it's slightly slower than regular function calls. That may not be a problem with a couple of function calls, but when it's done inside an algorithm, its overhead can grow polynomially. Consequently, if your list won't grow in size after initialization, you might want to use an array instead of a list in a local scope.

Normally, you should almost never think about these details. But when you know the difference, there are cases in which an array might be preferable to a list.

Lists are similar to StringBuilder. Both are dynamically growing data structures, but lists are less efficient in growth mechanics. Whenever a list decides that it needs to grow, it allocates a new array with a larger size and copies the existing contents to it. StringBuilder, on the other hand, keeps chunks of memory chained together instead, which doesn't require a copy operation. The buffer area for lists grows whenever the buffer limit is reached, but the size of the new buffer gets doubled every time, which means the need for growth gets reduced over time. Still, this is an example in which using a specific class for the task at hand is more efficient than using a generic one.

You can also get great performance from lists by specifying a capacity. If you don't specify a capacity to a list, it will start with an empty array. It will then increase its capacity to a few items. It will double its capacity after it's full. If you set a capacity while creating the list, you avoid unnecessary growth and copying operations altogether. Keep this in mind when you already know the maximum number of items the list will have beforehand.

That said, don't make a habit of specifying list capacity without knowing the reason. That might cause unnecessary memory overhead that can accumulate. Make a habit of making conscious decisions.

2.2.4   *Linked list*

Linked lists are lists where elements aren't consecutive in memory, but each element points to the address of the following item. They are useful for their O(1) insertion and removal performance. You can't access individual items by index because they can be stored anywhere in memory, and it's not possible to calculate it, but if you mostly access the beginning or the end of the list, or if you just need to enumerate the items, it can be just as fast. Otherwise, checking if an item exists in a linked list is an O(N) operation, like arrays and lists. Figure 2.5 shows a sample linked list layout.

Figure 2.5   Layout of a linked list

That doesn't mean a linked list is always faster than a regular list. Individual memory allocations for each element instead of allocating a whole block of memory in one shot and additional reference lookups can also hurt performance.

You might need a linked list whenever you need a queue or stack structure, but .NET covers that. So ideally, unless you're into systems programming, you shouldn't need to use a linked list in your daily work except for in job interviews. Unfortunately, interviewers love their puzzle questions with linked lists, so it's still important for you to become familiar with them.

No, you won't reverse a linked list

Answering coding questions in interviews is a rite of passage for software development positions. Most of the coding questions also cover some data structures and algorithms. Linked lists are part of the corpus, so there is a chance someone might ask you to reverse a linked list or invert a binary tree.

You will probably never perform those tasks in your actual job, but to give credit to the interviewer, they are testing your knowledge of data structures and algorithms to simply determine that you know what you're doing. They are trying to make sure that you're capable of making the right decision when a need arises to use the right data structure at the right place. They are also testing your analytical thinking and problem-solving ability, so it's important for you to think aloud and share your thought process with the interviewer.

You don't always need to solve the given question. An interviewer usually looks for someone who is passionate and knowledgeable about certain basic concepts and who can find their way around, even though they might get lost.

I, for example, usually followed up my coding questions to candidates at Microsoft with an extra step for them to find bugs in their code. That actually made them feel better because it felt like bugs were expected and they were not assessed based on how bug-free the code was, but on how they can identify bugs.

Linked lists were more popular in the ancient times of programming because memory efficiency took precedence. We couldn't afford to allocate kilobytes of memory just because our list needed to grow. We had to keep tight storage. A linked list was the perfect data structure for that. They are also still used frequently in operating system kernels because of their irresistible O(1) characteristic for insertion and removal operations.

2.2.5   *Queue*

A queue is a data structure that represents the most basic form of civilization. It allows you to read items from a list in the order of insertion. A queue can simply be an array as long as you keep separate spots for reading the next item and inserting the new one. If we added ascending numbers to a queue, it would resemble figure 2.6.

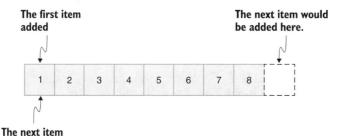

The first item added

The next item would be added here.

| 1 | 2 | 3 | 4 | 5 | 6 | 7 | 8 | |

The next item to be read

Figure 2.6   A high-level layout of a queue

The keyboard buffer on PCs in the MS-DOS era used a simple array of bytes to store key presses. The buffer prevented keystrokes from getting missed because of the slow or unresponsive software. When the buffer was full, the BIOS would beep so we would know that our keystrokes weren't being recorded anymore. Fortunately, .NET comes with an existing `Queue<T>` class that we can use without worrying about implementation details and performance.

2.2.6   *Dictionary*

Dictionaries, also known as *hashmaps* or sometimes *key/value things*, are among the most useful and the most used data structures. We tend to take their capabilities for granted. A dictionary is a container that can store a key and a value. It can later retrieve a value with a key in constant, aka O(1), time. That means they are extremely fast for data retrieval. Why are they so fast? What's the magic?

The magic lies in the word *hash*. *Hashing* is the term for generating a single number from arbitrary data. The number generated must be deterministic, which means that it must generate the same number for the same data, but it doesn't have to generate a unique value. There are many different ways to calculate a hash value. The hashing logic of an object resides in the `GetHashCode` implementation.

Hashes are nice because you get the same value every time, so you can use the hash values for lookups. If, for instance, you have an array of all possible hash values, you can look them up with an array index. But such an array would take about 16 gigabytes for each dictionary created because every `int` occupies four bytes and can have about four billion possible values.

Dictionaries allocate a much smaller array and rely on the even distribution of hash values. Instead of looking up the hash value, they look up "hash value mod array length." Let's say that a dictionary with integer keys allocates an array of six items to keep an index for them and the `GetHashCode()` method for an integer would just return its value. That means our formula to find out where an item would map to would simply be `value % 6`, since array indices start at zero. An array of numbers from 1 to 6 would be distributed as shown in figure 2.7.

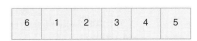

Figure 2.7 The distribution of items in a dictionary

What happens when we have more than the capacity of the dictionary? There will be overlaps, for sure, so dictionaries keep the overlapping items in a dynamically growing list. If we store items with keys from 1 to 7, the array would look like that in figure 2.8.

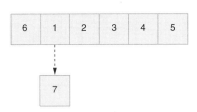

Figure 2.8 Storage of overlapping items in a dictionary

Why am I talking about this stuff? Because key lookup performance of a dictionary is O(1), normally, but lookup overhead of a linked list is O(N). That means that as the number of overlaps increases, lookup performance will slow down. If you had a `GetHashCode` function that always returned 4, for instance:[2]

```
public override int GetHashCode() {
    return 4; // chosen by fair dice roll
}
```

That means the internal structure of the dictionary would resemble figure 2.9 when you add items to it.

A dictionary is no better than a linked list if you have bad hash values. It can even have worse performance due to the extra plumbing the dictionary

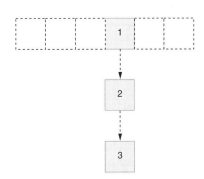

Figure 2.9 A dictionary when you screw up your `GetHashCode()`

---

[2] Inspired by this excellent xkcd cartoon about random numbers: https://xkcd.com/221.

uses to juggle these items. That brings us to the most important point: your `GetHashCode` function needs to be as unique as possible. If you're having many overlaps, your dictionaries will suffer, a suffering dictionary will make your application suffer, and a suffering application will make an entire company suffer. In the end, you will suffer. For want of a nail, a nation was lost.

Sometimes, you have to combine values of multiple properties in a class to calculate a unique hash value. For instance, repository names are unique per user on GitHub. That means any user can have a repository with the same name and the repository name itself isn't enough to make it unique. Suppose you use the name only: it would cause more collisions. That means you have to combine hash values. Similarly, if our website has unique values per topic, we would have the same problem.

To combine hash values efficiently, you have to know their ranges and deal with their bitwise representation. If you simply use an operator like addition or simple OR/XOR operations, you might still end up with many more collisions than you anticipated. You'd have to involve bit shifts, too. A proper `GetHashCode` function would use bitwise operations to get a good spread over the full 32 bits of an integer.

The code for such an operation might look like a hacking scene from a cheesy hacker movie. It's cryptic and hard to understand even for someone who is familiar with the concept. We're basically rotating one of the 32-bit integers by 16 bits so its lowest bytes are moved toward the middle and XORing ("^") that value together with the other 32-bit integer, hence lowering the chances of collisions a lot. It looks like this—scary:

```
public override int GetHashCode() {
    return (int)(((TopicId & 0xFFFF)<< 16)
        ^ (TopicId & 0xFFFF0000 >> 16)
        ^ PostId);
}
```

Luckily, with the advent of .NET Core and .NET 5, combining hash values in a way that gives the least collisions has been abstracted away behind `HashCode` class. To combine two values, all you have to do is this:

```
public override int GetHashCode() {
    return HashCode.Combine(TopicId, PostId);
}
```

Hash codes are used not only in dictionary keys, but also in other data structures like sets. Since it's far easier to write a proper `GetHashCode` with helper functions, you have no excuse to skip it. Keep an eye on it.

When should you not use `Dictionary`? If you only need to go over key-value pairs sequentially, a dictionary offers no benefits. It can, in fact, harm performance. Consider using a `List<KeyValuePair<K,V>>` instead, so you'll avoid unnecessary overhead.

2.2.7 *HashSet*

A set is like an array or a list except that it can only contain unique values. Its advantage over arrays or lists is that it has O(1) lookup performance like dictionary keys, thanks to the hash-based maps we just looked into. That means that if you need to perform a lot of checks to see if a given array or list contains an item, using a set might be faster. It's called `HashSet` in .NET, and it's free.

Because `HashSet` is fast for lookups and insertions, it's also suitable for intersection and union operations. It even comes with methods that provide the functionality. To get the benefits, you need to pay attention to your `GetHashCode()` implementations again.

2.2.8 *Stack*

Stacks are LIFO (Last In First Out) queues. They are useful when you want to save state and restore it in the reverse order that it's been saved. When you visit a Department of Motor Vehicles (DMV) office in real life, you sometimes need to use a stack. You first approach counter 5, and the employee at the counter checks your documents and sees that you're missing a payment, so they send you to counter 13. The employee at counter 13 sees that you're missing a photo in your documents and sends you to another counter, this time counter 47, to get your photo taken. Then you have to retrace your steps to counter 13, where you take the payment receipt and go back to counter 5 to get your driver's license. The list of counters and how you process them in order (LIFO) is a stack-like operation, and they are usually more efficient than the DMV.

A stack can be represented with an array. What's different is where you put the new items and where you read the next item from. Had we built a stack by adding numbers in ascending order, it'd look like figure 2.10.

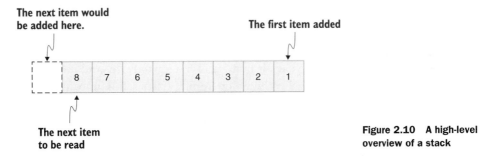

The next item would be added here.

The first item added

The next item to be read

Figure 2.10 A high-level overview of a stack

Adding to a stack is usually called *pushing*, and reading the next value from a stack is called *popping*. Stacks are useful for backtracking your steps. You might already be familiar with the *call stack* because it shows you not only where an exception occurred, but also which execution path it followed. Functions know where to return after they are done executing by using a stack. Before calling a function, the return address is added to the stack. When the function wants to return to its caller, the last address pushed onto the stack is read, and the CPU continues execution at that address.

2.2.9   *Call stack*

A *call stack* is the data structure where functions store the return addresses so the called functions know where to return to when they are done executing. There is one call stack per *thread*.

Every application runs in one or more separate processes. Processes allow memory and resource isolation. Every process has one or more threads. A thread is the unit of execution. All threads run parallel to each other on an operating system, hence the term *multithreading*. Even though you might only have a four-core CPU, the operating system can run thousands of threads in parallel. This can happen because most threads are waiting for something to complete most of the time, so it's possible to fill their slot with some other thread and have a sense of all threads running in parallel. That makes multitasking possible even on a single CPU.

There was a time when a process was both the container for application resources and the unit of execution in older UNIX systems. Although the approach was simple and elegant, it caused problems like *zombie processes*. Threads are more lightweight and have no such problem because they are bound to the execution's lifetime.

Every thread has its own call stack: a fixed amount of memory. By tradition, a stack grows from top to bottom in the process memory space, *top* meaning the end of the memory space and *bottom* meaning our famous null pointer: address zero. Pushing an item onto the call stack means putting the item there and decrementing the *stack pointer*.

Like every good thing, a stack has an end. It has a fixed size, so when it grows beyond that size, the CPU raises a `StackOverflowException`, something you'll encounter in your career whenever you accidentally call a function from itself. The stack is quite large, so you don't usually worry about hitting the limit in a normal case.

A call stack doesn't only hold return addresses, but also function parameters and local variables. Because local variables occupy so little memory, it's very efficient to use stacks for them as it doesn't require extra steps of memory management like allocation and deallocation. The stack is fast, but it has a fixed size, and it has the same lifetime as the function using it. When you return from a function, the stack space is given back. That's why it's only ideal to store a small amount of local data in it. Consequently, managed runtimes like C# or Java don't store class data in the stack and just store their references instead.

That's another reason why value types can have better performance over reference types in certain cases. Value types only exist on the stack when locally declared, although they are passed around with copying.

2.3   *What's the hype on types?*

Programmers take data types for granted. Some even argue that programmers are faster in *dynamically typed* languages like JavaScript or Python because they don't have to deal with intricate details like deciding the type of each variable.

NOTE *Dynamically typed* means that data types of variables or class members in a programming language can change during run time. You can assign a string to a variable and then assign an integer to the same variable in JavaScript because it's a dynamically typed language. A statically typed language like C# or Swift wouldn't allow that. We'll go into the details about these later.

Yes, specifying types for every variable, every parameter, and every member in the code is a chore, but you need to adopt a holistic approach to being faster. Being fast isn't solely about writing code, but about maintaining it, too. There could be a few cases when you may not really need to worry about maintenance because you just got fired and you couldn't care less. Apart from that, software development is a marathon, not a sprint.

Failing early is one of the best practices in development. Data types are one of the earliest defenses against development friction in coding. Types let you fail early and fix your mistakes before they become a burden. Aside from the obvious benefit of not confusing a string with an integer accidentally, you can make types work for you in other ways.

2.3.1 *Being strong on the type*

Most programming languages have types. Even the simplest programming languages like BASIC had types: strings and integers. Some of its dialects even had real numbers. There are a few languages called *typeless* like Tcl, REXX, Forth, and so forth. Those languages only operate on a single type: usually a string or an integer. Not having to think about types makes programming convenient, but it makes written programs slower and more prone to bugs.

Types are basically free checks for correctness, so understanding the underlying type system can help you tremendously in becoming a productive programmer. How programming languages implement types is strongly correlated with whether they are interpreted or compiled:

- *Interpreted programming languages* like Python or JavaScript let you run code in a text file immediately without the need for a compilation step. Because of their immediate nature, variables tend to have flexible types: you can assign a string to a previously integer variable, and you can even add strings and numbers together. These are usually called *dynamically typed languages* because of how they implement types. You can write code much faster in interpreted languages because you don't really need to declare types.

- *Compiled programming languages* tend to be stricter. How strict they are depends on how much pain the language designer wants to inflict on you. For example, the Rust language can be considered the *German engineering* of programming languages: extremely strict, perfectionist, and therefore error-free. The C language can also be considered German engineering, but more like a Volkswagen: it lets you break the rules and pay the price later. Both languages are statically typed. Once a variable is declared, its type cannot change, but Rust is called *strongly typed* like C#, while C is considered *weakly typed*.

Strongly typed and *weakly typed* mean how relaxed a language is in terms of assigning different types of variables to each other. In that sense, C is more relaxed: you can assign a pointer to an integer or vice versa without issues. On the other hand, C# is stricter: pointers/references and integers are incompatible types. Table 2.2 shows how various programming languages fall into these categories.

Table 2.2   Flavors of type strictness in programming languages

	Statically typed Variable type *cannot* change in runtime.	**Dynamically typed** Variable type *can* change in runtime.
Strongly typed Different types *cannot* be substituted for each other.	C#, Java, Rust, Swift, Kotlin, TypeScript, C++	Python, Ruby, Lisp
Weakly typed Different types *can* be substituted for each other.	Visual Basic, C	JavaScript, VBScript

Strict programming languages can be frustrating. Languages like Rust can even make you question life and why we exist in the universe. Declaring types and converting them explicitly when needed may look like a lot of bureaucracy. You don't need to declare types of every variable, argument, and member in JavaScript, for example. Why do we burden ourselves with explicit types if many programming languages can work without them?

The answer is simple: types can help us write code that is safer, faster, and easier to maintain. We can reclaim the time we lost while declaring types of variables, annotating our classes with the time we gained by having to debug fewer bugs, and having to solve fewer issues with performance.

Apart from the obvious benefits of types, they have some subtle benefits too. Let's go over them.

2.3.2   *Proof of validity*

Proof of validity is one of the less-known benefits of having predefined types. Suppose that you're developing a microblogging platform that only allows a certain number of characters in every post, and in return, you're not judged for being too lazy to write something longer than a sentence. In this hypothetical microblogging platform, you can mention other users in a post with the @ prefix and mention other posts with the # prefix followed by the post's identifier. You can even retrieve a post by typing its identifier in the search box. If you type in a username with the @ prefix in the search box, that user's profile will appear.

User input brings a new set of problems with validation. What happens if a user provides letters after the # prefix? What if they input a longer number than is allowed? It might seem like those scenarios work themselves out, but usually, your app crashes because somewhere in the code path, something that doesn't expect an invalid input will throw an exception. It's the worst possible experience for the user: they don't know what's gone wrong, and they don't even know what to do next. It can even become a security problem if you display that given input without sanitizing it.

Data validation doesn't provide a proof of validity throughout the code. You can validate the input in the client, but somebody, a third-party app, for example, can send a request without validation. You can validate the code that handles web requests, but another app of yours, such as your API code, can call your service code without necessary validation. Similarly, your database code can receive requests from multiple sources, like the service layer and a maintenance task, so you need to make sure that you're inserting the right records in the database. Figure 2.11 depicts at which points an application may need to validate input.

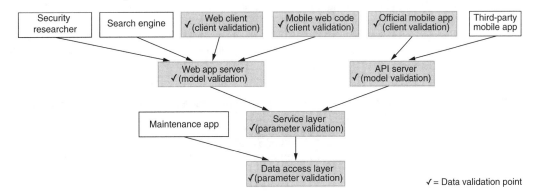

Figure 2.11 Unvalidated data sources and places where you need to validate data repetitively

That might eventually make you validate the input at multiple places around the code, and you need to make sure that you're consistent in validation, too. You don't want to end up with a post with an identifier of -1 or a user profile named ' OR 1=1-- (which is a basic SQL injection attack that we will examine in the chapter about security).

Types can carry over proof of validity. Instead of passing integers for blog post identifiers or strings for usernames, you can have classes or structs that validate their input on construction, which makes it impossible for them to contain an invalid value. It is simple, yet powerful. Any function that receives a post identifier as a parameter asks for a `PostId` class instead of an integer. This allows you to carry over proof of validity after the first validation in the constructor. If it's an integer, it needs to be validated; if it's a `PostId`, it has already been validated. There's no need to check its contents, because there is no way to create it without validation, as you can see in the following snippet. The only way to construct a `PostId` in the code snippet is to call its constructor, which validates its value and throws an exception if it fails. That means it's impossible to have an invalid `PostId` instance:

```
public class PostId
{
    public int Value { get; private set; }          ⊲──┐  Our value can't be changed
    public PostId(int id) {                             │  by external code.
        if (id <= 0) {
            throw new ArgumentOutOfRangeException(nameof(id));
        }
        Value = id;
    }
}
```

Constructor is the only way to create this object.

The style of code examples

Placement of curly braces is the second-most-debated topic in programming that hasn't been settled by consensus yet, right after tabs versus spaces. I prefer Allman style for most C-like languages, especially C# and Swift. In Allman style, every curly brace character resides on its own line. Swift officially recommends using 1TBS (One True Brace Style), aka improved K&R style, where an opening brace is on the same line with the declaration. People, however, still feel the need to leave extra blank lines after every block declaration because 1TBS is too cramped. When you add blank lines, it effectively becomes Allman style, but people can't bring themselves to admit it.

Allman style is the default for C# where every brace is on its own line. I find it much more readable than 1TBS or K&R. Java uses 1TBS, by the way.

I've had to format the code in 1TBS style because of the publisher's typesetting restrictions, but I suggest you consider Allman style when using C# not only because it's more readable, but because it's the most common style for C#.

However, when you decide to go that path, it's not as easy as the example I've shown. For example, comparing two different `PostId` objects with the same value wouldn't work as you expected because, by default, comparison only compares references, not the contents of the classes (I'll be talking about references versus values later in this chapter). You have to add a whole scaffolding around it to make it work without issues. Here is a quick checklist:

- You have to at least implement an override for the `Equals` method because some framework functions and some libraries can depend on it to compare two instances of your class.
- If you plan on comparing values yourself using equality operators (`==` and `!=`), you have to implement their *operator overloads* in the class.
- If you plan to use the class in a `Dictionary<K,V>` as a key, you have to override the `GetHashCode` method. I will explain how hashing and dictionaries are related later in this chapter.
- String formatting functions such as `String.Format` use the `ToString` method to get a string representation of the class suitable for printing.

> **Don't use operator overloading unless necessary**
>
> Operator overloading is a way to change how operators like ==, !=, +, and - in a programming language behave. Developers who learn about operator overloading might go overboard and tend to create their own language with weird behavior for irrelevant classes, like overloading a += operator to insert a record to a table with a syntax such as db += record. It's almost impossible to understand the intent of such code. It's also impossible to discover unless you read the documentation. There is no IDE function to discover which operators a type is overloading. Don't be the person who uses operator overloading needlessly. Even you will forget what it does and will beat yourself up over this. Use operator overloading only to provide alternatives to equality and typecasting operators, and only when needed. Don't waste time implementing them if they won't be needed.
>
> We'll be using operator overloading in some of the examples because it's required to make classes semantically equivalent to the values they represent. You'd expect a class to work with an == operator the same way the number it represents would.

Listing 2.2 shows a `PostId` class with all the necessary plumbing to make sure it works in all equality scenarios. We overrode `ToString()` so our class becomes compatible with string formatting and easier to inspect its value while debugging. We overrode `GetHashCode()` so it returns `Value` directly because the value itself can fit perfectly into an `int`. We overrode the `Equals()` method so equality checks in collections of this class work correctly in case we need unique values or we'd like to search against this value. We finally overrode `==` and `!=` operators so we can directly compare to `PostId` values without accessing their values.

NOTE An immutable class solely to represent values is called a *value type* in the streets. It's good to know colloquial names, but don't focus on them. Focus on their utility.

Listing 2.2 Full implementation of a class encompassing a value

```
public class PostId
{
    public int Value { get; private set; }
    public PostId(int id) {
        if (id <= 0) {
            throw new ArgumentOutOfRangeException(nameof(id));
        }
        Value = id;
    }
    public override string ToString() => Value.ToString();      System.Object
    public override int GetHashCode() => Value;                 overrides, using
    public override bool Equals(object obj) {                   arrow syntax notation
        return obj is PostId other && other.Value == Value;
    }
                                                                Overloading code for
    public static bool operator ==(PostId a, PostId b) {   ◁───  equality operators
        return a.Equals(b);
```

```
    }
    public static bool operator !=(PostId a, PostId b) {
        return !a.Equals(b);
    }
}
```

◁——— **Overloading code for equality operators**

The arrow syntax

The arrow syntax was introduced to C# in 6.0 and is equivalent to normal method syntax with a single return statement. You can opt for arrow syntax if the code is easier to read that way. It is not right or wrong to use arrow syntax—readable code is right, and unreadable code is wrong.

The method

```
public int Sum(int a, int b) {
    return a + b;
}
```

is equivalent to

```
public int Sum(int a, int b) => a + b;
```

It's not usually needed, but in case your class needs to be in a container that is sorted or compared, you have to implement these two additional features:

- You need to provide ordering by implementing IComparable<T> because equality itself isn't sufficient to determine the order. We didn't use it in listing 2.1 because identifiers are not ranked.

- If you plan on comparing values using less-than or greater-than operators, you have to implement related operator overloads (<, >, <=, >=) for them, too.

This can look like a lot of work when you can simply pass an integer around, but it pays off in large projects, especially when you are working in a team. You'll see more of the benefits in the following sections.

You don't always need to create new types to leverage a validation context. You can use inheritance to create base types that contain certain primitive types with common rules. For example, you can have a generic identifier type that can be adapted to other classes. You can simply rename the PostId class in listing 2.1 to DbId and derive all types from it.

Whenever you need a new type like PostId, UserId, or TopicId, you can inherit it from DbId and extend it as needed. Here we can have fully functional varieties of the same type of identifier to distinguish them better from other types. You can also add more code in the classes to specialize them in their own way:

```
public class PostId: DbId {
    public PostId(int id): base(id) { }
}
public class TopicId: DbId {
```

◁——— **We use inheritance to create new flavors of the same type.**

```
    public TopicId(int id) : base(id) { }
}
public class UserId: DbId {
    public UserId(int id): base(id) { }
}
```

We use inheritance to create
new flavors of the same type.

Having separate types for your design elements makes it easier to semantically catego-rize different uses of our `DbId` type if you're using them together and frequently. It also protects you from passing an incorrect type of an identifier to a function.

> **NOTE** Whenever you see a solution to a problem, make sure that you also know when not to use it. This reusability scenario is no exception. You may not need such elaborate work for your simple prototype—you may not even need a custom class. When you see that you're passing the same kind of value to func-tions frequently and you seem to be forgetting whether it needed validation, it might be beneficial to encompass it in a class and pass it around instead.

Custom data types are powerful because they can explain your design better than primitive types and can help you avoid repetitive validation, and therefore, bugs. They can be worth the hassle to implement. Moreover, the framework you're using might already be providing the types you need.

2.3.3 *Don't framework hard, framework smart*

.NET, like many other frameworks, comes with a set of useful abstractions for certain data types that are usually unknown or ignored. Custom text-based values like URLs, IP addresses, filenames, or even dates are stored as strings. We'll look at some of those ready-made types and how we can leverage them.

You may already know about .NET-based classes for those data types, but you might still prefer to use a string because it's simpler to handle. The issue with strings is that they lack proof of validation; your functions don't know if a given string is already vali-dated or not, causing either inadvertent failures or unnecessary revalidation code and thus slowing you down. Using a ready-made class for a specific data type is a better choice in those cases.

When the only tool you have is a hammer, every problem looks like a nail. The same applies to strings. Strings are great generalized storage for content, and they are so easy to parse, split, merge, or play around with. They are so tempting. But this con-fidence in strings makes you inclined to reinvent the wheel occasionally. When you start handling things with a string, you tend to do everything with string-processing functions even though that can be entirely unnecessary.

Consider this example: you're tasked to write a lookup service for a URL-shortening company called Supercalifragilisticexpialidocious, which is in financial trouble for unknown reasons, and you're Obi-wan, their only hope. Their service works like this:

1. User provides a long URL, such as

    ```
    https://llanfair.com/pwllgw/yngyll/gogerych/wyrndrobwll/llan/tysilio/
    ➥ gogo/goch.html
    ```

2. The service creates a short code for the URL and a new short URL, such as

   https://su.pa/mK61

3. Whenever a user navigates to the shortened URL from their web browser, they get redirected to the address in the long URL they provided.

The function you need to implement must extract the short code from a shortened URL. A string-based approach would look like this:

```
public string GetShortCode(string url)
{
    const string urlValidationPattern =
        @"^https?://([\w-]+.)+[\w-]+(/[\w- ./?%&=])?$";
    if (!Regex.IsMatch(url, urlValidationPattern)) {
        return null;
    }
    // take the part after the last slash
    string[] parts = url.Split('/');
    string lastPart = parts[^1];
    return lastPart;
}
```

Regular expression. It's used in string parsing and occult invocation rituals.

Not a valid URL

This is a new syntax introduced in C# 8.0 that refers to the second-last item in a range.

This code might look okay at first, but it already contains bugs, based on our hypothetical specification. The validation pattern for a URL is incomplete and allows invalid URLs. It doesn't take the possibility of multiple slashes in the URL path into account. It even unnecessarily creates an array of strings just to get the final portion of the URL.

> **NOTE** A bug can only exist against a specification. If you don't have any specification, you cannot claim anything is a bug. This lets companies avoid PR scandals by dismissing bugs with, "Oh, that's a feature." You don't need a written document for a specification either—it can exist only in your mind as long as you can answer the question, "Is this how this feature is supposed to work?"

More importantly, the logic isn't apparent from the code. A better approach might leverage the Uri class from the .NET Framework and look like this example:

```
public string GetShortCode(Uri url)
{
    string path = url.AbsolutePath;
    if (path.Contains('/')) {
        return null;
    }
    return path;
}
```

It's clear what we're expecting.

Look, ma, no regular expressions!

Not a valid URL

This time, we don't deal with string parsing ourselves. It's been handled already by the time our function gets called. Our code is more descriptive and is easier to write only because we just wrote Uri instead of string. Because parsing and validation happen earlier in the code, it becomes easier to debug, too. This book has a whole chapter about debugging, but the best debugging is not having to debug in the first place.

In addition to primitive data types like int, string, float, and so forth, .NET provides many other useful data types to use in our code. IPAddress is a better alternative to string for storing IP addresses, not just because it has validation in it, but also because it supports IPv6 that is in use today. It's unbelievable, I know. The class also has shortcut members for defining a local address:

```
var testAddress = IPAddress.Loopback;
```

This way, you avoid writing 127.0.0.1 whenever you need a loopback address, which makes you faster. If you make a mistake with the IP address, you catch it earlier than you would with a string.

Another such type is TimeSpan. It represents a duration, as the name implies. Durations are used almost everywhere in software projects, especially in caching or expiration mechanics. We tend to define durations as compile-time constants. The worst possible way is this:

```
const int cacheExpiration = 5; // minutes
```

It's not immediately clear that the unit of cache expiration is minutes. It's impossible to know the unit without looking at the source code. It's a better idea to incorporate it in the name at least, so your colleagues, or even yourself in the future, will know its type without looking at the source code:

```
public const int cacheExpirationMinutes = 5;
```

It's better this way, but when you need to use the same duration for a different function that receives a different unit, you'll have to convert it:

```
cache.Add(key, value, cacheExpirationMinutes * 60);
```

This is extra work. You have to remember to do this. It's prone to errors, too. You can mistype 60 and have a wrong value in the end and maybe spend days debugging it or try to optimize performance needlessly because of such a simple miscalculation.

TimeSpan is amazing in that sense. There is no reason for you to represent any duration in anything other than in TimeSpan, even when the function you're calling for doesn't accept TimeSpan as a parameter:

```
public static readonly TimeSpan cacheExpiration = TimeSpan.FromMinutes(5);
```

Look at that beauty! You already know it's a duration, and it's declared. What's better is that you don't have to know its unit anywhere else. For any function that receives a TimeSpan, you just pass it along. If a function receives a specific unit, say, minutes, as an integer, you can call it like this instead:

```
cache.Add(key, value, cacheExpiration.TotalMinutes);
```

And it gets converted to minutes. Brilliant!

Many more types are similarly useful, like DateTimeOffset, which represents a specific date and time like DateTime but includes the time zone information, so you don't lose data when suddenly your computer's or server's time zone information changes. In fact, you should always try to use DateTimeOffset over DateTime because it's also easily convertible to/from DateTime. You can even use arithmetic operators with TimeSpan and DateTimeOffset, thanks to operator overloading:

```
var now = DateTimeOffset.Now;
var birthDate =
    new DateTimeOffset(1976, 12, 21, 02, 00, 00,
        TimeSpan.FromHours(2));
TimeSpan timePassed = now - birthDate;
Console.WriteLine($"It's been {timePassed.TotalSeconds} seconds since I was
➥ born!");
```

> **NOTE**   Date and time handling is such a delicate concept and is easy to break, especially in global projects. That's why there are separate third-party libraries that cover the missing use cases, such as Noda Time by Jon Skeet.

.NET is like that gold pile that Uncle Scrooge jumps into and swims in. It's full of great utilities that make our lives easier. Learning about them might seem wasteful or boring, but it's much faster than trying to use strings or come up with our own makeshift implementations.

2.3.4   *Types over typos*

Writing code comments can be a chore, and I argue against doing it later in the book, although you should wait until you read that part before throwing your keyboard at me. Even without the code comments, your code doesn't have to lack descriptiveness. Types can help you to explain your code.

Consider that you encounter this snippet in the vast dungeons of your project's code base:

```
public int Move(int from, int to) {
    // ... quite a code here
    return 0;
}
```

What is this function doing? What is it moving? What kind of parameters is it taking? What kind of result is it returning? The answers to these questions are vague without types. You can try to understand the code or to look up the encompassing class, but that would take time. Your experience could be much better had it been named better:

```
public int MoveContents(int fromTopicId, int toTopicId) {
    // ... quite a code here
    return 0;
}
```

It's much better now, but you still have no way of knowing what kind of result it is returning. Is it an error code, is it the number of items moved, or is it the new topic identifier resulting from conflicts in the move operation? How can you convey this information without relying on code comments? With types, of course. Consider this code snippet instead:

```
public MoveResult MoveContents(int fromTopicId, int toTopicId) {
    // ... still quite a code here
    return MoveResult.Success;
}
```

It's slightly clearer. It doesn't add much because we already knew that the int was the result of the move function, but there is a difference—we now can explore what's in the MoveResult type to see what it is actually doing by simply pressing a key, F12 on Visual Studio and VS Code:

```
public enum MoveResult
{
    Success,
    Unauthorized,
    AlreadyMoved
}
```

We've got a much better idea now. Not only do the changes improve the understanding of the method's API, but they also improve the actual code itself in the function because instead of some constants or, worse, hardcoded integer values, you see a clear MoveResult.Success. Unlike constants in a class, enums constrain the possible values that can be passed around, and they come with their own type name, so you have a better chance of describing the intent.

Because the function receives integers as parameters, it needs to incorporate some validation since it's a publicly facing API. You can tell that it might even be needed in internal or private code because of how validation became pervasive. This would look better if there was validation logic in the original code:

```
public MoveResult MoveContents(TopicId from, TopicId to) {
    // ... still quite a code here
    return MoveResult.Success;
}
```

As you can see, types can work for you by moving code to its relevant place and making it easier to understand. Since the compiler checks whether you wrote a type's name correctly, they prevent you from including typos, too.

2.3.5 *To be nullable or non-nullable*

In the long run, all developers will encounter NullReferenceException. Although Tony Hoare, colloquially known as the inventor of *null*, calls creating it in the first place "the billion dollar mistake," it's not all hopeless.

The brief story of *null*

Null, or *nil* in some languages, is a value that symbolizes the absence of a value or the apathy of the programmer. It's usually synonymous with the value zero. Since a memory address with the value zero means an invalid region in memory, modern CPUs can catch this invalid access and convert it to a friendly exception message. In the medieval era of computing when null accesses weren't checked, computers used to freeze, get corrupted, or just get rebooted.

The problem isn't exactly null itself—we need to describe a missing value in our code anyway. It exists for a purpose. The problem is that all variables can be assigned null by default and never get checked if they are assigned to a null value unexpectedly, causing them to be assigned to null at the most unexpected places and to crash in the end.

JavaScript, as if it doesn't have enough issues with its type system, has two different nulls: null and undefined. Null symbolizes missing value, while undefined symbolizes missing assignment. I know, it hurts. You must accept JavaScript as it is.

C# 8.0 introduced a new feature called *nullable references*. It's a seemingly simple change: references can't be assigned null by default. That's it. Nullable references are probably the most significant change in the C# language since the introduction of generics. Every other feature about nullable references is related to this core change.

The confusing part about that name is that references were already nullable before C# 8.0. It should have been called *non-nullable references* to give programmers a better idea of what it means. I understand the logic in naming it because of how they introduced *nullable value types*, but many developers might feel it doesn't bring anything new to the table.

When all references were nullable, all functions that accepted references could receive two distinct values: a valid reference and null. Any function that didn't expect a null value would cause a crash when it tried to reference the value.

Making references non-nullable by default changed this. Functions can never receive null anymore as long as calling code also exists in the same project. Consider the following code:

```
public MoveResult MoveContents(TopicId from, TopicId to) {
    if (from is null) {
        throw new ArgumentNullException(nameof(from));
    }
    if (to is null) {
        throw new ArgumentNullException(nameof(to));
    }
    // .. actual code here
    return MoveResult.Success;
}
```

HINT   The is null syntax in the preceding code might look alien to you. I recently started using it over x == null after I read about it in a Twitter discussion by senior Microsoft engineers. Apparently, the is operator cannot be overloaded, so it's always guaranteed to return the correct result. You can similarly use `x is object` syntax instead of `x != null`. Non-nullable checks eliminate the need for null checks in your code, but external code can still call your code with nulls, for instance, if you're publishing a library. In that case, you might still need to perform null checks explicitly.

Why do we check for nulls if the code will crash either way?

If you don't check your arguments for null at the beginning of your function, the function continues to run until it references that null value. That means it can halt in an undesired state, like a half-written record, or may not halt but perform an invalid operation without you noticing. Failing as early as possible and avoiding unhandled states are always good ideas. Crashing isn't something you need to be afraid of: it's an opportunity for you to find bugs.

If you fail early, your stack trace for the exception will look cleaner. You'll know exactly which parameter caused the function to fail.

Not all null values need to be checked. You might be receiving an optional value, and null is the simplest way to express that intent. The chapter about error handling will discuss this in more detail.

You can enable null checks project-wide or per file. I always recommend enabling it project-wide for new projects because it encourages you to write correct code from the beginning, so you spend less time fixing your bugs. To enable it per file, you add a line saying `#nullable enable` at the beginning of the file.

> **PRO-TIP** Always end an enable/disable compiler directive with a `restore` counterpart rather than the opposite of enable/disable. This way you will not affect the global setting. This helps when you're fiddling with global project settings. You might miss valuable feedback otherwise.

With nullable checks enabled, your code looks like this:

```
#nullable enable
public MoveResult MoveContents (TopicId from, TopicId to) {
    // .. actual code here
    return MoveResult.Success;
}
#nullable restore
```

When you try to call `MoveResult` function with a null value or a nullable value, you will get a compiler warning right away instead of an error at a random time in production. You'll have identified the error even before trying the code out. You can choose to ignore the warnings and continue, but you never should.

Nullable references can be annoying at first. You cannot easily declare classes like you used to. Consider that we are developing a registration web page for a conference that receives the name and email of the recipient and records the results to the DB. Our class has a campaign source field that is a free-form string passed from the advertising network. If the string has no value, it means the page is accessed directly, not referred from an ad. Let's have a class like this:

```
#nullable enable
class ConferenceRegistration
{
    public string CampaignSource { get; set; }
    public string FirstName { get; set; }
    public string? MiddleName { get; set; }        ⊲——— Middle name is optional.
    public string LastName { get; set; }
    public string Email { get; set; }
    public DateTimeOffset CreatedOn { get; set; }  ⊲—┐ Having record creation
}                                                     │ dates in the database is
#nullable restore                                     │ good for auditing.
```

When you try to compile the class in the snippet, you'll receive a compiler warning for all the strings declared non-nullable, that is, all the properties except `MiddleName` and `CreatedOn`:

```
Non-nullable property '…' is uninitialized. Consider declaring the property
➥ as nullable.
```

The middle name is optional, so we declared `MiddleName` as nullable. That's why it didn't get a compiler error.

> **NOTE**   Never use empty strings to signify optionality. Use null for that purpose. It's impossible for your colleagues to understand your intention with an empty string. Are empty strings valid values, or do they indicate optionality? It's impossible to tell. Null is unambiguous.

About empty strings

Throughout your career, you will have to declare empty strings for purposes other than optionality. When you need to do that, avoid using the notation `""` to signify empty strings. Because of the many different environments in which code can be viewed, like your text editor, test runner output window, or your continuous integration web page, it's easy to confuse it with a string with a single space in it (`" "`). Explicitly declare empty strings with `String.Empty` to leverage existing types. You can also use it with the lowercase class name `string.Empty`, whichever your code conventions will let you do. Let the code convey your intent.

`CreatedOn`, on the other hand, is a struct, so the compiler just fills it with zeros. That's why it doesn't throw a compiler error, but still, it can be something we want to avoid.

A developer's first reaction to fix a compiler error is to apply whatever suggestion the compiler comes up with. In the previous example, that would be to declare the properties as nullable, but that changes our understanding. We suddenly make the properties for first name and last name optional too, which we shouldn't be doing. But we need to think about how we want to apply the optionality semantics.

If you want a property not to be null, you need to ask yourself several questions. First, "Does the property have a default value?"

If it does, you can assign the default value during the construction. That will give you a better idea about the behavior of the class when you're examining the code. If the field for campaign source has a default value, it can be expressed like this:

```
public string CampaignSource { get; set; } = "organic";
public DateTimeOffset CreatedOn { get; set; } = DateTimeOffset.Now;
```

That will remove the compiler warning, and it will convey your intent to whoever reads your code.

First name and last name cannot be optional, though, and they cannot have default values. No, don't try to put "John" and "Doe" for default values. Ask yourself this: "How do I want this class to be initialized?"

If you want your class to be initialized with a custom constructor so it won't allow invalid values *ever*, you can assign the property values in the constructor and declare them as `private set`, so they are impossible to change. We will discuss this more in the sections about immutability. You can signify optionality in the constructor with an optional parameter with a default value of null, too, as shown next.

Listing 2.3 A sample immutable class

```
class ConferenceRegistration
{
    public string CampaignSource { get; private set; }
    public string FirstName { get; private set; }          All properties
    public string? MiddleName { get; private set; }        are private set.
    public string LastName { get; private set; }
    public string Email { get; private set; }
    public DateTimeOffset CreatedOn { get; private set; } = DateTime.Now;

    public ConferenceRegistration(
        string firstName,
        string? middleName,
        string lastName,
        string email,                          Signify optionality
        string? campaignSource = null) {       with null.
        FirstName = firstName;
        MiddleName = middleName;
        LastName = lastName;
        Email = email;
        CampaignSource = campaignSource ?? "organic";
    }
}
```

I can hear you whining, "But that's too much work." I agree. Creating an immutable class shouldn't be this hard. Luckily, the C# team has introduced a new construct called *record types* in C# 9.0 to make this much easier, but if you can't use C# 9.0, you have to make a decision: do you want fewer bugs, or do you want to be done with it as quickly as possible?

Record types to the rescue

C# 9.0 brought in record types, which makes creating immutable classes extremely easy. The class in listing 2.3 can simply be expressed with code like this:

```
public record ConferenceRegistration(
    string CampaignSource,
    string FirstName,
    string? MiddleName,
    string LastName,
    string Email,
    DateTimeOffset CreatedOn);
```

It will automatically scaffold properties with the same name as the arguments we specify in the parameter list, and it will make the properties immutable, so the record code will behave exactly like the class shown in listing 2.3. You can also add methods and additional constructors in the body of a record block like a regular class instead of ending the declaration with a semicolon. It's phenomenal. Such a timesaver.

That's a tough decision because we humans are quite terrible at estimating the cost of future events and usually work with only the near future. That's the reason I've been able to write this book now—I'm obeying the shelter-in-place order in San Francisco due to the COVID-19 pandemic, because humankind has failed to foresee the future costs of a small outbreak in Wuhan, China. We are terrible estimators. Let's accept this fact.

Consider this: You have the chance to eliminate a whole class of bugs caused by missing null checks and incorrect state by simply having this constructor, or you can go ahead and leave it as is and deal with the consequences for every bug filed: bug reports, issue trackers, talking it out with PM, triaging and fixing the relevant bug, only to encounter another bug of the same class until you decide, "Okay, that's enough, I'll do it like Sedat told me to." Which path do you want to choose?

As I said before, this requires some kind of intuition about how many bugs you anticipate in some part of the code. You shouldn't blindly apply suggestions. You should have a sense of the future *churn*, that is, the amount of change on a piece of code. The more the code changes in the future, the more prone it is to bugs.

But let's say you did all that, and decided, "Nah, that will work okay, it's not worth the trouble." You can still get some level of null safety with keeping nullable checks in place but initializing your fields beforehand like this:

```
class ConferenceRegistration
{
    public string CampaignSource { get; set; } = "organic";
    public string FirstName { get; set; } = null!;
    public string? MiddleName { get; set; }
    public string LastName { get; set; } = null!;
    public string Email { get; set; } = null!;
    public DateTimeOffset CreatedOn { get; set; }
}
```

Notice null! as a new construct.

The bang operator (!) tells the compiler precisely "I know what I'm doing": in this case, "I will make sure that I will initialize those properties right after I create this class. If I don't, I accept that nullability checks won't work for me at all." Basically, you still retain nullability assurances if you keep your promise of initializing those properties right away.

That's thin ice to cross because it may not be possible to bring everyone in your team onto the same page about this, and they might still initialize the properties later. If you think you can manage the risks, you can stick to this. It can even be inevitable for some libraries such as Entity Framework, which requires a default constructor and settable properties on objects.

Maybe<T> is dead, long live Nullable<T>!

Because nullable types in C# used to have no compiler support to enforce their correctness and a mistake would crash the entire program, they were historically seen as an inferior way of signifying optionality. Because of that, people implemented their own optional types, called either Maybe<T> or Option<T>, without the risk of causing null reference exceptions. C# 8.0 makes compiler safety checks for null values first-class, so the era of rolling your own optional type is officially over. The compiler can both check and optimize nullable types better than ad hoc implementations. You also get syntactic support from the language with operators and pattern matching. Long live Nullable<T>!

Nullability checks help you think about your intentions for the code you're writing. You will have a clearer idea whether that value is truly optional or whether it doesn't need to be optional at all. It will reduce bugs and make you a better developer.

2.3.6 *Better performance for free*

Performance shouldn't be your first concern when you're writing a prototype, but having a general understanding of performance characteristics of types, data structures, and algorithms can move you toward a faster path. You can write faster code without knowing it. Using the specific type for the job instead of more generic ones can help you behind the scenes.

Existing types can use more efficient storage *for free*. A valid IPv6 string, for instance, can be up to 65 characters. An IPv4 address is at least seven characters long.

That means a string-based storage would occupy between 14 and 130 bytes, and when included with object headers, that makes it between 30 and 160 bytes. IPAddress type, on the other hand, stores an IP address as a series of bytes and uses between 20 and 44 bytes. Figure 2.12 shows the memory layout difference between string-based storage and a more "native" data structure.

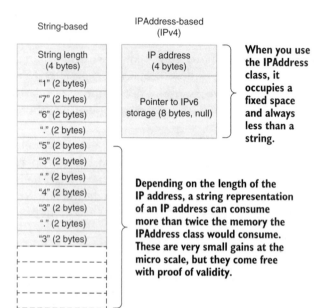

Figure 2.12   Storage differences of data types, excluding common object headers

It may not look like much, but remember, this comes for free. The longer the IP address gets, the more space savings you get. It also provides you proof of validation, so you can safely trust that the passed-along object holds a valid IP address throughout the code. Your code becomes easier to read because types also describe the intention behind the data.

On the other hand, we all know that there is no free lunch. What's the catch here? When should you not use it? Well, there is a small string-parsing overhead for the string to deconstruct it into bytes. Some code goes over the string to decide if it's an IPv4 or IPv6 address and parses it accordingly using some optimized code. On the other hand, because you'll have the string validated after parsing, it essentially removes the requirement of validation in the rest of your code, compensating for the small parsing overhead. Using the correct type from the get-go lets you avoid the overhead of trying to make sure the passed arguments are the correct type. Last but not least, preferring the correct type can also leverage value types in some cases where they're beneficial. We'll see more about the benefits of value types in the next section.

Performance and scalability aren't single-dimensional concepts. For example, optimizing data storage can actually lead to worse performance in some cases, as I'll explain in chapter 7. But with all the advantages of using the specific type for the job, using a specialized type for data is a no-brainer most of the time.

2.3.7 Reference types vs. value types

The distinction between reference types and value types is pretty much about how types are stored in memory. In simple terms, the contents of value types are stored in the call stack, whereas reference types are stored in *the heap*, and only a reference to their content is stored in the call stack instead. This is a simple example of how they look in code:

```
int result = 5;              ←┘  Primitive value type
var builder = new StringBuilder();     ←┘  Reference type
var date = new DateTime(1984, 10, 9);  ←───  All structs are value types.
string formula = "2 + 2 = ";  ←─┐
builder.Append(formula);          Primitive reference type
builder.Append(result);
builder.Append(date.ToString());       Outputs a mathematical
Console.WriteLine(builder.ToString());  ←┘  abomination
```

Java doesn't have value types except primitive ones like int. C# additionally lets you define your own value types. Knowing the difference between reference and value types can make you a more efficient programmer for free by making you use the correct type for the correct job. It's not hard to learn, either.

A *reference* is analogous to a managed *pointer*. A pointer is an address of memory. I usually imagine memory as an exceptionally long array of bytes, as figure 2.13 shows.

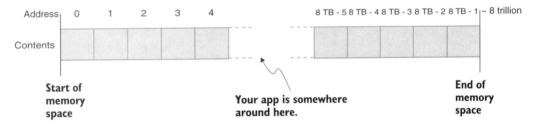

Figure 2.13 Memory layout of a 64-bit process that can address up to 8 TB

This isn't all of your RAM; this is just the memory layout of a single process. The contents of your physical RAM look much more complicated, but operating systems hide the fact that RAM is a mess by showing you a tidy, clean, contiguous area of memory for each process, which may not even exist on your RAM. That's why it's called *virtual memory*. As of 2020, nobody has close to 8 TB of RAM on their computers, yet you can access 8 TB of memory on a 64-bit operating system. I'm sure somebody in the future will be looking at this and laughing like I laugh at my old PC that had 1 MB of memory in the 1990s.

Why 8 TB? I thought 64-bit processors could address 16 exabytes!

They can. The reasons behind limiting user space are mostly practical. Creating virtual memory-mapping tables for a smaller memory range consumes fewer resources, and it's faster for the operating system. For example, switching between processes requires memory to be remapped in its entirety, and having a larger address space would make it slower. It will be possible to increase user space range in the future when 8 TB RAM becomes a common commodity, but until then, 8 TB is our horizon.

A pointer is basically a number that points to an address in memory. The advantage of using pointers instead of the actual data is to avoid unnecessary duplication, which can be quite expensive. We can just pass around gigabytes of data from function to function by simply passing around an address, aka a pointer. Otherwise, we would have to copy gigabytes of memory at every function call. We just copy a number instead.

Obviously, it doesn't make sense to use pointers for anything less than the size of the pointer itself. A 32-bit integer (int on C#) is just half the size of a pointer on a 64-bit system. Therefore, primitive types like int, long, bool, and byte are all considered value types. That means that instead of a pointer to their address, only their value is passed to functions.

A reference is synonymous with a pointer except that your access to its contents is managed by the .NET runtime. You can't know the value of a reference, either. This allows the garbage collector to move the memory pointed out by reference around as it needs, without you knowing it. You can also use pointers with C#, but that's only possible in an unsafe context.

Garbage collection

A programmer needs to track their allocation of memory and needs to free (deallocate) the allocated memory when they are done with it. Otherwise, your application's memory usage constantly increases, which is also known as a memory leak. Manually allocating and freeing memory is prone to bugs. A programmer might forget to free memory or, even worse, try to free already freed memory, which is the root of many security bugs.

One of the first proposed solutions to the problems with manual memory management was reference counting. It's a primitive form of garbage collection. Instead of leaving the initiative to free up memory to the programmer, the runtime would keep a secret counter for each allocated object. Every reference to the given object would increment the counter, and every time a variable referencing the object went out of scope, the counter would be decremented. Whenever the counter reached zero, that would mean there were no variables referencing the object, so it would be freed.

Reference counting works fine for many scenarios, but it has a couple of quirks: It's slow because every time a reference goes out of scope, it performs deallocation, which is usually less efficient than, say, freeing relevant blocks of memory together. It also creates a problem with cyclical references that requires extra work and diligence on the programmer's part to avoid.

Then, there's garbage collection, *mark and sweep garbage collection*, to be precise, since reference counting is a form of garbage collection, too. Garbage collection is a tradeoff between reference counting and manual memory management. With garbage collection, no separate reference counts are kept. Instead, a separate task goes over the entire object tree to find objects that are not referenced anymore and marks them as garbage. The garbage is kept for a while, and when it grows beyond a certain threshold, the garbage collector arrives and frees the unused memory in a single pass. That reduces the overhead of memory deallocation operations and memory fragmentation due to microdeallocations. Not keeping counters makes the code faster, too. The Rust programming language also introduced a novel memory management called *borrow checker* where the compiler can track exactly at which point an allocated memory is no longer needed. That means the memory allocation has zero extra cost in run time when you write it in Rust, but you pay the price by writing code in a specific way and getting lots of compiler errors until you figure out how things should be done.

C# allows complex value types called *structs*. A struct is remarkably similar to a class in definition, but unlike a class, it's passed by value everywhere. That means if you have a struct and you send it to a function, a copy of the struct gets created, and when that function passes it to another function, another copy will be created. *Structs are always copied.* Consider the following example.

Listing 2.4 Immutability example

```
struct Point
{
    public int X;
    public int Y;
    public override string ToString() => $"X:{X},Y:{Y}";
}

static void Main(string[] args) {
    var a = new Point() {
        X = 5,
        Y = 5,
    };
    var b = a;
    b.X = 100;
    b.Y = 200;
    Console.WriteLine(b);
    Console.WriteLine(a);
}
```

What do you think this program would write to console? When you assign a to b, the runtime creates a new copy of a. That means that when you modify b, you're modifying a new struct with a's values, not a itself. What if Point were a class? Then b would have the same reference as a, and changing the contents of a would mean changing b at the same time.

Value types exist because there are cases where they can be more efficient than reference types, in terms of both storage and performance. We have already discussed how a type with a size of a reference or less can be more efficiently passed by value. Reference types also incur a single level of indirection. Whenever you need to access the field of a reference type, the .NET runtime has to read the value of the reference first, then go to the address pointed out by the reference, and then read the actual value from there. For a value type, the runtime reads the value directly, making access faster.

Summary

- Computer science theory can be boring, but knowing some theory can make you a better developer.
- Types are normally known as boilerplate in strongly typed languages, but they can be used to write less code, too.
- .NET comes with better, more efficient data structures for certain data types that can easily make your code faster and more reliable.
- Using types can make your code more self-explanatory and therefore requires writing fewer comments.
- The nullable references feature introduced with C# 8.0 can make your code much more reliable and allow you to spend less time debugging your application.
- The difference between value types and reference types is significant, and knowing about it will make you a more efficient developer.
- Strings are more useful and more efficient if you know how their internals work.
- Arrays are fast and convenient, but they may not be the most suitable candidate for a publicly exposed API.
- Lists are great for growing lists, but arrays are more efficient if you don't intend to dynamically grow their contents.
- A linked list is a niche data structure, but knowing its characteristics can help you understand the tradeoffs of dictionaries.
- Dictionaries are great for fast key lookups, but their performance relies heavily on the correct implementation of GetHashCode().
- A list of unique values can be represented with a HashSet for awesome lookup performance.
- Stacks are great data structures for retracing your steps. The call stack is finite.
- Knowing how a call stack works also complements the performance implications of value and reference types.

Useful anti-patterns

This chapter covers

- Known bad practices that can be put to good use
- Anti-patterns that are, in fact, useful
- Identifying when to use a best practice versus its evil twin

Programming literature is full of best practices and design patterns. Some of them even seem indisputable and provoke people to give you the side-eye if you argue about them. They eventually turn into dogmas and are rarely questioned. Once in a while, someone writes a blog post about one, and if their article gets the approval of the Hacker News[1] community, it can be accepted as valid criticism and can open a door for new ideas. Otherwise, you can't even discuss them. If I had to send a single message to the world of programming, it would be to question all the things that are taught to you—their usefulness, their reason, their gain, and their cost.

Dogmas, immutable laws, create blind spots for us, and their size grows the longer we stick to them. Those blind spots can obscure some useful techniques that can even be more useful for certain use cases.

---

[1] Hacker News is a tech news–sharing platform where everyone is an expert about everything: https://news.ycombinator.com.

Anti-patterns, or *bad practices*, if you will, get a bad rap, and deservedly so, but that doesn't mean we should avoid them like radioactive material. I'll be going over some of those patterns that can help you more than their best practice counterparts. This way, you'll also be using the best practices and great design patterns with better understanding of how they help and when they aren't helpful. You'll see what you're missing in your blind spot and what kind of gems are there.

3.1 If it ain't broke, break it

One of the first things I learned at the companies where I worked—after where the restrooms were—was to avoid changing the code, aka *code churn*, at all costs. Every change you make carries the risk of creating a *regression*, which is a bug that breaks an already working scenario. Bugs are already costly, and fixing them takes time when they are part of a new feature. When it's a regression, that's worse than releasing a new feature with bugs—it's a step backward. Missing a shot in basketball is a bug. Scoring a goal on your own hoop, effectively scoring for your opponent, is a regression. Time is the most critical resource in software development, and losing time has the most severe penalty. Regressions lose the most time. It makes sense to avoid regressions and avoid breaking the code.

Avoiding changes can lead to a conundrum eventually, though, because if a new feature requires that something be broken and made again, it might cause resistance to its development. You can become accustomed to tiptoeing around existing code and trying to add everything in new code without touching existing code. Your effort to leave the code untouched can force you to create more code, which just increases the amount of code to maintain.

If you have to change existing code, that's a bigger problem. There is no tiptoeing around this time. It can be awfully hard to modify existing code because it is tightly coupled to a certain way of doing things, and changing it will oblige you to change many other places. This resistance of existing code to change is called *code rigidity*. That means the more rigid the code gets, the more of the code you have to break to manipulate it.

3.1.1 Facing code rigidity

Code rigidity is based on multiple factors, and one of them is too many dependencies in the code. *Dependency* can relate to multiple things: it can refer to a framework assembly, to an external library, or to another entity in your own code. All types of dependency can create problems if your code gets tangled up in them. Dependency can be both a blessing and a curse. Figure 3.1 depicts a piece of software with a terrible dependency graph. It violates the concern boundaries, and any break in one of the components would require changes in almost all of the code.

Why do dependencies cause problems? When you consider adding dependencies, consider also every component as a different customer or every layer as a different market segment with different needs. Serving multiple segments of customers is a

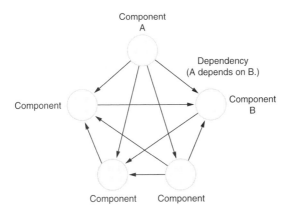

Figure 3.1   The occult symbol for dependency hell

greater responsibility than serving only a single type of customer. Customers have different needs, which might force you to cater to different needs unnecessarily. Think about these relationships when you are deciding on dependency chains. Ideally, try to serve as few types of customers as possible. This is the key to keeping your component or your entire layer as simple as possible.

We can't avoid dependencies. They are essential for reusing code. Code reuse is a two-clause contract. If component A depends on component B, the first clause is, "B will provide services to A." There is also a second clause that is often overlooked: "A will go through maintenance whenever B introduces a breaking change." Dependencies caused by code reuse are okay as long as you can keep the dependency chain organized and compartmentalized.

3.1.2   *Move fast, break things*

Why do you need to break that code, as in making it not even compile or fail the tests? Because intertwined dependencies cause rigidity in the code that makes it resistant to change. It's a steep hill that will make you slower over time, eventually bringing you to a halt. It's easier to handle breaks at the beginning, so you need to identify these issues and break your code, even when it's working. You can see how dependencies force your hand in figure 3.2.

A component with zero dependencies is the easiest to change. It's impossible to break anything else. If your component depends on one of your other components, that creates some rigidity because dependency implies a contract.

If you change the interface on B, that means you need to change A too. If you change the implementation of B without changing the interface, you can still break A because you break B. That becomes a bigger issue when you have multiple components that depend on a single component.

Changing A becomes harder because it needs a change in the dependent component and incurs a risk of breaking any of them. Programmers tend to assume that the more they reuse code, the more time they save. But at what cost? You need to consider this.

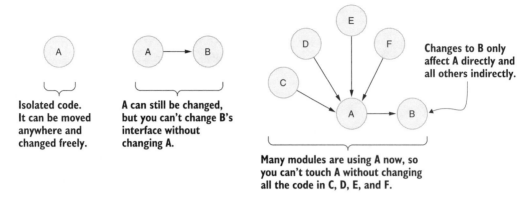

Figure 3.2   Resistance to change is proportional to dependencies.

3.1.3   *Respecting boundaries*

The first habit you must adopt is to avoid violating *abstraction boundaries* for dependencies. An abstraction boundary is the logical borders you draw around layers of your code, a set of the concerns of a given layer. For example, you can have web, business, and database layers in your code as abstractions. When you layer code like that, the database layer shouldn't know about the web layer or the business layer, and the web layer shouldn't know about the database, as figure 3.3 shows.

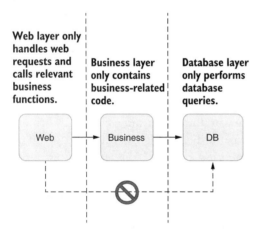

Figure 3.3   Violation of abstraction boundaries that you need to avoid

Why is stepping over boundaries a bad idea? Because it eliminates the benefits of an abstraction. When you pull the complexity of lower layers into higher layers, you become responsible for maintaining the impact of the changes everywhere on the lower layers. Think about a team whose members are responsible for their own layers. Suddenly, the developer of the web layer needs to learn SQL. Not only that, but the changes in the DB layer also need to be communicated now with more people than is necessary. It burdens the developer with unnecessary responsibilities. The time to reach a consensus among the people who need to be convinced increases exponentially. You lose time, and you lose the value of abstractions.

If you bump into such boundary issues, break the code, as in deconstruct it so it might stop working, remove the violation, refactor the code, and deal with the fallout. Fix other parts of the code that depend on it. You have to be vigilant about such issues and immediately cut them off, even at the risk of breaking the code. If the code makes you afraid to break it, it's badly designed code. That doesn't mean good code doesn't break, but when it does, it's much easier to glue the pieces back together.

The importance of tests

You need to be able to see if a change in code would cause a scenario to fail. You can rely on your own understanding of code for that, but your effectiveness will diminish as the code gets more complex over time.

In that sense, tests are simpler. Tests can be a list of instructions on a piece of paper, or they can be fully automated tests. Automated tests are usually preferable because you write them only once and don't waste your time executing them yourself. Thanks to testing frameworks, writing them is quite straightforward, too. We'll delve more into this subject in the chapter about testing.

3.1.4 *Isolating common functionality*

Does this all mean the web layer in figure 3.3 can't ever have common functionality with the DB? It can, of course. But such cases indicate a need for a separate component. For instance, both layers can rely on the common model classes. In that case, you'd have a relationship diagram like that shown in figure 3.4.

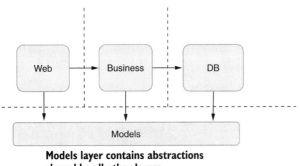

Models layer contains abstractions shared by all other layers.

Figure 3.4 Extracting common functionality without violating abstractions

Refactoring code can break your build process or make your tests fail, and theoretically, it's something you should never do. But I regard such violations as hidden breaks. They need immediate attention, and if they cause more breakage and more bugs in the process, that doesn't mean you caused the code to stop working: it means the bug that was already there has now manifested itself in a way that is easier to reason about.

Let's look at an example. Consider that you're writing an API for a chat app in which you can communicate only in emojis. Yes, it sounds horrible, but there was once a chat app in which you could send only "Yo" as a message.[2] Ours is an improvement over that, if nothing else.

We design the app with a web layer that accepts requests from mobile devices and calls the *business layer* (aka *logic layer*) that performs the actual operations. This kind of separation allows us to test the business layer without a web layer. We can also later use the same business logic in other platforms, such as a mobile website. Therefore, separating business logic makes sense.

NOTE *Business* in business logic or a business layer doesn't necessarily mean something related to a business, but is more like the core logic of the application with abstract models. Arguably, reading business-layer code should give you an idea about how the application works in higher-level terms.

A business layer doesn't know anything about databases or storage techniques. It calls on the database layer for that. The database layer encapsulates the database functionality in a DB-agnostic fashion. This kind of separation of concerns can make the testability of business logic easier because we can easily plug a mocked implementation of the storage layer into the business layer. More importantly, that architecture allows us to change a DB behind the scenes without changing a single line of code in the business layer, or in the web layer, for that matter. You can see how that kind of layering looks in figure 3.5.

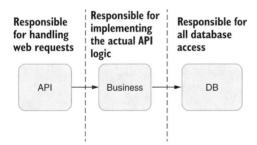

Figure 3.5   The basic architecture of our mobile app API

The downside is that every time you add a new feature to the API, you need to create a new business-layer class or method and a relevant database-layer class and methods. This seems like a lot of work, especially when the deadlines are tight and the feature is somewhat simple. "Why do I need to go through all this hassle for a simple SQL

---

[2]   The chat app called Yo in which you could only send a text containing "Yo" was once valued at $10 million. The company got shut down in 2016: https://en.wikipedia.org/wiki/Yo_(app).

query?" you might think. Let's go ahead and fulfill the fantasy of many developers and violate the existing abstractions.

3.1.5 Example web page

Suppose you receive a request from your manager to implement a new feature, a new statistics tab that shows how many messages the user sent and received in total. It's just two simple SQL queries on the backend:

```
SELECT COUNT(*) as Sent FROM Messages WHERE FromId=@userId
SELECT COUNT(*) as Received FROM Messages WHERE ToId=@userId
```

You can run these queries in your API layer. Even if you're not familiar with ASP.NET Core, web development, or SQL, for that matter, you should have no problem understanding the gist of the code in listing 3.1, which defines a model to return to the mobile app. The model is then automatically serialized into JSON. We retrieve a connection string to our SQL server database. We use that string to open a connection, run our queries against the database, and return the results.

The `StatsController` class in listing 3.1 is an abstraction over web handling wherein received query parameters are in function arguments, the URL is defined by the name of the controller, and the result is returned as an object. So, you would reach the code in listing 3.1 with a URL like https://yourwebdomain/Stats/Get?userId=123, and the MVC infrastructure maps the query parameters into function parameters and the returned object to a JSON result automatically. It makes writing web-handling code simpler because you don't really have to deal with URLs, query strings, HTTP headers, and JSON serialization.

Listing 3.1 Implementing a feature by violating abstractions

```
public class UserStats {                <--- Defines the model
  public int Received { get; set; }
  public int Sent { get; set; }
}

public class StatsController: ControllerBase {    <--- Our controller
  public UserStats Get(int userId) {
    var result = new UserStats();
    string connectionString = config.GetConnectionString("DB");
    using (var conn = new SqlConnection(connectionString)) {
      conn.Open();
      var cmd = conn.CreateCommand();
      cmd.CommandText =
        "SELECT COUNT(*) FROM Messages WHERE FromId={0}";
      cmd.Parameters.Add(userId);
      result.Sent = (int)cmd.ExecuteScalar();
      cmd.CommandText =
        "SELECT COUNT(*) FROM Messages WHERE ToId={0}";
      result.Received = (int)cmd.ExecuteScalar();
    }
```

Our API endpoint (annotation pointing to `public UserStats Get(int userId) {` ... `using (var conn = new SqlConnection(connectionString)) {`)

```
        return result;
    }
}
```

I probably spent five minutes writing this implementation. It looks straightforward. Why do we bother with abstractions? Just put everything in an API layer, right?

Such solutions can be okay when you're working on prototypes, which don't require a perfect design. But in a production system, you need to be careful about making such decisions. Are you allowed to break production? Is it okay if the site goes down for a couple of minutes? If these are okay, then feel free to use this. How about your team? Is the maintainer of the API layer okay with having these SQL queries all around the place? How about testing? How do you test this code and make sure that it runs correctly? How about new fields being added to this? Try to imagine the office the next day. How do you see people treating you? Do they hug you? Cheer you? Or do you find your desk and your chair decorated with tacks?

You added a dependency to the physical DB structure. If you need to change the layout of the Messages table or the DB technology you used, you'll have to go around all the code and make sure that everything works with the new DB or the new table layout.

3.1.6 *Leave no debt behind*

We programmers are not good at predicting future events and their costs. When we make certain unfavorable decisions just for the sake of meeting a deadline, we make it even harder to meet the next one because of the mess we've created. Programmers commonly call this *technical debt.*

Technical debts are conscious decisions. The unconscious ones are called *technical ineptitude.* The reason they are called debts is because either you pay them back later, or the code will come looking for you in an unforeseen future and break your legs with a tire iron.

There are many ways technical debt can accumulate. It might look easier just to pass an arbitrary value instead of taking the trouble to create a constant for it. "A string seems to work fine there," "No harm will come from shortening a name," "Let me just copy everything and change some of its parts," "I know, I'll just use regular expressions." Every small bad decision will add seconds to your and your team's performance. Your throughput will degrade cumulatively over time. You will get slower and slower, getting less satisfaction from your work and less positive feedback from management. By being the wrong kind of lazy, you are dooming yourself to failure. Be the right kind of lazy: serve your future laziness.

The best way to deal with technical debt is to procrastinate with it. You have a larger job ahead of you? Use this as an opportunity to get yourself warmed up. It might break the code. That's good—use it as an opportunity to identify rigid parts of the code, get them granular, flexible. Try to tackle it, change it, and then if you think it doesn't work well enough, undo all your changes.

3.2 *Write it from scratch*

If changing code is risky, writing it from scratch must be orders of magnitude riskier. It essentially means any untested scenario might be broken. Not only does it mean writing everything from scratch, but fixing all the bugs from scratch, too. It's regarded as a seriously cost-inefficient method for fixing design deficiencies.

However, that's only true for code that already works. For code that you already have been working on, starting anew can be a blessing. How, you might ask? It's all related to the spiral of desperation when writing new code. It goes like this:

1. You start with a simple and elegant design.
2. You start writing code.
3. Then some edge cases that you didn't think of appear.
4. You start revising your design.
5. Then you notice that the current design doesn't work for the requirements.
6. You start tweaking the design again, but you avoid redoing it because it would cause too many changes. Every line adds to your shame.
7. Your design is now a Frankenstein's monster of ideas and code mashed together. Elegance is lost, simplicity is lost, and all hope is lost.

At that point, you've entered a loop of sunk-cost fallacy. The time you spent already with your existing code makes you averse to redoing it. But because it can't solve the main issues, you spend days trying to convince yourself that the design might work. Maybe you do fix it at some point, but it might lose you weeks, just because you dug yourself into a hole.

3.2.1 *Erase and rewrite*

I say, *start from scratch*: rewrite it. Toss away everything you already did and write every bit from scratch. You can't imagine how refreshing and fast that will be. You might think writing it from scratch would be hugely inefficient and you'd be spending double the time, but that's not the case because you've already done it once. You already know your way around the problem. The gains in redoing a task resembles something like those shown in figure 3.6.

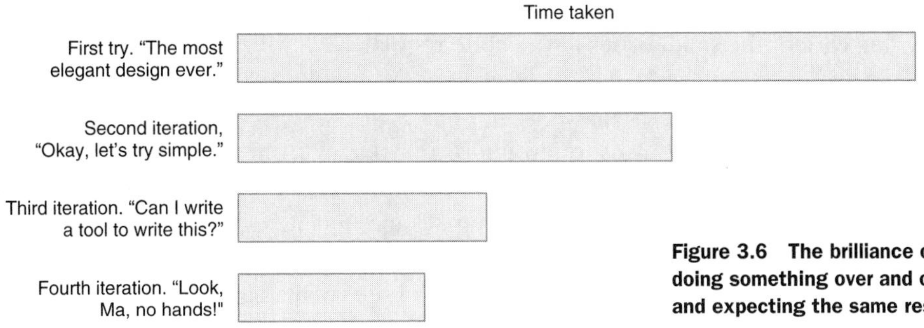

Figure 3.6 The brilliance of doing something over and over and expecting the same results

It's hard to overstate the gains in speed when you're doing something the second time. Unlike the hackers depicted in movies, most of your time is spent looking at the screen: not writing stuff, but thinking about things, considering the right way of doing things. Programming isn't about crafting things as much as it's about navigating the maze of a complex decision tree. When you restart the maze from the beginning, you already know possible mishaps, familiar pitfalls, and certain designs you've reached in your previous attempt.

If you feel stuck developing something new, write it from scratch. I'd say don't even save the previous copy of your work, but you might want to in case you're not really sure if you can do it again really quickly. Okay, then save a copy somewhere, but I assure you, most of the time, you won't even need to look at your previous work. It's already in your mind, guiding you much faster, and without going into the same spiral of desperation this time.

More importantly, when you start from scratch, you'll know if you're following the wrong path much earlier in your process than you previously did. Your pitfall radar will come installed this time. You'll have gained an innate sense of developing that certain feature the right way. Programming this way is a lot like playing console games like *Marvel's Spider-Man* or *The Last of Us*. You die constantly and start that sequence again. You die, you respawn. You become better with this repetition, and the more you repeat, the better you become at programming. Doing it from scratch improves how you develop that single feature, yes, but it also improves your development skills in general for all the future code you will be writing.

Don't hesitate to throw your work away and write it from scratch. Don't fall for the sunk-cost fallacy.

3.3   *Fix it, even if it ain't broke*

There are ways to deal with code rigidity, and one of them is to keep the code churning so it doesn't solidify—as far as the analogy goes. Good code should be easy to change, and it shouldn't give you a list of a thousand places that you need to change to make the change you need. Certain changes can be performed on code that aren't necessary but can help you in the long term. You can make it a regular habit to keep your dependencies up to date, keeping your app fluid, and identify the most rigid parts that are hard to change. You can also improve the code as a *gardening activity*, taking care of the small issues in the code regularly.

3.3.1   *Race toward the future*

You'll inevitably be using one or more packages from the package ecosystem, and you'll leave them as is because they keep working for you. The problem with this is that when you need to use another package and it requires a later version of your package, the upgrade process can be much more painful than gradually upgrading your packages and staying current. You can see such a conflict in figure 3.7.

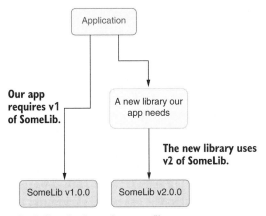

Our app requires v1 of SomeLib.

The new library uses v2 of SomeLib.

Both libraries have the same filename, SomeLib.dll, and v2 is incompatible with v1. It creates a hard-to-resolve situation, losing you a lot of time.

Figure 3.7   Unfixable version conflicts

Most of the time, package maintainers only think about the upgrade scenarios between two major versions, rather than multiple in-between versions. For example, the popular Elasticsearch search library requires major version upgrades to be performed one by one; it doesn't support upgrading from one version to another directly.

.NET supports *binding redirects* to avoid the problem of multiple versions of the same package, to a certain degree. A binding redirect is a directive in application configuration that causes .NET to forward calls to an older version of an assembly to its newer version, or vice versa. Of course, this only works when both packages are compatible. You don't normally need to deal with binding redirects yourself because Visual Studio can do that for you if you have already selected Automatically Generate Binding Redirects in the project properties screen.

Keeping your packages up to date periodically will have two important benefits. First, you'll have spread the effort of upgrading to the current version out over the maintenance period. Every step will be less painful. Second, and more importantly, every minor upgrade might break your code or your design in small or subtle ways that you will need to fix to move to the future. This may sound undesirable, but it will make you improve the code and design in small steps as long as you have tests in place.

You might have a web application that uses Elasticsearch for search operations and Newtonsoft.Json for parsing and producing JSON. They are among the most common libraries out there. The problem starts when you need to upgrade the Newtonsoft.Json package to use a new feature, but Elasticsearch uses the old one. But to upgrade Elasticsearch, you need to change the code that handles Elasticsearch, too. What do you do?

Most packages only support single-version upgrades. Elasticsearch, for example, expects you to upgrade from 5 to 6, and it has guidelines on how to do that. It doesn't have guidelines for upgrading from 5 to 7. You'll have to apply each individual upgrade step separately. Some upgrades also require you to change code significantly. Elasticsearch 7 almost makes you write the code from scratch.

You might as well stay in the older versions under the safety of unchanged code, but not only does the support for older versions end at some point, but the documentation and code examples don't stay around forever, either. Stack Overflow gets filled with the answers about the newer versions because people use the latest version when they start a new project. Your support network for the older version fades over time. That makes it even harder to upgrade with every passing year, which pushes you into a downward spiral of desperation.

My solution to this problem is to join the race toward the future. Keep the libraries up to date. Make it a regular habit to upgrade libraries. This will break your code occasionally, and thanks to that, you'll find out which part of your code is more fragile, and you can add more test coverage.

The key idea is that upgrades may cause your code to break, but letting them have microbreaks will prevent huge roadblocks that become really hard to tackle. You are not only investing in a fictional future gain, but you are also investing in the flexing of dependencies of your app, letting it break and mending it so it doesn't break as easily with the next change, regardless of package upgrades. The less resistant your app is to change, the better it is in terms of design and ease of maintenance.

3.3.2 *Cleanliness is next to codeliness*

What I liked first about computers was their determinism. What you wrote would happen the same way all the time, guaranteed. Code that's working would always work. I found comfort in that. How naive of me. In my career, I've seen many instances of bugs that could only be observed occasionally based on the speed of your CPU or the time of the day. The first truth of the streets is, "Everything changes." Your code will change. Requirements will change. Documentation will change. The environment will change. It's impossible for you to keep running code stable just by not touching it.

Since we've gotten that out of the way, we can relax and say that it's okay to touch code. We shouldn't be afraid of change because it will happen anyway. That means that you shouldn't hesitate to improve working code. Improvements can be small: adding some necessary comments, removing some unnecessary ones, naming things better. Keep the code alive. The more changes you make on some code, the less resistant it becomes to future change. That's because changes will cause breaks and breaks will let you identify weak parts and make them more manageable. You should develop an understanding of how and where your code breaks. Eventually, you'll have an innate sense of what kind of change would be the least risky.

You can call this kind of code-improvement activity *gardening*. You are not necessarily adding features or fixing bugs, but the code should be slightly improved when you're done with it. Such a change can let the next developer who visits the code understand it better or improve the test coverage on the code, as if Santa left some gifts overnight or the bonsai at the office was mysteriously alive.

Why should you bother doing a chore that will never be recognized by anyone in your career? Ideally, it should be recognized and rewarded, but that may not be always the case. You can even get some backlash from your peers because they may not like the change you made. You can even break their workflow without breaking the code. You can turn it into a worse design than what the original developer intended while you're trying to improve it.

Yes, and that's expected. The only way to become mature about how to handle code is to change lots of it. Make sure that your changes are easily reversible so in case you upset someone, you can take your changes back. You will also learn how to communicate with your peers about changes that might impact them. Good communication is the greatest skill you can improve in software development.

The greatest benefit of trivial code improvements is that it puts you into the programming state of mind very quickly. Large work items are the heaviest mental dumbbells. You usually don't know where to start and how to handle such a large change. The pessimism of "Oh, that will be so hard to do that I'll just suffer through this" makes you postpone starting the project. The more you postpone it, the more you will dread coding it.

Making minor improvements to code is a trick to get your mental wheels turning so you can warm up enough to tackle a larger problem. Because you're already coding, your brain resists switching gears less than if you try to switch from browsing social media to coding. Relevant cognitive parts will have already been fired and are ready for a larger project.

If you can't find anything to improve, you can get help from code analyzers. They are great tools for finding minor issues in the code. Make sure you customize the options of the code analyzer you use to avoid offending people as much as possible. Talk to your peers about what they think about it. If they think that they can't be bothered to fix the issues, promise them to fix the first batch yourself and use that as an opportunity to warm up. Otherwise, you can use a command-line alternative or Visual Studio's own code analysis features to run code analysis without violating your team's coding guidelines.

You don't even have to apply the changes you make because they are only for warming you up to coding. For example, you may not be sure if you can apply a certain fix, it might look risky, but you have already done so much. But as you have learned, throw it away. You can always start from scratch and do it again. Don't worry much about throwing away your work. If you are keen on it, keep a backup, but I wouldn't really worry about it.

If you know that your team will be okay with the changes you made, then publish them. The satisfaction of improvement, however small, can motivate you to make larger changes.

3.4   *Do repeat yourself*

Repetition and *copy-paste programming* are concepts that are looked down on in the circles of software development. Like every sane recommendation, they've eventually turned into a religion, causing people to suffer.

The theory goes like this: you write a piece of code. You need the same piece of code somewhere else in the code. A beginner's inclination would be to just copy and paste the same code and use it. It's all good so far. Then you find a bug in the copy-pasted code. Now, you need to change the code in two separate places. You need to keep them in sync. That will create more work and cause you to miss deadlines.

It makes sense, right? The solution to the problem is usually to put the code in a shared class or module and use it in both parts of the code instead. So, when you change the shared code, you would be changing it magically everywhere it's referenced, saving you a great deal of time.

It's all good so far, but it doesn't last forever. The problems begin to appear when you apply this principle to everything imaginable, and blindly, at that. One minor detail you miss when you try to refactor code into reusable classes is that you are inherently creating new dependencies, and dependencies influence your design. Sometimes they can even force your hand.

The biggest problem with shared dependencies is that the parts of the software that use the shared code can diverge in their requirements. When this happens, a developer's reflex is to cater to different needs while using the same code. That means adding optional parameters, conditional logic to make sure that the shared code can serve two different requirements. This makes the actual code more complicated, eventually causing more problems than it solves. At some point, you start thinking about a more complicated design than copy-pasted code.

Consider an example in which you are tasked to write an API for an online shopping website. The client needs to change the shipping address for the customer, which is represented by a class called `PostalAddress` like this:

```
public class PostalAddress {
  public string FirstName { get; set; }
  public string LastName { get; set; }
  public string Address1 { get; set; }
  public string Address2 { get; set; }
  public string City { get; set; }
  public string ZipCode { get; set; }
  public string Notes { get; set; }
}
```

You need to apply some normalization to the fields, such as capitalization, so they look decent even when the user doesn't provide the correct input. An update function might look like a sequence of normalization operations and the update on the database:

```
public void SetShippingAddress(Guid customerId,
  PostalAddress newAddress) {
  normalizeFields(newAddress);
```

```
    db.UpdateShippingAddress(customerId, newAddress);
}

private void normalizeFields(PostalAddress address) {
  address.FirstName = TextHelper.Capitalize(address.FirstName);
  address.LastName = TextHelper.Capitalize(address.LastName);
  address.Notes = TextHelper.Capitalize(address.Notes);
}
```

Our capitalize method would work by making the first character uppercase and the rest of the string lowercase:

```
public static string Capitalize(string text) {
  if (text.Length < 2) {
    return text.ToUpper();
  }
  return Char.ToUpper(text[0]) + text.Substring(1).ToLower();
}
```

Now, this seems to work for shipping notes and names: "gunyuz" becomes "Gunyuz" and "PLEASE LEAVE IT AT THE DOOR" becomes "Please leave it at the door," saving the delivery person some anxiety. After you run your application for a while, you want to normalize city names, too. You add it to the `normalizeFields` function:

```
address.City = TextHelper.Capitalize(address.City);
```

It's all good so far, but when you start to receive orders from San Francisco, you notice that they are normalized to "San francisco." Now you have to change the logic of your capitalization function so that it capitalizes every word, so the city name becomes "San Francisco." It will also help with the names of Elon Musk's kids. But then you notice the delivery note becomes, "Please Leave It At The Door." It's better than all upper-case, but the boss wants it perfect. What do you do?

The easiest change that touches the least code might seem to be to change the `Capitalize` function so that it receives an additional parameter about behavior. The code in listing 3.2 receives an additional parameter called `everyWord` that specifies if it's supposed to capitalize every word or only the first word. Please note that you didn't name the parameter `isCity` or something like that because what you're using it for isn't the problem of the `Capitalize` function. Names should explain things in the terms of the context they are in, not the caller's. Anyway, you split the text into words if `everyWord` is true and capitalize each word individually by calling yourself for each word and then join the words back into a new string.

Listing 3.2 Initial implementation of the `Capitalize` function

```
public static string Capitalize(string text,
  bool everyWord = false) {        ⟵──┐
  if (text.Length < 2) {                │ Newly introduced parameter
```

```
      return text;
    }
    if (!everyWord) {
      return Char.ToUpper(text[0]) + text.Substring(1).ToLower();
    }
    string[] words = text.Split(' ');
    for (int i = 0; i < words.Length; i++) {
      words[i] = Capitalize(words[i]);
    }
    return String.Join(" ", words);
  }
```

> **The case that handles only the first letter**

> **Capitalizes every word by calling the same function**

It has already started to look complicated, but bear with me—I really want you to be convinced about this. Changing the behavior of the function seems like the simplest solution. You just add a parameter and `if` statements here and there, and there you go. This creates a bad habit, almost a reflex, to handle every small change this way and can create an enormous amount of complexity.

Let's say you also need capitalization for filenames to download in your app, and you already have a function that corrects letter cases, so you just need the filenames capitalized and separated with an underscore. For example, if the API received *invoice report*, it should turn into `Invoice_Report`. Because you already have a capitalize function, your first instinct will be to modify its behavior slightly again. You add a new parameter called `filename` because the behavior you are adding doesn't have a more generic name, and you check the parameter at the places where it matters. When converting to upper- and lowercase, you must use culture invariant versions of `ToUpper` and `ToLower` functions so the filenames on Turkish computers don't suddenly become `?nvoice_Report` instead. Notice the dotted "I" in `?nvoice_Report`? Our implementation would now look like that shown in the following listing.

> **Listing 3.3   A Swiss army knife function that can do anything**

```
public static string Capitalize(string text,
    bool everyWord = false, bool filename = false) {      ◁—— Your new parameter
    if (text.Length < 2) {
      return text;
    }
    if (!everyWord) {
      if (filename) {                                      ◁—— Filename-specific code
        return Char.ToUpperInvariant(text[0])
          + text.Substring(1).ToLowerInvariant();
      }
      return Char.ToUpper(text[0]) + text.Substring(1).ToLower();
    }
    string[] words = text.Split(' ');
    for (int i = 0; i < words.Length; i++) {
      words[i] = Capitalize(words[i]);
    }
    string separator = " ";
    if (filename) {
```

```
      separator = "_";              ◁─── Filename-specific code
    }
    return String.Join(separator, words);
  }
```

Look what a monster you've created. You violated your principle of crosscutting concerns and made your `Capitalize` function aware of your file-naming conventions. It suddenly became part of a specific business logic, rather than staying generic. Yes, you are reusing code as much as possible, but you are making your job in the future really hard.

Notice that you also created a new case that isn't even in your design: a new file-name format where not all words are capitalized. It's exposed through the condition where `everyWord` is `false` and `filename` is `true`. You didn't intend this, but now you have it. Another developer might rely on the behavior, and that's how your code becomes spaghetti over time.

I propose a cleaner approach: *repeat yourself.* Instead of trying to merge every single bit of logic into the same code, try to have separate functions with perhaps slightly repetitive code. You can have separate functions for each use case. You can have one that capitalizes only the first letter, you can have another one that capitalizes every word, and you can have another one that actually formats a filename. They don't even have to reside next to each other—the code about the filename can stay closer to the business logic it's required for. You instead have these three functions that convey their intent much better. The first one is named `CapitalizeFirstLetter` so its function is clearer. The second one is `CapitalizeEveryWord`, which also explains what it does better. It calls `CapitalizeFirstLetter` for every word, which is much easier to understand than trying to reason about recursion. Finally, you have `FormatFilename`, which has an entirely different name because capitalization isn't the only thing it does. It has all the capitalization logic implemented from scratch. This lets you freely modify the function when your filename formatting conventions change without needing to think about how it would impact your capitalization work, as shown in the next listing.

Listing 3.4 Repeated work with much better readability and flexibility

```
public static string CapitalizeFirstLetter(string text) {
  if (text.Length < 2) {
    return text.ToUpper();
  }
  return Char.ToUpper(text[0]) + text.Substring(1).ToLower();
}

public static string CapitalizeEveryWord(string text) {
  var words = text.Split(' ');
  for (int n = 0; n < words.Length; n++) {
    words[n] = CapitalizeFirstLetter(words[n]);
  }
  return String.Join(" ", words);
}
```

```
public static string FormatFilename(string filename) {
  var words = filename.Split(' ');
  for (int n = 0; n < words.Length; n++) {
    string word = words[n];
    if (word.Length < 2) {
      words[n] = word.ToUpperInvariant();
    } else {
      words[n] = Char.ToUpperInvariant(word[0]) +
        word.Substring(1).ToLowerInvariant();
    }
  }
  return String.Join("_", words);
}
```

This way, you won't have to cram every possible bit of logic into a single function. This gets especially important when requirements diverge between callers.

3.4.1 Reuse or copy?

How do you decide between reusing the code and replicating it somewhere else? The greatest factor would be how you frame the caller's concerns, that is, describing the caller's requirements for what they actually are. When you describe the requirements of the function where a filename needs to be formatted, you become biased by the existence of a function that is quite close to what you want to do (capitalization) and that immediately signals to your brain to use that existing function. If the filename would be capitalized exactly the same way, it might still make sense, but the difference in requirements should be a red flag.

Three things are hard in computer science: cache invalidation, naming things, and off-by-one errors.[3] Naming things correctly is one of the most important factors when understanding conflicting concerns in code reuse. The name Capitalize frames the function in a correct way. We could have called it NormalizeName when we first created it, but it would have prevented us from reusing it in other fields. What we did was to name things as closely as possible to their actual functionality. This way, our function can serve all the different purposes without creating confusion, and more importantly, it explains its job better wherever it's used. You can see how different naming approaches affect describing the actual behavior in figure 3.8.

We could go deeper with the actual functionality, like, "This function converts first letters of each word in a string to uppercase and converts all the remaining letters to lowercase," but that's hard to fit into a name. Names should be as short and as unambiguous as possible. Capitalize works in that sense.

Awareness of concerns for a piece of code is an important skill to have. I usually assign personalities to functions and classes to categorize their concerns. I'd say, "This function doesn't care about this," as if it were a person. You can similarly get an understanding

---

[3] This is Leon Bambrick's excellent variation (https://twitter.com/secretGeek/status/7269997868) of the famous quote by Phil Karlton, who said it without the "off-by-one errors" part.

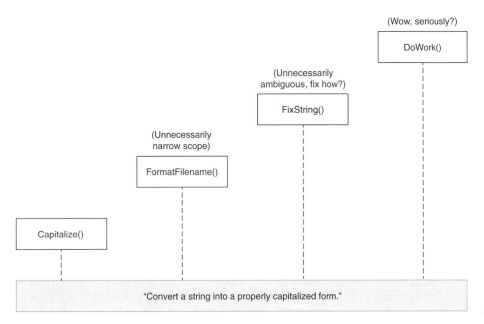

Figure 3.8   Pick a name as close as possible to the actual functionality.

of the concerns of a piece of code. That's why we named the parameter to capitalize every word `everyWord` instead of `isCity` because the function just doesn't care if it's a city or not. It isn't the function's concern.

When you name things closer to their circle of concern, their usage patterns become more apparent. Then why did we end up naming the filename-formatting function `FormatFilename`? Shouldn't we have called it `CapitalizeInvariantAndSep-arateWithUnderscores`? No. Functions can do multiple things, but they only perform a single task, and they should be named after that task. If you feel the need to use the conjunctions "and" or "or" in your function's name, either you're naming it wrong or you are putting too much responsibility on your function.

Name is just one aspect of the concerns of code. Where the code resides, its module, its class, can also be an indication of how to decide whether to reuse it.

3.5   *Invent it here*

There is a common Turkish expression that literally translates to "Don't come up with an invention now." It means, "Don't cause us trouble by trying a novel thing now, we don't have time for that." Reinventing the wheel is problematic. That pathology even has its own name in computer science circles: *Not Invented Here Syndrome*. It specifically addresses a type of person who cannot sleep at night if they don't invent an already invented product themselves.

It's certainly a lot of work to go to great lengths to create something from scratch when there is a known and working alternative. It's prone to errors, too. The problem arises when reusing existing stuff becomes the norm and creating something becomes unreachable. The calcification of this perspective eventually turns into the motto "never invent anything." You shouldn't let yourself be afraid of inventing things.

First, an inventor has a questioning mindset. If you keep questioning things, you will inevitably become an inventor. When you explicitly prevent yourself from asking questions, you start to become dull and you turn yourself into a menial worker. You should avoid that attitude because it's impossible for someone without a questioning mindset to optimize their work.

Secondly, not all inventions have alternatives. Your own abstractions are also inventions—your classes, your design, the helper functions you come up with. They are all productivity enhancements, yet they require invention.

I always wanted to write a website that provides Twitter statistics reports about my followers and people I follow. The problem is that I don't want to learn how the Twitter API works. I know there are libraries out there that handle this, but I also don't want to learn how *they* work, or more importantly, I don't want their implementation to influence my design. If I use a certain library, it will bind me to the API of that library, and if I want to change the library, I will need to rewrite code everywhere.

The way to deal with these issues involves invention. We come up with our dream interface and put it as an abstraction in front of the library we use. This way, we avoid binding ourselves to a certain API design. If we want to change the library we use, we just change our abstraction, not everything in our code. I currently have no idea how the Twitter web API works, but I imagine that it is a regular web request with something to identify the authorization to access the Twitter API. That means getting an item from Twitter.

A programmer's first reflex is to find a package and check out the documentation on how it works to integrate it into their code. Instead of doing that, invent a new API yourself and use it, which eventually calls the library that you're using behind the scenes. Your API should be the simplest possible for your requirements. Become your own customer.

First, go over the requirements of an API. A web-based API provides a user interface on the web to give permissions to an application. It opens up a page on Twitter that asks for permissions and redirects back to the app if the user confirms. That means we need to know which URL to open for authorization and which URL to redirect back to. We can then use the data in the redirected page to make additional API calls later.

We shouldn't need anything else after we authorize. So, I imagine an API for this purpose like that shown next.

Listing 3.5   Our imaginary Twitter API

```
public class Twitter {
  public static Uri GetAuthorizationUrl(Uri callbackUrl) {      Static functions
    string redirectUrl = "";                                     that handle the
    // … do something here to build the redirect url             authorization flow
    return new Uri(redirectUrl);
  }
```

```
    public static TwitterAccessToken GetAccessToken(      ◁──┐   Static functions
      TwitterCallbackInfo callbackData) {                     │   that handle the
      // we should be getting something like this             │   authorization flow
      return new TwitterAccessToken();
    }

    public Twitter(TwitterAccessToken accessToken) {
      // we should store this somewhere
    }

    public IEnumerable<TwitterUserId> GetListOfFollowers(   ◁──┐   The actual functionality
      TwitterUserId userId) {                                   │   we want
      // no idea how this will work
    }
}

public class TwitterUserId {              ◁──────┐
  // who knows how twitter defines user ids        │
}                                                  │
                                                   │
public class TwitterAccessToken {         ◁──────┤   Classes to define
  // no idea what this will be                     │   Twitter's concepts
}                                                  │
                                                   │
public class TwitterCallbackInfo {        ◁──────┘
  // this neither
}
```

We invented something from scratch, a new Twitter API, even though we know little about how the Twitter API actually works. It might not be the best API for general use, but our customers are ourselves, so we have the luxury of designing it to fit our needs. For instance, I don't think I'll need to handle how the data is transferred in chunks from the original API, and I don't care if it makes me wait and blocks the running code, which may not be desirable in a more generic API.

> **NOTE** This approach to having your own convenient interfaces that act as an adapter is, unsurprisingly, called *adapter pattern* in the streets. I avoid emphasizing names over actual utility, but in case somebody asks you, now you know it.

We can later extract an interface from the classes we defined, so we don't have to depend on concrete implementations, which makes testing easier. We don't even know if the Twitter library we're going to use supports replacing their implementation easily. You may occasionally encounter cases where your dream design doesn't really fit with the design of the actual product. In that case, you need to tweak your design, but that's a good sign—it means your design also represents your understanding of the underlying technology.

So, I might have lied a little. Don't write a Twitter library from scratch. But don't stray from the inventor's mindset, either. Those go hand in hand, and you should stick with both.

3.6   *Don't use inheritance*

Object-oriented programming (OOP) fell on the programming world like an anvil in the 1990s, causing a paradigm shift from structured programming. It was considered revolutionary. The decades-old problem of how to reuse code had finally been resolved.

The most emphasized feature of OOP was inheritance. You could define code reuse as a set of inherited dependencies. Not only did this allow simpler code reuse, but also simpler code modification. To create new code that has a slightly different behavior, you didn't need to think about changing the original code. You just derived from it and overrode the relevant member to have modified behavior.

Inheritance caused more problems than it solved in the long run. *Multiple inheritance* was one of the first issues. What if you had to reuse the code from multiple classes and they all had the method with the same name, and perhaps with the same signature? How would it work? What about the diamond dependency problem shown in figure 3.9? It would be really complicated, so very few programming languages went ahead and implemented it.

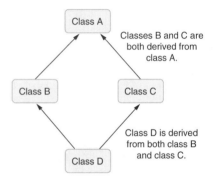

Figure 3.9   Diamond dependency problem—how should class D behave?

Aside from multiple inheritance, a greater problem with inheritance is that of strong dependency, also known as *tight coupling*. As I have already discussed, dependencies are the root of all evil. Because of its nature, inheritance binds you to a concrete implementation, which is considered a violation of one of the well-regarded principles of object-oriented programming, the *dependency inversion principle*, which states that code should never depend on the concrete implementation, but on an abstraction.

Why is there such a principle? Because when you are bound to a concrete implementation, your code becomes rigid and immovable. As we have seen, rigid code is very hard to test or modify.

Then how do you reuse code? How do you inherit your class from an abstraction? It's simple—it's called *composition*. Instead of inheriting from a class, you receive its abstraction as a parameter in your constructor. Think of your components as lego pieces that support each other rather than as a hierarchy of objects.

With regular inheritance, the relationship between common code and its variations is expressed with an ancestor/descendant model. In contrast, composition thinks of the common function as a separate component.

On SOLID principles

There is a famous acronym, SOLID, that stands for five principles of object-oriented programming. The problem is that SOLID feels like it was invented to make a meaningful word rather than to make us better programmers. I don't think all its principles carry the same importance, and some may not matter at all. I strongly oppose embracing a set of principles without being convinced of their value.

The *single-responsibility principle*, the S of SOLID, says a class should be responsible for one thing only as opposed to one class doing multiple things, aka *God classes*. That's a bit vague because it's we who define what one thing entails. Can we say a class with two methods is still responsible for one thing anymore? Even a God class is responsible for one thing at a certain level: being a God class. I'd replace this with the *clear-name principle*: the name of a class should explain its function with as little vagueness as possible. If the name is too long or too vague, the class needs to be split into multiple classes.

The *open-closed principle* states that a class should be open for extension but closed for modification. It means that we should design our classes so that their behavior can be modified externally. This is, again, very vague and can even be unnecessarily time consuming. Extensibility is a design decision and may not be desirable, practical, or even safe at times. It feels like the advice to "use the racing tires" of programming. I would instead say, "Treat extensibility as a feature."

The *Liskov substitution principle*, coined by Barbara Liskov, states that a program's behavior shouldn't change if one of the classes used is replaced with a derived class. Although the advice is sound, I don't think it matters in daily programming work. It feels like the advice "Don't have bugs" to me. If you break an interface's contract, the program will have bugs. If you design a bad interface, the program will also have bugs. That's the natural order of things. Perhaps this can be turned into simpler and more actionable advice like "Stick to the contract."

The *interface segregation principle* favors smaller and goal-specific interfaces over generalized, broadly scoped interfaces. This is unnecessarily complicated and vague, if not just plain wrong, advice. There could be cases where broadly scoped interfaces are more suitable for the job, and overly granular interfaces can create too much overhead. Splitting interfaces shouldn't be based on scope, but on the actual requirements of the design. If a single interface isn't suitable for the job, feel free to split it, not to satisfy some granularity criteria.

The *dependency inversion principle* is the final one. Again, it's not a very good name. Just call it *depend on abstractions*. Yes, depending on concrete implementations creates tight coupling, and we've already seen its undesirable effects. But that doesn't mean you should start creating interfaces for every dependency you have. I say the opposite: prefer depending on abstractions when you prefer flexibility and you see value in it, and depend on the concrete implementation in cases where it just doesn't matter. Your code should adapt to your design, not the other way around. Feel free to experiment with different models.

Composition is more like a client-server relationship than a parent-child one. You call reused code by its reference instead of inheriting its methods in your scope. You can construct the class you're depending on in your constructor, or even better, you can receive it as a parameter, which would let you use it as an external dependency. That allows you to make that relationship more configurable and flexible.

Receiving it as a parameter has the extra advantage of making it easier to unit test the object by injecting mock versions of the concrete implementations. I'll discuss dependency injection more in chapter 5.

Using composition over inheritance can require writing substantially more code because you might need to define dependencies with interfaces instead of concrete references, but it would also free the code from dependencies. You still need to weigh the pros and cons of composition before you use it.

3.7   *Don't use classes*

Make no mistake—classes are great. They do their job and then get out of the way. But as I discussed in chapter 2, they incur a small reference indirection overhead and occupy slightly more indirection compared to value types. These issues won't matter most of the time, but it's important for you to know their pros and cons to understand the code and how you can impact it by making wrong decisions.

Value types can be, well, valuable. The primitive types that come with C# such as int, long, and double are already value types. You can also compose your own value types with constructs like enum and struct.

3.7.1   *Enum is yum!*

Enums are great for holding discrete ordinal values. Classes can also be used to define discrete values, but they lack certain affordances that enums have. A class is still, of course, better than hardcoding values.

If you're writing code that handles the response of a web request that you make in your app, you may need to deal with different numerical response codes. Say that you're querying weather information from the National Weather Service for a user's given location, and you write a function to retrieve the required information. In listing 3.6, we're using RestSharp for API requests and Newtonsoft.JSON to parse the response if the request is successful by checking whether the HTTP status code is successful. Notice that we're using a hardcoded value (200) on the if line to check for the status code. We then use the Json.NET library to parse the response into a dynamic object to extract the information we need.

> **Listing 3.6   Function that returns NWS temperature forecast for a given coordinate**

```
static double? getTemperature(double latitude,
  double longitude) {
  const string apiUrl = "https://api.weather.gov";
  string coordinates = $"{latitude},{longitude}";
  string requestPath = $"/points/{coordinates}/forecast/hourly";
```

```
                var client = new RestClient(apiUrl);
                var request = new RestRequest(requestPath);    │ Send the request to NWS.
                var response = client.Get(request);     ◁──────┘
                if (response.StatusCode == 200) {        ◁─────── Check for successful HTTP status code.
                  dynamic obj = JObject.Parse(response.Content);  ◁───┐
  Yay,             var period = obj.properties.periods[0];        │ We parse JSON here.
result!  └─▷      return (double)period.temperature;
                }
                return null;
            }
```

The greatest problem with hardcoded values is humans' inability to memorize numbers. We're not good at it. We don't understand them at first sight with the exception of the number of zeros on our paychecks. They are harder to type than simple names because it's hard to associate numbers with mnemonics, and yet they are easier to make a typo in. The second problem with hardcoded values is that values can change. If you use the same value everywhere else, that means changing everything else just to change a value.

The second problem with numbers is that they lack intent. A numeric value like 200 can be anything. We don't know what it is. So don't hardcode values.

Classes are one way to encapsulate values. You can encapsulate HTTP status codes in a class like this:

```
class HttpStatusCode {
  public const int OK = 200;
  public const int NotFound = 404;
  public const int ServerError = 500;
  // ... and so on
}
```

This way, you can change the line that checks for a successful HTTP request with some code like this:

```
if (response.StatusCode == HttpStatusCode.OK) {
…
}
```

That version looks way more descriptive. We immediately understand the context, what the value means, and what it means in which context. It's perfectly descriptive.

Then, what are enums for? Can't we use classes for this? Consider that we have another class for holding values:

```
class ImageWidths {
  public const int Small = 50;
  public const int Medium = 100;
  public const int Large = 200;
}
```

Now this code would compile, and more importantly, it would return true:

```
return HttpStatusCode.OK == ImageWidths.Large;
```

That's something you probably don't want. Suppose we wrote it with an `enum` instead:

```
enum HttpStatusCode {
  OK = 200,
  NotFound = 404,
  ServerError = 500,
}
```

That's way easier to write, right? Its usage would be the same in our example. More importantly, every `enum` type you define is distinct, which makes the values type-safe, unlike our example with classes with `consts`. An `enum` is a blessing in our case. If we tried the same comparison with two different `enum` types, the compiler would throw an error:

```
error CS0019: Operator '==' cannot be applied to operands of type
➡ 'HttpStatusCode' and 'ImageWidths'
```

Awesome! Enums save us time by not allowing us to compare apples to oranges during compilation. They convey intent as well as classes that contain values. Enums are also value types, which means they are as fast as passing around an integer value.

3.7.2   *Structs rock!*

As chapter 2 points out, classes have a little storage overhead. Every class needs to keep an object header and virtual method table when instantiated. Additionally, classes are allocated on the heap, and they are garbage collected.

That means .NET needs to keep track of every class instantiated and get them out of memory when not needed. That's a very efficient process—most of the time, you don't even notice it's there. It's magical. It requires no manual memory management. So, no, you don't have to be scared of using classes.

But as we've seen, it's good to know when you can take advantage of a free benefit when it's available. Structs are like classes. You can define properties, fields, and methods in them. Structs can also implement interfaces. However, a struct cannot be inherited and also cannot inherit from another struct or class. That's because structs don't have a virtual method table or an object header. They are not garbage collected because they are allocated on the call stack.

As I discussed in chapter 2, a call stack is just a contiguous block of memory with only its top pointer moving around. That makes a stack a very efficient storage mechanism because cleanup is fast and automatic. There is no possibility of fragmentation because it's always LIFO (Last In First Out).

If a stack is that fast, why don't we use it for everything? Why is there heap or garbage collection? That's because a stack can only live for the lifetime of the function. When your function returns, anything on the function's stack frame is gone, so other functions can use the same stack space. We need the heap for the objects that outlive functions.

Also, a stack is limited in size. That's why there is a whole website named Stack Overflow: because your application will crash if you overflow the stack. Respect the stack—know its limits.

Structs are lightweight classes. They are allocated on stacks because they are value types. That means that assigning a struct value to a variable means copying its contents since no single reference represents it. You need to keep this in mind because copying is slower than passing around references for any data larger than the size of a pointer.

Although structs are value types themselves, they can still contain reference types. If, say, a struct contains a string, it's still a reference type inside a value type, similar to how you can have value types inside a reference type. I will illustrate this in the figures throughout this section.

If you have a struct that contains only an integer value, it occupies less space in general than a reference to a class that contains an integer value, as figure 3.10 shows. Consider that our struct and class variants are about holding identifiers, as I discussed in chapter 2. Two flavors of the same structure would look like those in the following listing.

Listing 3.7 Similarity of class and struct declarations

```
public class Id {
  public int Value { get; private set; }

  public Id (int value) {
    this.Value = value;
  }
}

public struct Id {
  public int Value { get; private set; }

  public Id (int value) {
    this.Value = value;
  }
}
```

The only difference in the code is struct versus class keywords, but observe how they differ in how they are stored when you create them in a function like this:

```
var a = new Id(123);
```

Figure 3.10 shows how they are laid out.

Because structs are value types, assigning one to another also creates another copy of the whole content of the struct instead of just creating another copy of the reference:

```
var a = new Id(123);
var b = a;
```

In this case, figure 3.11 shows how structs can be efficient for storage of small types.

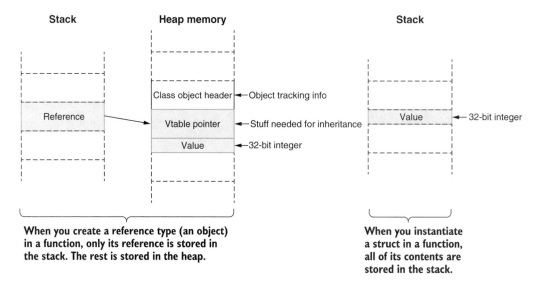

When you create a reference type (an object) in a function, only its reference is stored in the stack. The rest is stored in the heap.

When you instantiate a struct in a function, all of its contents are stored in the stack.

Figure 3.10   The difference between how classes and structs are laid out in memory

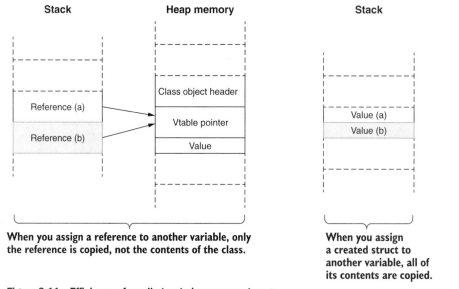

When you assign a reference to another variable, only the reference is copied, not the contents of the class.

When you assign a created struct to another variable, all of its contents are copied.

Figure 3.11   Efficiency of small structs in memory storage

Although stack storage is temporary during the execution of the function, it's minuscule compared to the heap. A stack is 1 megabyte in size in .NET, while a heap can contain terabytes of data. A stack is fast, but if you fill it with large structs, it can fill up easily. Furthermore, copying large structs is also slower than only copying a reference. Consider that we'd like to keep some user information along with our identifiers. Our implementation would look like the next listing.

Listing 3.8 Defining a larger class or a struct

```
public class Person {
  public int Id { get; private set; }
  public string FirstName { get; private set; }
  public string LastName { get; private set; }
  public string City { get; private set; }

  public Person(int id, string firstName, string lastName,
    string city) {
    Id = id;
    FirstName = firstName;
    LastName = lastName;
    City = city;
  }
}
```

> We can make a class a struct by changing the "class" word here to "struct."

The only difference between the two definitions is the `struct` and `class` keywords. Yet creating and assigning one from another has a profound impact on how things work behind the scenes. Consider this simple code where `Person` can be either a struct or a class:

```
var a = new Person(42, "Sedat", "Kapanoglu", "San Francisco");
var b = a;
```

After you assign a to b, the difference in resulting memory layouts is shown in figure 3.12.

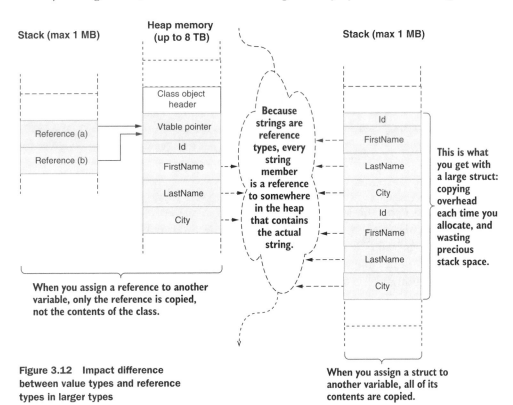

Figure 3.12 Impact difference between value types and reference types in larger types

A call stack can be extremely fast and efficient for storing things. They are great for working with small values with less overhead because they are not subject to garbage collection. Because they are not reference types, they cannot be null, either, which makes null reference exceptions impossible with structs.

You can't use structs for everything, as is apparent by how they are stored: you can't share a common reference to them, which means you can't change a common instance from different references. That's something we do a lot unconsciously and never think about. Consider if we wanted the struct to be mutable and used `get;` `set;` modifiers instead of `get;` `private set;`. That means we could modify the `struct` on the fly. Look at the example shown next.

Listing 3.9   A mutable struct

```
public struct Person {
  public int Id { get; set; }
  public string FirstName { get; set; }
  public string LastName { get; set; }
  public string City { get; set; }

  public Person(int id, string firstName, string lastName,
    string city) {
    Id = id;
    FirstName = firstName;
    LastName = lastName;
    City = city;
  }
}
```

Consider this piece of code with a mutable struct:

```
var a = new Person(42, "Sedat", "Kapanoglu", "San Francisco");
var b = a;
b.City = "Eskisehir";
Console.WriteLine(a.City);
Console.WriteLine(b.City);
```

What do you think the output would be? If it were a class, both lines would show "Eskisehir" as the new city. But since we have two separate copies, it would print "San Francisco" and "Eskisehir." Because of this, it's always a great idea to make structs almost immutable so they can't be accidentally changed later and cause bugs.

Although you should prefer composition over inheritance for code reuse, inheritance can also be useful when the given dependency is contained. Classes can provide you better flexibility than structs in those cases.

Classes can provide more efficient storage when they are larger in size because only their references will be copied in an assignment. In light of all this, feel free to use structs for small, immutable value types that have no need for inheritance.

3.8 Write bad code

Best practices come from bad code, and yet bad code can also emerge from the blind application of best practices. Structured, object-oriented, and even functional programming are all developed to make developers write better code. When best practices are taught, some bad practices are also singled out as "evil" and are completely banished. Let's visit some of them.

3.8.1 Don't use If/Else

If/Else is one of the first constructs you learn about programming. It is the expression of one of the fundamental parts of computers: logic. We love If/Else. It lets us express the logic of our program in a flowchart-like way. But that kind of expression can also make code less readable.

Like many programming constructs, If/Else blocks make the code in the conditionals indented. Suppose that we want to add some functionality to our Person class from the last section to process a record in the DB. We want to see if the City property of the Person class was changed and to change it in the DB too if the Person class points to a valid record. This is quite a stretched implementation. There are better ways to do these things, but I want to show you how the code can turn out, rather than its actual functionality. I draw a shape for you in the following listing.

Listing 3.10 An example of an If/Else festival in the code

```
public UpdateResult UpdateCityIfChanged() {
  if (Id > 0) {
    bool isActive = db.IsPersonActive(Id);
    if (isActive) {
      if (FirstName != null && LastName != null) {
        string normalizedFirstName = FirstName.ToUpper();
        string normalizedLastName = LastName.ToUpper();
        string currentCity = db.GetCurrentCityByName(
          normalizedFirstName, normalizedLastName);
        if (currentCity != City) {
          bool success = db.UpdateCurrentCity(Id, City);
          if (success) {
            return UpdateResult.Success;
          } else {
            return UpdateResult.UpdateFailed;
          }
        } else {
          return UpdateResult.CityDidNotChange;
        }
      } else {
        return UpdateResult.InvalidName;
      }
    } else {
      return UpdateResult.PersonInactive;
    }
  } else {
```

```
        return UpdateResult.InvalidId;
    }
}
```

Even if I explained what the function did step by step, it's impossible to come back to this function five minutes later and not be confused again. One reason for the confusion is too much indentation. People are not accustomed to reading things in indented format, with the small exception of Reddit users. It's hard to determine which block a line belongs to, what the context is. It's hard to follow the logic.

The general principle to avoid unnecessary indentation is exiting the function as early as possible and avoiding using else when the flow already implies an else. Listing 3.11 shows how return statements already imply the end of the code flow, eliminating the need for else.

Listing 3.11 Look, Ma, no elses!

```
public UpdateResult UpdateCityIfChanged() {
    if (Id <= 0) {
        return UpdateResult.InvalidId;               ◁────┐
    }
    bool isActive = db.IsPersonActive(Id);
    if (!isActive) {
        return UpdateResult.PersonInactive;          ◁────┤
    }
    if (FirstName is null || LastName is null) {
        return UpdateResult.InvalidName;             ◁────┤
    }
    string normalizedFirstName = FirstName.ToUpper();
    string normalizedLastName = LastName.ToUpper();      No code runs
    string currentCity = db.GetCurrentCityByName(        after a return.
        normalizedFirstName, normalizedLastName);
    if (currentCity == City) {
        return UpdateResult.CityDidNotChange;        ◁────┤
    }
    bool success = db.UpdateCurrentCity(Id, City);
    if (!success) {
        return UpdateResult.UpdateFailed;            ◁────┤
    }
    return UpdateResult.Success;                     ◁────┘
}
```

The technique used here is called following the *happy path*. The *happy path* in code is the part of the code that runs if nothing else goes wrong. It's what ideally happens during execution. Since the happy path summarizes a function's main work, it must be the easiest part to read. By converting the code in else statements into early return statements, we allow the reader to identify the happy path much more easily than having matryoshka dolls of if statements.

Validate early, and return as early as possible. Put the exceptional cases inside `if` statements, and try to put your happy path outside of the blocks. Familiarize yourself with these two shapes to make your code more readable and maintainable.

3.8.2 *Use goto*

The entire theory of programming can be summarized with memory, basic arithmetic, and `if` and `goto` statements. A `goto` statement transfers the execution of the program directly to an arbitrary destination point. They are hard to follow, and using them has been discouraged since Edsger Dijkstra wrote a paper titled "Go to statement is considered harmful" (https://dl.acm.org/doi/10.1145/362929.362947). There are many misconceptions about Dijkstra's paper, first and foremost its title. Dijkstra titled his paper "A case against the GO TO statement," but his editor, also the inventor of the Pascal language, Niklaus Wirth, changed the title, which made Dijkstra's stance more aggressive and turned the war against `goto` into a witch hunt.

This all happened before the 1980s. Programming languages had ample time to create new constructs to address the functions of the `goto` statement. The `for`/`while` loops, `return`/`break`/`continue` statements, and even exceptions were created to address specific scenarios that were previously only possible with `goto`. Former BASIC programmers will remember the famous error-handling statement `ON ERROR GOTO`, which was a primitive exception-handling mechanism.

Although many modern languages don't have a `goto` equivalent anymore, C# does, and it works great for a single scenario: eliminating redundant exit points in a function. It's possible to use a `goto` statement in an easy-to-understand fashion and make your code less prone to bugs while saving you time. It's like a three-combo hit on *Mortal Kombat.*

An exit point is each statement in a function that causes it to return to its caller. Every `return` statement is an exit point in C#. Eliminating exit points in the older era of programming languages was more important than it is now because manual cleanup was a more prominent part of a programmer's daily life. You had to remember what you allocated and what you needed to clean up before you returned.

C# provides great tools for structured cleanup such as `try`/`finally` blocks and `using` statements. There may be cases where neither works for your scenario and you can use `goto` for cleanup too, but it actually shines more in eliminating redundancy. Let's say we're developing the shipment address entry form for an online shopping web page. Web forms are great for demonstrating the multilevel validation that happens with them. Assume that we'd like to use ASP.NET Core for that. That means we need to have a `submit` action for our form. Its code might look like that in listing 3.12. We have model validation that happens in the client, but at the same time, we need some server validation with our form so we can check whether the address is really correct using USPS API. After the check, we can try to save the information to the database, and if that succeeds, we redirect the user to the billing information page. Otherwise, we need to display the shipping address form again.

Listing 3.12   A shipping address form handling code with ASP.NET Core

```
[HttpPost]
public IActionResult Submit(ShipmentAddress form) {
  if (!ModelState.IsValid) {
    return RedirectToAction("Index", "ShippingForm", form);      ◁
  }
  var validationResult = service.ValidateShippingForm(form);
  if (validationResult != ShippingFormValidationResult.Valid) {
    return RedirectToAction("Index", "ShippingForm", form);      ◁         Redundant
  }                                                                        exit points
  bool success = service.SaveShippingInfo(form);
  if (!success) {
    ModelState.AddModelError("", "Problem occurred while " +
      "saving your information, please try again");
    return RedirectToAction("Index", "ShipingForm", form);       ◁
  }
  return RedirectToAction("Index", "BillingForm");      ◁——— The happy path
}
```

I have already discussed some of the issues with copy-paste, but the multiple exit points in listing 3.12 pose another problem. Did you notice the typo in the third `return` statement? We accidentally deleted a character without noticing, and since it's in a string, that bug is impossible to detect unless we encounter a problem when saving the form in the production or we build elaborate tests for our controllers. Duplication can cause problems in these cases. The `goto` statement can help you merge the `return` statements under a single `goto` label, as listing 3.13 shows. We create a new label for our error case under our happy path and reuse it at multiple places in our function using `goto`.

Listing 3.13   Merging common exit points into a single `return` statement

```
[HttpPost]
public IActionResult Submit2(ShipmentAddress form) {
  if (!ModelState.IsValid) {
    goto Error;                                                  ◁
  }
  var validationResult = service.ValidateShippingForm(form);
  if (validationResult != ShippingFormValidationResult.Valid) {
    goto Error;                                                  ◁         The infamous
  }                                                                        goto!
  bool success = service.SaveShippingInfo(form);
  if (!success) {
    ModelState.AddModelError("", "Problem occurred while " +
      "saving your shipment information, please try again");
    goto Error;                                                  ◁
  }
  return RedirectToAction("Index", "BillingForm");
Error:                                                                     Common
  return RedirectToAction("Index", "ShippingForm", form);        ◁         exit code
}
```

Destination label

The great thing about this kind of consolidation is that if you ever want to add more in
your common exit code, you only need to add it to a single place. Let's say you want to
save a cookie to the client when there is an error. All you need to do is to add it after
the Error label, as shown next.

Listing 3.14 Ease of adding extra code to common exit code

```
[HttpPost]
public IActionResult Submit3(ShipmentAddress form) {
  if (!ModelState.IsValid) {
    goto Error;
  }
  var validationResult = service.ValidateShippingForm(form);
  if (validationResult != ShippingFormValidationResult.Valid) {
    goto Error;
  }
  bool success = service.SaveShippingInfo(form);
  if (!success) {
    ModelState.AddModelError("", "Problem occurred while " +
      "saving your information, please try again");
    goto Error;
  }
  return RedirectToAction("Index", "BillingForm");
Error:                                                            The code that
  Response.Cookies.Append("shipping_error", "1");    ◁──┘ saves the cookie
  return RedirectToAction("Index", "ShippingForm", form);
}
```

By using goto, we actually kept our code style more readable with fewer indents, saved
ourselves time, and made it easier to make changes in the future because we only have
to change it once.

A statement like goto can still perplex a colleague who is not used to the syntax.
Luckily, C# 7.0 introduced local functions that can be used to perform the same work,
perhaps in a way that's easier to understand. We declare a local function called error
that performs the common error return operation and returns its result instead of
using goto. You can see it in action in the next listing.

Listing 3.15 Using local functions instead of goto

```
[HttpPost]
public IActionResult Submit4(ShipmentAddress form) {
  IActionResult error() {                            ◁─── Our local function
    Response.Cookies.Append("shipping_error", "1");
    return RedirectToAction("Index", "ShippingForm", form);
  }
  if (!ModelState.IsValid) {        ┌ Common error
    return error();              ◁──┘ return cases
  }
  var validationResult = service.ValidateShippingForm(form);
  if (validationResult != ShippingFormValidationResult.Valid) {
```

```
    return error();
  }
  bool success = service.SaveShippingInfo(form);
  if (!success) {
    ModelState.AddModelError("", "Problem occurred while " +
      "saving your information, please try again");
    return error();
  }
  return RedirectToAction("Index", "BillingForm");
}
```

Common error return cases

Using local functions also allows us to declare error handling at the top of the function, which is the norm with modern programming languages like Go, with statements like `defer`, although in our case, we have to explicitly call the `error()` function to execute it.

3.9 *Don't write code comments*

A Turkish architect called Sinan lived in the sixteenth century. He built the famous Suleymaniye Mosque in Istanbul and countless other buildings. There is a story about his prowess in architecture. As the story goes, hundreds of years after Sinan passed, a group of architects started restoration work on one of his buildings. There was a keystone in one of the archways that they needed to replace. They carefully removed the stone block and found a small glass vial wedged between blocks that contained a note. The note said, "This keystone would last only three hundred years. If you're reading this note, it must have broken down or you are trying to repair it. There is only one right way to put a new keystone back in correctly." The note continued with the technical details of how to replace the keystone properly.

Sinan the architect could be the first person in history who used code comments correctly. Consider the opposite case where the building had writings everywhere on it. Doors would have the text, "This is a door." Windows would have "Window" written over them. Between every brick there would be a glass vial with a note in it saying, "These are bricks."

You don't need to write code comments if your code is sufficiently self-explanatory. Conversely, you can hurt the readability of code with extraneous comments. Don't write code comments just for the sake of writing comments. Use them wisely and only when necessary.

Consider the example in the next listing. If we had gone overboard with code comments, it could have looked like this.

Listing 3.16   Code comments everywhere!

```
/// <summary>
/// Receive a shipment address model and update it in the
/// database and then redirect the user to billing page if
/// it's successful.
/// </summary>
```

These are already explained by the function's context and declaration.

```
/// <param name="form">The model to receive.</param>
/// <returns>Redirect result to the entry form if
/// there is an error, or redirect result to the
/// billing form page if successful.</returns>
[HttpPost]
public IActionResult Submit(ShipmentAddress form) {
  // Our common error handling code that saves the cookie
  // and redirects back to the entry form for
  // shipping information.
  IActionResult error() {
    Response.Cookies.Append("shipping_error", "1");
    return RedirectToAction("Index", "ShippingForm", form);
  }
  // check if the model state is valid
  if (!ModelState.IsValid) {
    return error();
  }
  // validate the form with server side validation logic.
  var validationResult = service.ValidateShippingForm(form);
  // is the validation successful?
  if (validationResult != ShippingFormValidationResult.Valid) {
    return error();
  }
  // save shipping information
  bool success = service.SaveShippingInfo(form);
  if (!success) {
    // failed to save. report the error to the user.
    ModelState.AddModelError("", "Problem occurred while " +
      "saving your information, please try again");
    return error();
  }
  // go to the billing form
  return RedirectToAction("Index", "BillingForm");
}
```

These are already explained by the function's context and declaration.

Literally a repetition of the following code

Again, completely unnecessary

Another repetition

Come on!

Really? We've come to this now?

No kidding, Sherlock.

I would never have guessed.

The code we're reading tells us a story even without the comments. Let's go over the same code without comments and find the hidden hints in it (figure 3.13).

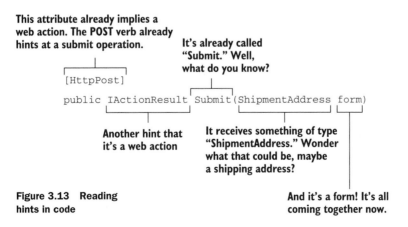

This attribute already implies a web action. The POST verb already hints at a submit operation.

It's already called "Submit." Well, what do you know?

```
[HttpPost]
public IActionResult Submit(ShipmentAddress form)
```

Another hint that it's a web action

It receives something of type "ShipmentAddress." Wonder what that could be, maybe a shipping address?

Figure 3.13 Reading hints in code

And it's a form! It's all coming together now.

This might look like a lot of work. You're trying to bring the pieces together just to understand what the code does. It does get better over time. You will spend less effort the better you get at it. There are things that you can do to improve the life of the poor soul who reads your code, and even yourself six months later, because after six months, it might as well be somebody else's code.

3.9.1 *Choose great names*

I touched on the importance of good names at the beginning of this chapter, about how our names should represent or summarize the functionality as closely as possible. Functions shouldn't have ambiguous names like *Process, DoWork, Make,* and so forth unless the context is absolutely clear. That might sometimes require you to type longer names than usual, but it's usually possible to create good names and still keep them concise.

The same applies for variable names. Reserve single-letter variable names only for loop variables (i, j, and n) and coordinates like x, y, and z where they are obvious. Otherwise, always pick a descriptive name, and avoid abbreviations. It's still okay to use well-known initialisms like HTTP and JSON or well-known abbreviations like ID and DB, but don't shorten words. You only type the variable name once anyway. Code completion can take care of the rest later. The benefits of descriptive names are tremendous. Most importantly, they save you time. When you pick a descriptive name, you don't have to write a full-sentence comment to explain it wherever it's used. Consult the convention documentation of the programming language you're using. Microsoft's guideline for .NET naming conventions, for example, is a great starting point for C#: https://docs.microsoft.com/en-us/dotnet/standard/design-guidelines/naming-guidelines.

3.9.2 *Leverage functions*

Small functions are easier to understand. Try to keep a function small enough to fit in a developer's screen. Scrolling back and forth is terrible for understanding what a code does. You should be able to see everything the function does right in front of you.

How do you shorten a function? Beginners might be inclined to put as much as possible on a single line to make the function more compressed. No! Never put multiple statements on a single line. Always have at least one line per statement. You can even have blank lines in a function to group relevant statements together. In light of this, let's look at our function in the next listing.

Listing 3.17 Using blank lines to separate logical parts of a function

```
[HttpPost]
public IActionResult Submit(ShipmentAddress form) {
  IActionResult error() {
    Response.Cookies.Append("shipping_error", "1");        Error-handling
    return RedirectToAction("Index", "ShippingForm", form);  code part
  }
```

```
  if (!ModelState.IsValid) {          MVC Model
    return error();                   validation part
  }
  var validationResult = service.ValidateShippingForm(form);
  if (validationResult != ShippingFormValidationResult.Valid) {   Server-side model
    return error();                                                 validation part
  }
  bool success = service.SaveShippingInfo(form);
  if (!success) {
    ModelState.AddModelError("", "Problem occurred while " +
      "saving your information, please try again");     Saving part and the
    return error();                                      successful case
  }
  return RedirectToAction("Index", "BillingForm");
}
```

You may ask how this helps make the function smaller. Yes, in fact, it makes the function bigger. But identifying logical parts of a function lets you refactor those parts into meaningful functions, which is the key to having small functions and descriptive code at the same time. You can refactor the same code into even more digestible chunks if the logic isn't straightforward enough to understand. In listing 3.18, we extract parts of the logic in our Submit function by using what we identified as logical parts. We basically have a validation part, an actual saving part, a save-error-handling part, and a successful response. We only leave those four parts in the body of the function.

Listing 3.18 Keeping only the descriptive functionality in the function

```
[HttpPost]
public IActionResult Submit(ShipmentAddress form) {
  if (!validate(form)) {
    return shippingFormError();         Validation
  }
  bool success = service.SaveShippingInfo(form);      Saving
  if (!success) {
    reportSaveError();         Error handling
    return shippingFormError();
  }
  return RedirectToAction("Index", "BillingForm");      Successful response
}

private bool validate(ShipmentAddress form) {
  if (!ModelState.IsValid) {
    return false;
  }
  var validationResult = service.ValidateShippingForm(form);
  return validationResult == ShippingFormValidationResult.Valid;
}

private IActionResult shippingFormError() {
  Response.Cookies.Append("shipping_error", "1");
  return RedirectToAction("Index", "ShippingForm", form);
}
```

```
private void reportSaveError() {
  ModelState.AddModelError("", "Problem occurred while " +
    "saving your information, please try again");
}
```

The actual function is so simple that it almost reads like an English sentence—well, maybe a hybrid of English and Turkish, but still very readable. We achieved greatly descriptive code without writing a single line of comment, and that's the key you need to keep in mind if you ever ask if it's too much work. It's less work than writing paragraphs of comments. You'll also thank yourself by shaking your left hand with your right hand when you learn that you don't need to keep comments and the actual code in sync for the comments to remain useful over the lifetime of the project. This is way better.

Extracting functions may look like a chore, but it's in fact a breeze with development environments like Visual Studio. You just select the part of the code that you want to extract and press Ctrl-. (the period key) or choose the light bulb icon appearing next to the code and select Extract Method. All you need to do is to give it a name.

When you extract those pieces, you also open a door to reusing those pieces of code in the same file, which can save you time when you're writing a billing form if the error-handling semantics aren't any different.

This all may sound like I'm against code comments. It's exactly the opposite. Avoiding unnecessary comments makes useful comments shine like jewels. It's the only way to make comments useful. Think like Sinan when you're writing comments: "Will someone need an explanation for this?" If it needs an explanation, be as clear as possible, be elaborate, even draw ASCII diagrams if necessary. Write as many paragraphs as you need, just so the developers working on the same code don't have to come to your desk and ask you what that piece of code does or fix it incorrectly because you forgot to explain yourself. It comes down to you to fix the code correctly when the production goes down. You owe this to yourself as much as to everybody else.

There are cases where you must write comments whether they are useful or not, such as public APIs, because users may not have access to the code. But that also doesn't mean that having written comments makes your code easy to understand. You still need to write clean code with small, easy-to-digest pieces.

Summary

- Avoid creating rigid code by avoiding violating logical dependency boundaries.
- Don't be afraid of doing a job from scratch because the next time you do it, it'll go much faster.
- Break the code when there are dependencies that might tie your shoelaces together in the future, and fix it.
- Avoid digging yourself a legacy hole by keeping the code up to date and fixing the problems it causes regularly.
- Repeat the code instead of reusing it to avoid violating logical responsibilities.

- Invent smart abstractions so the future code you write takes less time. Use abstractions as investments.
- Don't let the external libraries you use dictate your design.
- Prefer composition over inheritance to avoid binding your code to a specific hierarchy.
- Try to keep a code style that is easy to read from the top down.
- Exit early from functions and avoid using `else`.
- Use `goto` or, even better, a local function to keep common code in one place.
- Avoid frivolous, redundant code comments that make it impossible to distinguish the tree from the forest.
- Write self-descriptive code by leveraging good naming for variables and functions.
- Divide functions into easy-to-digest sub-functions to keep the code as descriptive as possible.
- Write code comments when they are useful.

Tasty testing 4

Many software developers would liken testing to writing a book: it's tedious, nobody likes doing it, and it rarely pays off. Compared to coding, testing is considered a second-class activity, not doing *the real work*. Testers are subjected to a preconception that they have it too easy.

The reason for the dislike of testing is that we developers see it as disconnected from building software. From a programmer's perspective, building software is all about writing code, whereas from a manager's vantage point, it's all about setting the right course for the team. Similarly, for a tester, it's all about the quality of the product. We consider testing an external activity because of our perception that it's not part of software development, and we want to be involved as little as possible.

Testing can be integral to a developer's work and can help them along the way. It can give you assurances that no other understanding of your code can give you. It can save you time, and you don't even need to hate yourself for it. Let's see how.

4.1 Types of tests

Software testing is about increasing confidence in the behavior of software. This is important: tests never guarantee a behavior, but they increase its likelihood quite a lot, as in orders of magnitude. There are many ways to categorize types of testing, but the most important distinction is how we run or implement it because it affects our time economy the most.

4.1.1 Manual testing

Testing can be a manual activity, and it usually is for developers, who test their code by running it and inspecting its behavior. Manual tests have their own types too, like end-to-end testing, which means testing every supported scenario on a software from beginning to end. End-to-end testing's value is enormous, but it's time consuming.

Code reviews can be considered a way of testing, albeit a weak one. You can understand what the code does and what it will do when it's run to a certain extent. You can vaguely see how it fulfills the requirements, but you can't tell for sure. Tests, based on their types, can provide different levels of assurance about how the code will work. In that sense, a code review can be considered a type of test.

What's a code review?

The main purpose of a code review is to examine code before it gets pushed to the repository and to find potential bugs in it. You could do it in a physical meeting or use a website like GitHub. Unfortunately, over the course of years, it has turned into many different things, ranging from a rite of passage that completely destroys the developer's self-esteem to a pile of a software architects' unwarranted quotes from articles they read.

The most important part of a code review is that it's the last moment when you can criticize the code without having to fix it yourself. After a piece of code passes the review, it becomes everyone's code because you all have approved it. You can always say, "I wish you'd said that in the code review, Mark," whenever someone brings up your terrible $O(N^2)$ sort code and then put your headphones back on. Just kidding—you should feel ashamed for writing an $O(N^2)$ sort code, especially after reading this book, but you still blame Mark! You should know better. Get along with your colleagues. You'll need them.

Ideally, code reviews are not about code style or formatting, because automated tools called either *linters* or *code analysis tools* can check for those issues. It should be mainly about bugs and the technical debt that the code might introduce to other developers. Code review is async pair programming; it's a cost-efficient way to keep everyone on the same page and put their collective minds into identifying potential problems.

4.1.2   Automated tests

You are a programmer; you have the gift of writing code. That means you can make the computer do things for you, and that includes testing. You can write code that tests your code, so you don't have to. Programmers usually focus on creating tooling only for the software they're developing, not on the development process itself, but that's equally important.

Automated tests can differ vastly in terms of their scope and, more importantly, in how much they increase your confidence in the behavior of the software. The smallest kinds of automated tests are *unit tests*. They are also the easiest to write because they test only a single unit of code: a public function. It needs to be public because testing is supposed to examine externally visible interfaces rather than the internal details of a class. The definition of a unit can sometimes change in the literature, be it a class or a module or another logical arrangement of those, but I find functions are convenient as the target units.

The problem with unit tests is that even though they let you see if units work okay, they can't guarantee if they work okay *together*. Consequently, you have to test whether they get along together too. Those tests are called *integration tests*. Automated UI tests are usually also integration tests if they run the production code to build the correct user interface.

4.1.3   Living dangerously: Testing in production

I had once bought a poster of a famous meme for one of our developers. It said, "I don't always test code, but when I do, I do it in *production*." I hung it on the wall right behind his monitor so he would always remember not to do that.

> **DEFINITION**   In software lingo, the term *production* means a live environment accessed by actual users where any change affects the actual data. Many developers confuse it with their computer. There is *development* for that. *Development* as a name for a runtime environment means code running locally on your machine and not affecting any data that harms production. As a precaution to harming production, there is sometimes a production-like remote environment that is similar to production. It's sometimes called *staging*, and it doesn't affect actual data that is visible to your site's users.

Testing in production, aka live code, is considered a bad practice; no wonder such a poster exists. The reason is because by the time you find a failure, you might have already lost users or customers. More importantly, when you break production, there is a chance that you might break the workflow of the whole development team. You can easily understand that it has happened by the disappointed looks and raised eyebrows you get if you're in an open office setting, along with text messages saying, "WTF!!!!???," Slack notification numbers increasing like KITT's[1] speedometer, or the steam coming out of your boss's ears.

---

[1] KITT, standing for Knight Industries Two Thousand, is a self-driving car equipped with voice recognition. It was depicted in the 1980s sci-fi TV series *Knight Rider*. It's normal that you don't understand this reference since anybody who did is probably dead, with the possible exception of David Hasselhoff. That guy is immortal.

Like any bad practice, testing in production isn't always bad. If the scenario you introduce isn't part of a frequently used, critical code path, you might get away with testing in production. That's why Facebook had the mantra "Move fast and break things," because they let the developers assess the impact of the change to the business. They later dropped the slogan after the 2016 US elections, but it still has some substance. If it's a small break in an infrequently used feature, it might be okay to live with the fallout and fix it as soon as possible.

Even not testing your code can be okay if you think breaking a scenario isn't something your users would abandon the app for. I managed to run one of the most popular websites in Turkey myself with zero automated tests in its first years, with a lot of errors and a lot of downtime, of course, because, hello: no automated tests!

4.1.4 *Choosing the right testing methodology*

You need to be aware of certain factors about a given scenario that you are trying to implement or change to decide how you want to test it. Those are mainly risk and cost. It's similar to what we used to calculate in our minds when our parents assigned us a chore:

- Cost
  - How much time do you need to spend to implement/run a certain test?
  - How many times will you need to repeat it?
  - If the code that is tested changes, who will know to test it?
  - How hard is it to keep the test reliable?
- Risk
  - How likely is this scenario to break?
  - If it breaks, how badly will it impact the business? How much money would you lose, aka, "Would this get me fired if it breaks?"
  - If it breaks, how many other scenarios will break along with it? For example, if your mailing feature stops working, many features that depend on it will be broken, too.
  - How frequently does the code change? How much do you anticipate it will change in the future? Every change introduces a new risk.

You need to find a sweet spot that costs you the least and poses the least risk. Every risk is an implication of more cost. In time, you will have a map of mental tradeoffs for how much cost a test introduces and how much risk it poses, as figure 4.1 shows.

Never say "It works on my computer" loudly to someone. That's for your internal thinking only. There will never be some code that you can describe by saying, "Well, it didn't work on my computer, but I was weirdly optimistic!" Of course, it works on your computer! Can you imagine deploying something that you cannot even run yourself? You can use it as a mantra while you're thinking about whether a feature should be tested as long as there is no chain of accountability. If nobody makes you answer for

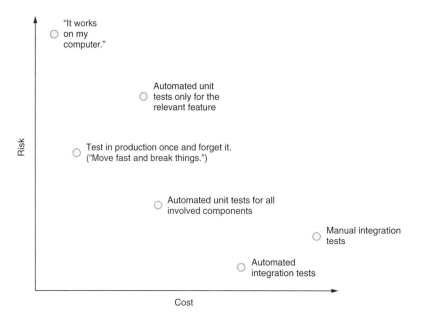

Figure 4.1   An example of a mental model to assess different testing strategies

your mistakes, then go for it. That means the (excess) budget of the company you're working for makes it possible for your bosses to tolerate those mistakes.

If you need to fix your own bugs, though, the "It works on my computer" mentality puts you into a very slow and time-wasting cycle because of the delay between the deployment and the feedback loops. One basic problem with developer productivity is that interruptions cause significant delays. The reason is *the zone.* I have already discussed how warming up to the code can get your productivity wheels turning. That mental state is sometimes called *the zone.* You're in the zone if you're in that productive state of mind. Similarly, getting interrupted can cause those wheels to stop and take you out of the zone, so you have to warm up again. As figure 4.2 shows, automated tests alleviate this problem by keeping you in the zone until you reach a certain degree of confidence about a feature's completion. It shows you two different cycles of how expensive "It works on my computer" can be for both the business and the developer. Every time you get out of the zone, you need extra time to reenter it, which sometimes can even be longer than the time required to test your feature manually.

You can achieve a quick iteration cycle similar to automated tests with manual tests, but they just take more time. That's why automated tests are great: they keep you in the zone and cost you the least time. Arguably, writing and running tests can be considered disconnected activities that might push you out of the zone. Still, running unit tests is extremely fast and is supposed to end in seconds. Writing tests is a slightly disconnected activity, but it still makes you think about the code you've written. You might even consider it a recap exercise. This chapter is mostly about unit testing in general because it is in the sweet spot of cost versus risk in figure 4.1.

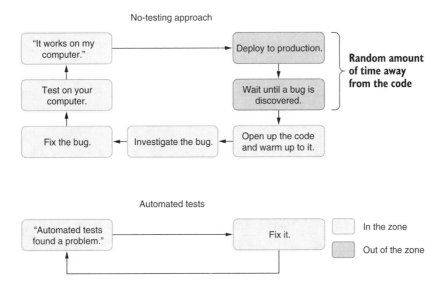

Figure 4.2   The expensive development cycle of "It works on my computer" versus automated tests

4.2   *How to stop worrying and love the tests*

Unit testing is about writing test code that tests a single unit of your code, usually a function. You will encounter people who argue about what constitutes a unit. Basically, it doesn't matter much as long as you can test a given unit in isolation. You can't test a whole class in a single test anyway. Every test actually tests only a single scenario for a function. Thus, it's usual to have multiple tests even for a single function.

Test frameworks make writing tests as easy as possible, but they are not necessary. A test suite can simply be a separate program that runs the tests and shows the results. As a matter of fact, that was the only way to test your program before test frameworks became a thing. I'd like to show you a simple piece of code and how unit testing has evolved over time so you can write tests for a given function as easily as possible.

Let's imagine that you are tasked with changing how the post dates are displayed on a microblogging website called Blabber. The post dates were displayed as a full date, and according to the new social media fashion, it's more favorable to use acronyms that show a duration since the post was created in seconds, minutes, hours, and so forth. You need to develop a function that gets a `DateTimeOffset` and converts it into a string that shows the time span in text is expressed as "3h" for three hours, "2m" for two minutes, or "1s" for one second. It should show only the most significant unit. If the post is three hours, two minutes, and one second old, it should only show "3h."

Listing 4.1 shows such a function. In this listing, we define an *extension method* to the `DateTimeOffset` class in .NET, so we can call it wherever we want, like a native method of `DateTimeOffset`.

Avoid polluting code completion with extension methods

C# provides a nice syntax to define additional methods for a type even if you don't have access to its source. If you prefix the first parameter of a function with the `this` keyword, it starts to appear in that type's method list in code completion. It's so convenient that developers like extension methods a lot and tend to make everything an extension method instead of a static method. Say, you have a simple method like this:

```
static class SumHelper {
   static int Sum(int a, int b) => a + b;
}
```

To call this method, you have to write `SumHelper.Sum(amount, rate);` and, more importantly, you must know that there is a class called `SumHelper`. You can write it as an extension method instead like this:

```
static class SumHelper {
   static decimal Sum(this int a, int b) => a + b;
}
```

Now you can call the method like this:

```
int result = 5.Sum(10);
```

It looks good, but there's a problem. Whenever you write an extension method for a well-known class like `string` or `int`, you introduce it to code completion, which is the dropdown you see on Visual Studio when you type a dot after an identifier. It can be extremely annoying to struggle to find the method you're looking for in the list of completely irrelevant methods.

Do not introduce a purpose-specific method into a commonly used .NET class. Do that only for generic methods that will be used commonly. For example, a `Reverse` method in a `string` class can be okay, but `MakeCdnFilename` wouldn't be. `Reverse` can be applicable in any context, but `MakeCdnFilename` would only be needed when you must, well, make a filename suitable for the content delivery network you're using. Other than that, it's a nuisance for you and every developer in your team. Don't make people hate you. More importantly, don't make yourself hate you. In those cases, you can perfectly use a static class and a syntax like `Cdn.MakeFilename()`.

Don't create an extension method when you can make the method part of the class. It only makes sense to do that when you want to introduce a new functionality beyond a dependency boundary. For example, you might have a web project that uses a class defined in a library that doesn't depend on web components. Later, you might want to add a specific functionality to that class related to web functionality in the web project. It's better to introduce a new dependency only to the extension method in the web project, rather than making the library depend on your web components. Unnecessary dependencies can tie your shoelaces together.

We calculate the interval between current time and the post time and check its fields to determine the most significant unit of the interval and return the result based on it.

Listing 4.1   A function that converts a date to a string representation of the interval

```
public static class DateTimeExtensions {
  public static string ToIntervalString(
    this DateTimeOffset postTime) {
    TimeSpan interval = DateTimeOffset.Now - postTime;
    if (interval.TotalHours >= 1.0) {
      return $"{(int)interval.TotalHours}h";
    }
    if (interval.TotalMinutes >= 1.0) {
      return $"{(int)interval.TotalMinutes}m";
    }
    if (interval.TotalSeconds >= 1.0) {
      return $"{(int)interval.TotalSeconds}s";
    }
    return "now";
  }
}
```

This defines an extension method to the **DateTimeOffset** class.

Calculate the interval.

It's possible to write this code more briefly or performant, but not when it sacrifices readability.

We have a vague spec about the function, and we can start writing some tests for it. It'd be a good idea to write possible inputs and expected outputs in a table to ensure the function works correctly, as in table 4.1.

Table 4.1   A sample test specification for our conversion function

Input	Output
< 1 second	"now"
< 1 minute	"<seconds>s"
< 1 hour	"<minutes>m"
>= 1 hour	"<hours>h"

If DateTimeOffset is a class, we should also be testing for the case when we pass null, but because it's a struct, it cannot be null. That saved us one test. Normally, you don't really need to create a table like that, and you can usually manage with a mental model of it, but whenever you're in doubt, by all means write it down.

Our tests should consist of calls with different DateTimeOffsets and comparisons with different strings. At this point, test reliability becomes a concern because Date-Time.Now always changes, and our tests are not guaranteed to run in a specific time. If another test was running or if something slowed the computer down, you can easily fail the test for the output now. That means our tests will be flaky and can fail occasionally.

That indicates a problem with our design. A simple solution would be to make our function deterministic by passing a TimeSpan instead of a DateTimeOffset and calculating the difference in the caller instead. As you can see, writing tests around your code helps you identify design problems too, which is one of the selling points of a test-driven development (TDD) approach. We didn't use TDD here because we know

we can just go ahead and change the function easily, as in the following listing, to
receive a TimeSpan directly.

Listing 4.2   Our refined design

```
public static string ToIntervalString(
  this TimeSpan interval) {          ⭠———— We receive a TimeSpan instead.
  if (interval.TotalHours >= 1.0) {
    return $"{(int)interval.TotalHours}h";
  }
  if (interval.TotalMinutes >= 1.0) {
    return $"{(int)interval.TotalMinutes}m";
  }
  if (interval.TotalSeconds >= 1.0) {
    return $"{(int)interval.TotalSeconds}s";
  }
  return "now";
}
```

Our test cases didn't change, but our tests will be much more reliable. More importantly, we decoupled two different tasks, calculating the difference between two dates
and converting an interval to a string representation. Deconstructing concerns in
code can help you achieve better designs. It can also be a chore to calculate differences, and you can have a separate wrapper function for that.

   Now how do we make sure our function works? We can simply push it to production and wait a couple minutes to hear any screams. If not, we're good to go. By the
way, is your résumé up to date? No reason, just asking.

   We can write a program that tests the function and see the results. An example
program would be like that in listing 4.3. It's a plain console application that references our project and uses the Debug.Assert method in the System.Diagnostics
namespace to make sure it passes. It ensures that the function returns expected values. Because asserts run only in Debug configuration, we also ensure that the code
isn't run in any other configuration at the beginning with a compiler directive.

Listing 4.3   Primitive unit testing

```
#if !DEBUG
#error asserts will only run in Debug configuration      ⭠———   We need the preprocessor
#endif                                                           statement to make asserts
using System;                                                    work.
using System.Diagnostics;
namespace DateUtilsTests {
  public class Program {
    public static void Main(string[] args) {
      var span = TimeSpan.FromSeconds(3);
      Debug.Assert(span.ToIntervalString() == "3s",         Test case for
"3s case failed");                                          seconds
      span = TimeSpan.FromMinutes(5);
      Debug.Assert(span.ToIntervalString() == "5m",         Test case for
"5m case failed");                                          minutes
```

```
      span = TimeSpan.FromHours(7);
      Debug.Assert(span.ToIntervalString() == "7h",
"7h case failed");
      span = TimeSpan.FromMilliseconds(1);
      Debug.Assert(span.ToIntervalString() == "now",
"now case failed");
    }
  }
}
```

Test case for hours

Test case for less than a second

So why do we need unit test frameworks? Can't we write all tests like this? We could, but it would take more work. In our example, you'll note the following:

- There is no way to detect if any of the tests failed from an external program, such as a build tool. We need special handling around that. Test frameworks and test runners that come with them handle that easily.
- The first failing test would cause the program to terminate. That will cost us time if we have many more failures. We will have to run tests again and again and thus wasting more time. Test frameworks can run all tests and report the failures all together, like compiler errors.
- It's impossible to run certain tests selectively. You might be working on a specific feature and want to debug the function you wrote by debugging the test code. Test frameworks allow you to debug specific tests without having to run the rest.
- Test frameworks can produce a code-coverage report that helps you identify missing test coverage on your code. That's not possible by writing ad hoc test code. If you happen to write a coverage analysis tool, you might as well work on creating a test framework.
- Although those tests don't depend on each other, they run sequentially, so running the whole test suite takes a long time. Normally, that's not a problem with a small number of test cases, but in a medium-scale project, you can have thousands of tests that take different amounts of times. You can create threads and run the tests in parallel, but that's too much work. Test frameworks can do all of that with a simple switch.
- When an error happens, you only know that there is a problem, but you have no idea about its nature. Strings are mismatched, so, what kind of mismatch is it? Did the function return null? Was there an extra character? Test frameworks can report these details too.
- Anything other than using .NET-provided `Debug.Assert` will require us writing extra code: a scaffolding, if you will. If you start down that path, using an existing framework is much better.
- You'll have the opportunity to join never-ending debates about which test framework is better and to feel superior for completely wrong reasons.

Now, let's try writing the same tests with a test framework, as in listing 4.4. Many test frameworks look alike, with the exception of xUnit, which was supposedly developed by extraterrestrial life-forms visiting Earth, but in principle, it shouldn't matter which framework you're using, with the exception of slight changes in the terminology. We're using NUnit here, but you can use any framework you want. You'll see how much clearer the code is with a framework. Most of our test code is actually pretty much a text version of our input/output table, as in table 4.1. It's apparent what we're testing, and more importantly, although we only have a single test method, we have the capability to run or debug each test individually in the test runner. The technique we used in listing 4.4 with `TestCase` attributes is called a *parameterized test*. If you have a specific set of inputs and outputs, you can simply declare them as data and use it in the same function over and over, avoiding the repetition of writing a separate test for each test. Similarly, by combining `ExpectedResult` values and declaring the function with a return value, you don't even need to write `Asserts` explicitly. The framework does it automatically. It's less work!

You can run these tests in a Test Explorer window of Visual Studio: View → Test Explorer. You can also run a `dotnet` test from the command prompt, or you can even use a third-party test runner like NCrunch. The test results in Visual Studio's Test Explorer will look like those in figure 4.3.

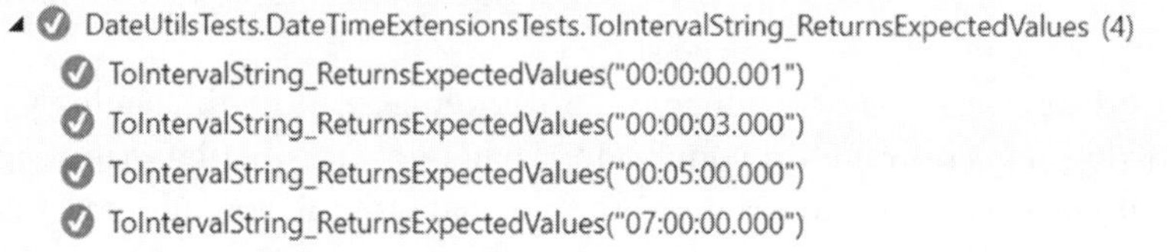

▲ ✅ DateUtilsTests.DateTimeExtensionsTests.ToIntervalString_ReturnsExpectedValues (4)

   ✅ ToIntervalString_ReturnsExpectedValues("00:00:00.001")

   ✅ ToIntervalString_ReturnsExpectedValues("00:00:03.000")

   ✅ ToIntervalString_ReturnsExpectedValues("00:05:00.000")

   ✅ ToIntervalString_ReturnsExpectedValues("07:00:00.000")

Figure 4.3   Test results that you can't take your eyes off

Listing 4.4   Test framework magic

```
using System;
using NUnit.Framework;
namespace DateUtilsTests {
  class DateUtilsTest {
    [TestCase("00:00:03.000", ExpectedResult = "3s")]
    [TestCase("00:05:00.000", ExpectedResult = "5m")]
    [TestCase("07:00:00.000", ExpectedResult = "7h")]
    [TestCase("00:00:00.001", ExpectedResult = "now")]
    public string ToIntervalString_ReturnsExpectedValues(        Converting a string
      string timeSpanText) {                                     to our input type
      var input = TimeSpan.Parse(timeSpanText);   ◄─────────
      return input.ToIntervalString();   ◄────────
    }                                          No assertions!
  }
}
```

You can see how a single function is actually broken into four different functions during the test-running phase and how its arguments are displayed along with the test name in figure 4.3. More importantly, you can select a single test, run it, or debug it. And if a test fails, you see a brilliant report that exactly tells what's wrong with your code. Say you accidentally wrote *nov* instead of *now*. The test error would show up like this:

```
Message:
      String lengths are both 3. Strings differ at index 2.
      Expected: "now"
      But was:  "nov"
      ------------^
```

Not only do you see that there is an error, but you also see a clear explanation about where it happened.

It's a no-brainer to use test frameworks, and you will get to love writing tests more when you're aware of how they save you extra work. They are NASA preflight check lights, "system status nominal" announcements, and they are your little nanobots doing their work for you. Love tests, love test frameworks.

4.3 Don't use TDD or other acronyms

Unit testing, like every successful religion, has split into factions. Test-driven development (TDD) and behavior-driven development (BDD) are some examples. I've come to believe that there are people in the software industry who really love to create new paradigms and standards to be followed without question, and there are people who just love to follow them without question. We love prescriptions and rituals because all we need to do is to follow them without thinking too much. That can cost us a lot of time and make us hate testing.

The idea behind TDD is that writing tests before actual code can guide you to write better code. TDD prescribes that you should write tests for a class first before writing a single line of code of that class, so the code you write constitutes a guideline for how to implement the actual code. You write your tests. It fails to compile. You start writing actual code, and it compiles. Then you run tests, and they fail. Then you fix the bugs in your code to make the tests pass. BDD is also a test-first approach with differences in the naming and layout of tests.

The philosophy behind TDD and BDD isn't complete rubbish. When you think about how some code should be tested first, it can influence how you think about its design. The problem with TDD isn't the mentality but the practice, the ritualistic approach: write tests, and because the actual code is still missing, get a compiler error (wow, really, Sherlock?); after writing the code, fix the test failures. I hate errors. They make me feel unsuccessful. Every red squiggly line in the editor, every STOP sign in the Errors list window, and every warning icon is a cognitive load, confusing and distracting me.

When you focus on the test before you write a single line of code, you start thinking more about tests than your own problem domain. You start thinking about better ways to write tests. Your mental space gets allocated to the task of writing tests, the test framework's syntactic elements, and the organization of tests, rather than the production code itself. That's not the goal of testing. Tests shouldn't make you think. Tests should be the easiest piece of code you can write. If that's not the case, you're doing it wrong.

Writing tests before writing code triggers the sunk-cost fallacy. Remember how in chapter 3 dependencies made your code more rigid? Surprise! Tests depend on your code too. When you have a full-blown test suite at hand, you become disinclined to change the design of the code because that would mean changing the tests too. It reduces your flexibility when you're prototyping code. Arguably, tests can give you some ideas about whether the design really works, but only in isolated scenarios. You might later discover that a prototype doesn't work well with other components and change your design before you write any tests. That could be okay if you spend a lot of time on the drawing board when you're designing, but that's not usually the case in the streets. You need the ability to quickly change your design.

You can consider writing tests when you believe you're mostly done with your prototype and it seems to be working out okay. Yes, tests will make your code harder to change then, but at the same time, they will compensate for that by making you confident in the behavior of your code, letting you make changes more easily. You'll effectively get faster.

4.4 Write tests for your own good

Yes, writing tests improves the software, but it also improves your living standards. I already discussed how writing tests first can constrain you from changing your code's design. Writing tests last can make your code more flexible because you can easily make significant changes later, without worrying about breaking the behavior after you forget about the code completely. It frees you. It works as insurance, almost the inverse of the sunk-cost fallacy. The difference in writing tests after is that you are not discouraged in a rapid iteration phase like prototyping. You need to overhaul some code? The first step you need to take is to write tests for it.

Writing tests after you have a good prototype works as a recap exercise for your design. You go over the whole code once again with tests in mind. You can identify certain problems that you didn't find when you were prototyping your code.

Remember how I pointed out that doing small, trivial fixes in the code can get you warmed up for large coding tasks? Well, writing tests is a great way to do that. Find missing tests and add them. It never hurts to have more tests unless they're redundant. They don't have to be related to your upcoming work. You can simply blindly add test coverage, and who knows, you might find bugs while doing so.

Tests can act as a specification or documentation if they're written in a clear, easy-to-understand way. Code for each test should describe the input and the expected output of a function by how it's written and how it's named. Code may not be the best way to describe something, but it's a thousand times better than having nothing at all.

Do you hate it when your colleagues break your code? Tests are there to help. Tests enforce the contract between the code and the specification that developers can't break. You won't have to see comments like this:

```
// When this code was written,
// only God and I knew what it did.
// Now only God knows.²
```

Tests assure you that a fixed bug will remain fixed and won't appear again. Every time you fix a bug, adding a test for it will ensure you won't have to deal with that bug again, ever. Otherwise, who knows when another change will trigger it again? Tests are critical timesavers when used this way.

Tests improve both the software and the developer. Write tests to be a more efficient developer.

4.5 Deciding what to test

That is not halted which can eternal run,
And with strange eons, even tests may be down.

—H. P. Codecraft

Writing one test and seeing it pass is only half of the story. It doesn't mean your function works. Will it fail when the code breaks? Have you covered all the possible scenarios? What should you be testing for? If your tests don't help you find bugs, they are already failures.

One of my managers had a manual technique to ensure that his team wrote reliable tests: he removed random lines of code from the production code and ran tests again. If your tests passed, that meant you failed.

There are better approaches to identify what cases to test. A specification is a great starting point, but you rarely have those in the streets. It might make sense to create a specification yourself, but even if the only thing you have is code, there are ways to identify what to test.

4.5.1 Respect boundaries

You can call a function that receives a simple integer with four billion different values. Does that mean that you have to test whether your function works for each one of those? No. Instead, you should try to identify which input values cause the code to diverge into a branch or cause values to overflow and then test values around those.

Consider a function that checks whether a birth date is of legal age for the registration page of your online game. It's trivial for anyone who was born 18 years before (assuming 18 is the legal age for your game): you just subtract the years and check whether it's at least 18. But what if that person turned 18 last week? Are you going to

---

² That infamous comment is a derivative joke originally attributed to the author John Paul Friedrich Richter who lived in the 19th century. He didn't write a single line of code—only comments (https://quoteinvestigator .com/2013/09/24/god-knows/).

deprive that person of enjoying your pay-to-win game with mediocre graphics? Of course not.

Let's define a function `IsLegalBirthdate`. We use a `DateTime` class instead of `DateTimeOffset` to represent a birth date because birth dates don't have time zones. If you were born on December 21 in Samoa, your birthday is December 21 everywhere in the world, even in American Samoa, which is 24 hours ahead of Samoa despite being only a hundred miles away. I'm sure there is intense discussion there every year about when to have relatives over for Christmas dinner. Time zones are weird.

Anyway, we first calculate the year difference. The only time we need to look at exact dates is for the year of that person's 18th birthday. If it's that year, we check the month and the day. Otherwise, we only check whether the person is older than 18. We use a constant to signify legal age instead of writing the number everywhere because writing the number is susceptible to typos, and when your boss comes asking you, "Hey, can you raise the legal age to 21?," you only have one place to edit it out in this function. You also avoid having to write `// legal age` next to every `18` in the code to explain it. It suddenly becomes self-explanatory. Every conditional in the function—which encompasses `if` statements, `while` loops, `switch` cases, and so forth—causes only certain input values to exercise the code path inside. That means we can split the range of input values based on the conditionals, depending on the input parameters. In the example in listing 4.5, we don't need to test for all possible `DateTime` values between January 1 of the year AD 1 and December 31, 9999, which is about 3.6 million. We only need to test for 7 different inputs.

Listing 4.5   The bouncer's algorithm

```
public static bool IsLegalBirthdate(DateTime birthdate) {
  const int legalAge = 18;
  var now = DateTime.Now;
  int age = now.Year - birthdate.Year;
  if (age == legalAge) {
    return now.Month > birthdate.Month          Conditionals
      || (now.Month == birthdate.Month          in the code
        && now.Day > birthdate.Day);
  }
  return age > legalAge;
}
```

The seven input values are listed in table 4.2.

Table 4.2   Partitioning input values based on conditionals

	Year difference	Month of birth date	Day of birth date	Expected result
1	= 18	= Current month	< Current day	true
2	= 18	= Current month	= Current day	false
3	= 18	= Current month	> Current day	false

Table 4.2 Partitioning input values based on conditionals *(continued)*

	Year difference	Month of birth date	Day of birth date	Expected result
4	= 18	< Current month	Any	true
5	= 18	> Current month	Any	false
6	> 18	Any	Any	true
7	< 18	Any	Any	false

We suddenly brought down our number of cases from 3.6 million to 7, simply by identifying conditionals. Those conditionals that split the input range are called *boundary conditionals* because they define the boundaries for input values for possible code paths in the function. Then we can go ahead and write tests for those input values, as shown in listing 4.6. We basically create a clone of our test table in our inputs and convert it to a DateTime and run through our function. We can't hardcode DateTime values directly into our input/output table because a birth date's legality changes based on the current time.

We could convert this to a TimeSpan-based function as we did before, but legal age isn't based on an exact number of days—it's based on an absolute date-time instead. Table 4.2 is also better because it reflects your mental model more accurately. We use -1 for less than, 1 for greater than, and 0 for equality, and prepare our actual input values using those values as references.

Listing 4.6 Creating our test function from table 4.2

```
[TestCase(18,  0, -1, ExpectedResult = true)]
[TestCase(18,  0,  0, ExpectedResult = false)]
[TestCase(18,  0,  1, ExpectedResult = false)]
[TestCase(18, -1,  0, ExpectedResult = true)]
[TestCase(18,  1,  0, ExpectedResult = false)]
[TestCase(19,  0,  0, ExpectedResult = true)]
[TestCase(17,  0,  0, ExpectedResult = false)]
public bool IsLegalBirthdate_ReturnsExpectedValues(
  int yearDifference, int monthDifference, int dayDifference) {
  var now = DateTime.Now;
  var input = now.AddYears(-yearDifference)      ┐ Preparing our
    .AddMonths(monthDifference)                  │ actual input here
    .AddDays(dayDifference);                      ┘
  return DateTimeExtensions.IsLegalBirthdate(input);
}
```

We did it! We narrowed down the number of possible inputs and identified exactly what to test in our function to create a concrete test plan.

Whenever you need to find out what to test in a function, you're supposed to start with a specification. In the streets, however, you'll likely figure out that a specification has never existed or was obsolete a long time ago, so the second-best way would be to start with boundary conditions. Using parameterized tests also helps us focus on what to test rather than on writing repetitive test code. It's occasionally inevitable that we have to create a new function for each test, but specifically with data-bound tests like this one, parameterized tests can save you considerable time.

4.5.2   Code coverage

Code coverage is magic, and like magic, it's mostly stories. Code coverage is measured by injecting every line of your code with callbacks to trace how far the code called by a test executes and which parts it misses. That way, you can find out which part of the code isn't exercised and therefore is missing tests.

Development environments rarely come with code-coverage measurement tools out of the box. They are either in astronomically priced versions of Visual Studio or other paid third-party tools like NCrunch, dotCover, and NCover. Codecov (https://codecov.io) is a service that can work with your online repository, and it offers a free plan. Free code-coverage measurement locally in .NET was possible only with the Coverlet library and code-coverage reporting extensions in Visual Studio Code when this book was drafted.

Code-coverage tools tell you which parts of your code ran when you ran your tests. It's quite handy to see what kind of test coverage you're missing to exercise all code paths. It's not the only part of the story, and it's certainly not the most effective. You can have 100% code coverage and still have missing test cases. I'll discuss them later in the chapter.

Assume that we comment out the tests that call our `IsLegalBirthdate` function with a birth date that is exactly 18 years old, as in the following listing.

Listing 4.7   Missing tests

```
//[TestCase(18,   0, -1, ExpectedResult = true)]
//[TestCase(18,   0,  0, ExpectedResult = false)]
//[TestCase(18,   0,  1, ExpectedResult = false)]      Commented-out
//[TestCase(18,  -1,  0, ExpectedResult = true)]       test cases
//[TestCase(18,   1,  0, ExpectedResult = false)]
[TestCase(19,   0,  0, ExpectedResult = true)]
[TestCase(17,   0,  0, ExpectedResult = false)]
public bool IsLegalBirthdate_ReturnsExpectedValues(
  int yearDifference, int monthDifference, int dayDifference) {
  var now = DateTime.Now;
  var input = now.AddYears(-yearDifference)
    .AddMonths(monthDifference)
    .AddDays(dayDifference);
  return DateTimeExtensions.IsLegalBirthdate(input);
}
```

In this case, a tool like NCrunch, for example, would show the missing coverage, as in figure 4.4. The coverage circle next to the return statement inside the `if` statement is grayed out because we never call the function with a parameter that matches the condition `age == legalAge`. That means we're missing some input values.

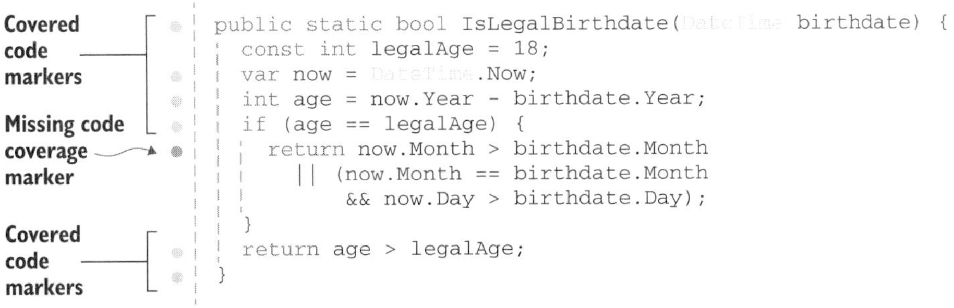

```
Covered          ●   public static bool IsLegalBirthdate(DateTime birthdate) {
code                     const int legalAge = 18;
markers          ●       var now = DateTime.Now;
                 ●       int age = now.Year - birthdate.Year;
Missing code     ●       if (age == legalAge) {
coverage         ●         return now.Month > birthdate.Month
marker                       || (now.Month == birthdate.Month
                                   && now.Day > birthdate.Day);
                         }
Covered          ●       return age > legalAge;
code             ●   }
markers
```

Figure 4.4   Missing code coverage

When you uncomment those commented-out test cases and run tests again, code coverage shows that you have 100% code coverage, as figure 4.5 shows.

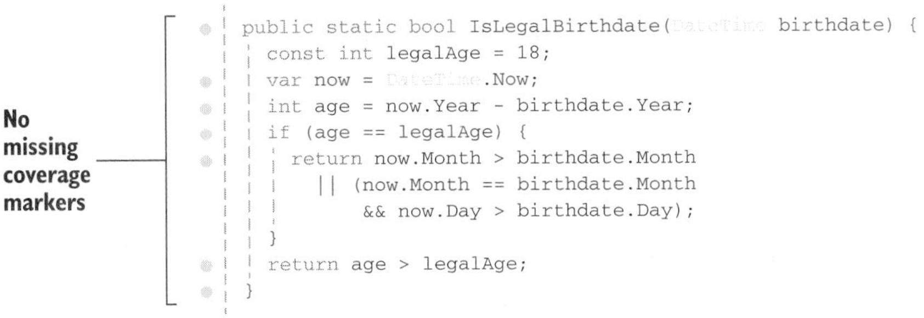

```
                 ●   public static bool IsLegalBirthdate(DateTime birthdate) {
                         const int legalAge = 18;
                 ●       var now = DateTime.Now;
                 ●       int age = now.Year - birthdate.Year;
                 ●       if (age == legalAge) {
No               ●         return now.Month > birthdate.Month
missing                      || (now.Month == birthdate.Month
coverage                           && now.Day > birthdate.Day);
markers                  }
                 ●       return age > legalAge;
                 ●   }
```

Figure 4.5   Full code coverage

Code-coverage tools are a good starting point, but they are not fully effective in showing actual test coverage. You should still have a good understanding of the range of input values and boundary conditionals. One-hundred percent code coverage doesn't mean 100% test coverage. Consider the following function where you need to return an item from list by index:

```
public Tag GetTagDetails(byte numberOfItems, int index) {
  return GetTrendingTags(numberOfItems)[index];
}
```

Calling that function GetTagDetails(1, 0); would succeed, and we would immediately achieve 100% code coverage. Would we have tested all the possible cases? No. Our input coverage would be nowhere close to that. What if numberOfItems is zero and index is non-zero? What happens if index is negative?

These concerns mean that we shouldn't be focusing solely on code coverage and trying to fill all the gaps. Instead, we should be conscious about our test coverage by taking all possible inputs into account and being smart about the boundary values. That said, they are not mutually exclusive: you can use both approaches at the same time.

4.6   *Don't write tests*

Yes, testing is helpful, but nothing's better than completely avoiding writing tests. How do you get away without writing tests and still keep your code reliable?

4.6.1   *Don't write code*

If a piece of code doesn't exist, it doesn't need to be tested. Deleted code has no bugs. Think about this when you're writing code. Is it worth writing tests for? Maybe you don't need to write that code at all. For example, can you use an existing package instead of implementing it from scratch? Can you leverage an existing class that does the exact same thing you are trying to implement? For example, you might be tempted to write custom regular expressions for validating URLs when all you need to do is to leverage the `System.Uri` class.

Third-party code isn't guaranteed to be perfect or always suitable for your purposes, of course. You might later discover that the code doesn't work for you, but it's usually worth taking that risk before trying to write something from scratch. Similarly, the same code base you're working on might have the code doing the same job implemented by a colleague. Search your code base to see if something's there.

If nothing works, be ready to implement your own. Don't be scared of reinventing the wheel. It can be very educational, as I discussed in chapter 3.

4.6.2   *Don't write all the tests*

The famous *Pareto principle* states that 80% of consequences are the results of 20% of the causes. At least, that's what 80% of the definitions say. It's more commonly called the *80/20 principle*. It's also applicable in testing. You can get 80% reliability from 20% test coverage if you choose your tests wisely.

Bugs don't appear homogeneously. Not every code line has the same probability of producing a bug. It's more likely to find bugs in more commonly used code and code with high churn. You can call those areas of the code where a problem is more likely to happen *hot paths*.

That's exactly what I did with my website. It had no tests whatsoever even after it became one of the most popular Turkish websites in the world. Then I had to add tests because too many bugs started to appear with the text markup parser. The markup was custom and it barely resembled Markdown, but I developed it before Markdown was even a vitamin in the oranges Dave Gruber ate. Because parsing logic was complicated and prone to bugs, it became economically infeasible to fix every issue after deploying to production. I developed a test suite for it. That was before the advent of test frameworks, so I had to develop my own. I incrementally added more tests as more bugs appeared because I hated creating the same bugs, and we developed a quite extensive test suite later, which saved us thousands of failing production deployments. Tests just work.

Even just viewing your website's home page provides a good amount of code coverage because it exercises many shared code paths with other pages. That's called *smoke testing* in the streets. It comes from the times when they developed the first prototype of the computer and just tried to turn it on to see if smoke came out of it. If there was no smoke, that was pretty much a good sign. Similarly, having good test coverage for critical, shared components is more important than having 100% code coverage. Don't spend hours just to add test coverage for a single line in a rudimentary constructor that isn't covered by tests if it won't make much difference. You already know that code coverage isn't the whole story.

4.7 Let the compiler test your code

With a strongly typed language, you can leverage the type system to reduce the number of test cases you'll need. I've already discussed how nullable references can help you avoid null checks in the code, which also reduces the need to write tests for null cases. Let's look at a simple example. In the previous section, we validated that the person who wants to register is at least 18 years old. We now need to validate if the chosen username is valid, so we need a function that validates usernames.

4.7.1 Eliminate null checks

Let our rule for a username be lowercase alphanumeric characters, up to eight characters long. A regular expression pattern for such a username would be `"^[a-z0-9]{1,8}$"`. We can write a username class, as in listing 4.8. We define a `Username` class to represent all usernames in the code. We avoid having to think about where we should validate our input by passing this to any code that requires a username.

To make sure that a username is never invalid, we validate the parameter in the constructor and throw an exception if it's not in the correct format. Apart from the constructor, the rest of the code is boilerplate to make it work in comparison scenarios. Remember, you can always derive such a class by creating a base `StringValue` class and writing minimal code for each string-based value class. I wanted to keep implementations duplicate in the book to clarify what the code entails. Notice the use of the `nameof` operator instead of hardcoded strings for references to parameters. It lets you keep names in sync after renaming. It can also be used for fields and properties and is especially useful for test cases where data is stored in a separate field and you have to refer to it by its name.

Listing 4.8 A username value type implementation

```
public class Username {
  public string Value { get; private set; }
  private const string validUsernamePattern = @"^[a-z0-9]{1,8}$";

  public Username(string username) {
    if (username is null) {
      throw new ArgumentNullException(nameof(username));
    }
    if (!Regex.IsMatch(username, validUsernamePattern)) {
      throw new ArgumentException(nameof(username),
```

We validate the username here, once and for all.

```
          "Invalid username");
      }
      this.Value = username;
   }

   public override string ToString() => base.ToString();
   public override int GetHashCode() => Value.GetHashCode();
   public override bool Equals(object obj) {
      return obj is Username other && other.Value == Value;
   }
   public static implicit operator string(Username username) {
      return username.Value;
   }
   public static bool operator==(Username a, Username b) {
      return a.Value == b.Value;
   }
   public static bool operator !=(Username a, Username b) {
      return !(a == b);
   }
}
```

Our usual boilerplate to make a class comparable

Myths around regular expressions

Regular expressions are one of the most brilliant inventions in the history of computer science. We owe them to the venerable Stephen Cole Kleene. They let you create a text parser out of a couple of characters. The pattern "light" matches only the string "light" while "[ln]ight" matches both "light" and "night." Similarly, "li(gh){1,2}t" matches only the words "light" and "lighght," which is not a typo but a single-word Aram Saroyan poem.

Jamie Zawinski famously said, "Some people, when confronted with a problem, think 'I know, I'll use regular expressions.' Now they have two problems." The phrase *regular expression* implies certain parsing characteristics. Regular expressions are not context aware, so you can't use a single regular expression to find the innermost tag in an HTML document or to detect unmatched closing tags. That means they are not suitable for complicated parsing tasks. Still, you can use them to parse text with a non-nested structure.

Regular expressions are surprisingly performant for the cases they suit. If you need extra performance, you can precompile them in C# by creating a `Regex` object with the option `RegexOptions.Compiled`. That means custom code that parses a string based on your pattern will be created on demand. Your pattern turns into C# and eventually into machine code. Consecutive calls to the same `Regex` object will reuse the compiled code, gaining you performance for multiple iterations.

Despite how performant they are, you shouldn't use regular expressions when a simpler alternative exists. If you need to check whether a string is a certain length, a simple `"str.Lengthv== 5"` will be way faster and more readable than `"Regex.IsMatch (@"^.{5}$", str)"`. Similarly, the `string` class contains many performant methods for common string-check operations like `StartsWith`, `EndsWith`, `IndexOf`, `Last-IndexOf`, `IsNullOrEmpty`, and `IsNullOrWhiteSpace`. Always prefer provided methods over regular expressions for their specific use cases.

That said, it's also important for you to know at least the basic syntax of regular expressions because they can be powerful in a development environment. You can manipulate code in quite complicated ways that can save you hours of work. All popular text editors support regular expressions for find-and-replace operations. I'm talking about operations like "I want to move hundreds of bracket characters in the code to the next line only when they appear next to a line of code." You can think about correct regular expression patterns for a couple of minutes as opposed to doing it manually for an hour.

Testing the constructor of Username would require us to create three different test methods, as shown in listing 4.9: one for nullability because a different exception type is raised; one for non-null but invalid inputs; and finally, one for the valid inputs, because we need to make sure that it also recognizes valid inputs as valid.

Listing 4.9 Tests for the Username class

```
class UsernameTest {
  [Test]
  public void ctor_nullUsername_ThrowsArgumentNullException() {
    Assert.Throws<ArgumentNullException>(
      () => new Username(null));
  }

  [TestCase("")]
  [TestCase("Upper")]
  [TestCase("toolongusername")]
  [TestCase("root!!")]
  [TestCase("a b")]
  public void ctor_invalidUsername_ThrowsArgumentException(string username) {
    Assert.Throws<ArgumentException>(
      () => new Username(username));
  }

  [TestCase("a")]
  [TestCase("1")]
  [TestCase("hunter2")]
  [TestCase("12345678")]
  [TestCase("abcdefgh")]
  public void ctor_validUsername_DoesNotThrow(string username) {
    Assert.DoesNotThrow(() => new Username(username));
  }
}
```

Had we enabled nullable references for the project Username class was in, we wouldn't need to write tests for the null case at all. The only exception would be when we're writing a public API, which may not run against a nullable-references-aware code. In that case, we'd still need to check against nulls.

Similarly, declaring Username a struct when suitable would make it a value type, which would also remove the requirement for a null check. Using correct types and correct structures for types will help us reduce the number of tests. The compiler will ensure the correctness of our code instead.

Using specific types for our purposes reduces the need for tests. When your registration function receives a Username instead of a string, you don't need to check whether the registration function validates its arguments. Similarly, when your function receives a URL argument as a Uri class, you don't need to check whether your function processes the URL correctly anymore.

4.7.2   Eliminate range checks

You can use unsigned integer types to reduce the range of possible invalid input values. You can see unsigned versions of primitive integer types in table 4.3. There you can see the varieties of data types with their possible ranges that might be more suitable for your code. It's also important that you keep in mind whether the type is directly compatible with int because it's the go-to type of .NET for integers. You probably have already seen these types, but you might not have considered that they can save you having to write extra test cases. For example, if your function needs only positive values, then why bother with int and checking for negative values and throwing exceptions? Just receive uint instead.

Table 4.3   Alternative integer types with different value ranges

Name	Integer type	Value range	Assignable to int without loss?
int	32-bit signed	-2147483648..2147483647	Duh
uint	32-bit unsigned	0..4294967295	No
long	64-bit signed	-9223372036854775808..9223372036854775807	No
ulong	64-bit unsigned	0..18446744073709551615	No
short	16-bit signed	-32768..32767	Yes
ushort	16-bit unsigned	0..65535	Yes
sbyte	8-bit signed	-128..127	Yes
byte	8-bit unsigned	0..255	Yes

When you use an unsigned type, trying to pass a negative constant value to your function will cause a compiler error. Passing a variable with a negative value is possible only with explicit type casting, which makes you think about whether the value you have is really suitable for that function at the call site. It's not the function's responsibility to validate for negative arguments anymore. Assume that a function needs to return trending tags in your microblogging website up to only a specified number of tags. It receives a number of items to retrieve rows of posts, as in listing 4.10.

Also in listing 4.10, a GetTrendingTags function returns items by taking the number of items into account. Notice that the input value is a byte instead of int because we don't have any use case more than 255 items in the trending tag list. That actually immediately eliminates the cases where an input value can be negative or too large. We don't even need to validate the input anymore. This results in one fewer test case and a much better range of input values, which reduces the area for bugs immediately.

> **Listing 4.10 Receiving posts only belonging to a certain page**

```
using System;
using System.Collections.Generic;
using System.Linq;

namespace Posts {
  public class Tag {
    public Guid Id { get; set; }
    public string Title { get; set; }
  }

  public class PostService {
    public const int MaxPageSize = 100;
    private readonly IPostRepository db;

    public PostService(IPostRepository db) {
      this.db = db;
    }

    public IList<Tag> GetTrendingTags(byte numberOfItems) {      ◁──┘ We chose byte
      return db.GetTrendingTagTable()                                  instead of int.
        .Take(numberOfItems)         ◁────── A byte or a ushort can be
        .ToList();                           passed as safely as int too.
    }
  }
}
```

Two things are happening here. First, we chose a smaller data type for our use case. We don't intend to support billions of rows in a trending tag box. We don't even know what that would look like. We have narrowed down our input space. Second, we chose byte, an unsigned type, which cannot be negative. That way, we avoided a possible test case and a potential problem that might cause an exception. LINQ's Take function doesn't throw an exception with a List, but it can when it gets translated to a query for a database like Microsoft SQL Server. By changing the type, we avoid those cases, and we don't need to write tests for them.

Note that .NET uses int as the de facto standard type for many operations like indexing and counting. Opting for a different type might require you to cast and convert values into ints if you happen to interact with standard .NET components. You need to make sure that you're not digging yourself into a hole by being pedantic. Your quality of life and the enjoyment you get from writing code are more important than a certain one-off case you're trying to avoid. For example, if you need more than 255 items in the future, you'll have to replace all references to bytes with shorts or ints, which can be time consuming. You need to make sure that you are saving yourself from writing tests for a worthy cause. You might even find writing additional tests more favorable in many cases than dealing with different types. In the end, it's only your comfort and your time that matter, despite how powerful it is to use types for hinting at valid value ranges.

4.7.3 *Eliminate valid value checks*

There are times we use values to signify an operation in a function. A common example is the fopen function in the C programming language. It takes a second string parameter that symbolizes the open mode, which can mean *open for reading*, *open for appending*, *open for writing*, and so forth.

Decades after C, the .NET team has made a better decision and created separate functions for each case. You have separate File.Create, File.OpenRead, and File.OpenWrite methods, avoiding the need for an extra parameter and for parsing that parameter. It's impossible to pass along the wrong parameter. It's impossible for functions to have bugs in parameter parsing because there is no parameter.

It's common to use such values to signify a type of operation. You should consider separating them into distinct functions instead, which can both convey the intent better and reduce your test surface.

One common technique in C# is to use Boolean parameters to change the logic of the running function. An example is to have a sorting option in the trending tags retrieval function, as in listing 4.11. Assume that we need trending tags in our tag management page, too, and that it's better to show them sorted by title there. In contradiction with the laws of thermodynamics, developers tend to constantly lose entropy. They always try to make the change with the least entropy without thinking about how much of a burden it will be in the future. The first instinct of a developer can be to add a Boolean parameter and be done with it.

Listing 4.11 Boolean parameters

```
public IList<Tag> GetTrendingTags(byte numberOfItems,
  bool sortByTitle) {                          ←——  Newly added parameter
    var query = db.GetTrendingTagTable();
    if (sortByTitle) {                         ←——  Newly introduced conditional
      query = query.OrderBy(p => p.Title);
    }
    return query.Take(numberOfItems).ToList();
}
```

The problem is that if we keep adding Booleans like this, it can get really complicated because of the combinations of the function parameters. Let's say another feature required trending tags from yesterday. We add that in with other parameters in the next listing. Now, our function needs to support combinations of sortByTitle and yesterdaysTags too.

Listing 4.12 More Boolean parameters

```
public IList<Tag> GetTrendingTags(byte numberOfItems,
  bool sortByTitle, bool yesterdaysTags) {        ←—— More parameters!
  var query = yesterdaysTags
    ? db.GetTrendingTagTable()                    More
    : db.GetYesterdaysTrendingTagTable();         conditionals!
  if (sortByTitle) {
    query = query.OrderBy(p => p.Title);
  }
  return query.Take(numberOfItems).ToList();
}
```

There is an ongoing trend here. Our function's complexity increases with every Boolean parameter. Although we have three different use cases, we have four flavors of the function. With every added Boolean parameter, we are creating fictional versions of the function that no one will use, although someone might someday and then get into a bind. A better approach is to have a separate function for each client, as shown next.

Listing 4.13 Separate functions

```
public IList<Tag> GetTrendingTags(byte numberOfItems) {        ←
  return db.GetTrendingTagTable()
    .Take(numberOfItems)
    .ToList();
}

public IList<Tag> GetTrendingTagsByTitle(
  byte numberOfItems) {
  return db.GetTrendingTagTable()                We separate functionality
    .OrderBy(p => p.Title)                       by function names instead
    .Take(numberOfItems)                              of parameters.
    .ToList();
}

public IList<Tag> GetYesterdaysTrendingTags(byte numberOfItems) {  ←
  return db.GetYesterdaysTrendingTagTable()
    .Take(numberOfItems)
    .ToList();
}
```

You now have one less test case. You get much better readability and slightly increased performance as a free bonus. The gains are minuscule, of course, and unnoticeable for a single function, but at points where the code needs to scale, they can make a difference without you even knowing it. The savings will increase exponentially when you avoid trying to pass state in parameters and leverage functions as much as possible. You might still be irked by repetitive code, which can easily be refactored into common functions, as in the next listing.

Listing 4.14   **Separate functions with common logic refactored out**

```
private IList<Tag> toListTrimmed(byte numberOfItems,
  IQueryable<Tag> query) {                              Common
  return query.Take(numberOfItems).ToList();            functionality
}

public IList<Tag> GetTrendingTags(byte numberOfItems) {
  return toListTrimmed(numberOfItems, db.GetTrendingTagTable());
}

public IList<Tag> GetTrendingTagsByTitle(byte numberOfItems) {
  return toListTrimmed(numberOfItems, db.GetTrendingTagTable()
    .OrderBy(p => p.Title));
}

public IList<Tag> GetYesterdaysTrendingTags(byte numberOfItems) {
  return toListTrimmed(numberOfItems,
    db.GetYesterdaysTrendingTagTable());
}
```

Our savings are not impressive here, but such refactors can make greater differences in other cases. The important takeaway is to use refactoring to avoid code repetition and combinatorial hell.

The same technique can be used with `enum` parameters that are used to dictate a certain operation to a function. Use separate functions, and you can even use function composition, instead of passing along a shopping list of parameters.

4.8   Naming tests

There is a lot in a name. That's why it's important to have good coding conventions in both production and test code, although they shouldn't necessarily overlap. Tests with good coverage can serve as specifications if they're named correctly. From the name of a test, you should be able to tell

- The name of the function being tested
- Input and initial state
- Expected behavior
- Whom to blame

I'm kidding about the last one, of course. Remember? You already green-lit that code in the code review. You have no right to blame someone else anymore. At best, you can share the blame. I commonly use an "A_B_C" format to name tests, which is quite different than what you're used to naming your regular functions. We used a simpler naming scheme in previous examples because we were able to use the `TestCase` attribute to describe the initial state of the test. I use an additional `ReturnsExpectedValues`, but you can simply suffix the function name with `Test`. It's better if you don't use the function name alone because that might confuse you when it appears in code completion lists. Similarly, if the function doesn't take any input or doesn't depend on any initial state, you can skip the part describing that. The purpose here is to allow you to spend less time dealing with tests, not to put you through a military drill about naming rules.

Say your boss asked you to write a new validation rule for a registration form to make sure registration code returns failure if the user hasn't accepted the policy terms. A name for such a test would be `Register_LicenseNotAccepted_ShouldReturnFailure`, as in figure 4.6.

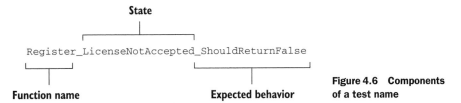

Figure 4.6 Components of a test name

That's not the only possible naming convention. Some people prefer creating inner classes for each function to be tested and name tests with only state and expected behavior, but I find that unnecessarily cumbersome. It's important that you pick the convention that works best for you.

Summary

- It's possible to overcome the disdain for writing tests by not writing many of them in the first place.
- Test-driven development and similar paradigms can make you hate writing tests even more. Seek to write tests that spark joy.
- The effort to write tests can be significantly shortened by test frameworks, especially with parameterized, data-driven tests.
- The number of test cases can be reduced significantly by properly analyzing the boundary values of a function input.
- Proper use of types can let you avoid writing many unnecessary tests.
- Tests don't just ensure the quality of the code. They can also help you improve your own development skills and throughput.
- Testing in production can be acceptable as long as your résumé is up to date.

Rewarding refactoring

This chapter covers

- Getting comfortable with refactoring
- Incremental refactoring on large changes
- Using tests to make code changes faster
- Dependency injection

In chapter 3, I discussed how resistance to change caused the downfall of the French royal family and software developers. Refactoring is the art of changing the structure of the code. According to Martin Fowler,[1] Leo Brodie coined the term in his book *Thinking Forth* back in 1984. That makes the term as old as *Back to the Future* and *Karate Kid,* my favorite movies when I was a kid.

Writing great code is usually only half of being an efficient developer. The other half is being agile in transforming code. In an ideal world, we should be writing and changing code at the speed of thought. Hitting keys, nailing the syntax, memorizing keywords, and changing the coffee filter are all obstacles between your ideas and the product. Since it'll probably take a while before we get AI to do programming work for us, it's a good idea to polish our refactoring skills.

---

[1] Etymology of Refactoring, Martin Fowler, https://martinfowler.com/bliki/EtymologyOfRefactoring.html.

IDEs are instrumental in refactoring. You can rename a class with a single keystroke (F2 on Visual Studio for Windows) and rename all the references to it instantly. You can even access most of the refactoring options with a single keystroke. I strongly recommend familiarizing yourself with keyboard shortcuts for the features that you frequently use on your favorite editor. The time savings will accumulate, and you'll look cool to your colleagues.

5.1 Why do we refactor?

Change is inevitable, and code change is doubly so. Refactoring serves purposes other than simply changing the code. It lets you

- *Reduce repetition and increase code reuse.* You can move a class that can be reused by other components to a common location so those other components can start using it. Similarly, you can extract methods from the code and make them available for reuse.
- *Bring your mental model and the code closer.* Names are important. Some names may not be as easily understandable as others. Renaming things is part of the refactoring process and can help you achieve a better design that more closely matches your mental model.
- *Make the code easier to understand and maintain.* You can reduce code complexity by splitting long functions into smaller, more maintainable ones. Similarly, a model can be easier to understand if complex data types are grouped in smaller, atomic parts.
- *Prevent certain classes of bugs from appearing.* Certain refactoring operations, like changing a class to a `struct`, can prevent bugs related to nullability, as I discussed in chapter 2. Similarly, enabling nullable references on a project and changing data types to non-nullable ones can prevent bugs that are basically refactoring operations.
- *Prepare for a significant architectural change.* Big changes can be performed faster if you prepare the code for the change beforehand. You will see how that can happen in the next section.
- *Get rid of the rigid parts of the code.* Through dependency injection, you can remove dependencies and have a loosely coupled design.

Most of the time, we developers see refactoring as a mundane task that is part of our programming work. Refactoring is also separate external work that you do even if you're not writing a single line of code. You can even do it for the purpose of reading the code because it's hard to grasp. Richard Feynman once said, "If you want to truly learn a subject, write a book about it." In a similar vein, you can truly learn about a piece of code by refactoring it.

Simple refactoring operations need no guidance at all. You want to rename a class? Go ahead. Extract methods or interfaces? These are no-brainers. They are even on the right-click menu for Visual Studio, which can also be brought up with Ctrl-. on Windows.

Most of the time, refactoring operations don't affect code reliability at all. However, when it comes to a significant architectural change in the code base, you might need some advice.

5.2   *Architectural changes*

It's almost never a good idea to perform a large architectural change in one shot. That's not because it's technically hard, but mostly because large changes generate a large number of bugs and integration problems due to the long and broad nature of the work. By integration problems, I mean that if you're working on a large change, you need to work on it for a long time without being able to integrate changes from other developers (see figure 5.1). That puts you in a bind. Do you wait until you're done with your work and manually apply every change that's been made on the code in that timeframe and fix all the conflicts yourself, or do you tell your team members to stop working until you finish your changes? This is mostly a problem when you're refactoring. You don't have the same problem when you're developing a new feature because the possibility of conflicting with other developers is far less: the feature itself does not exist in the first place. That's why an incremental approach is better.

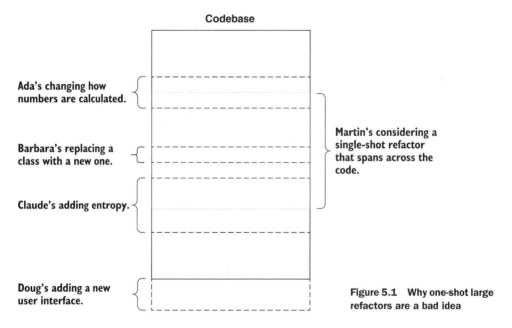

Figure 5.1   Why one-shot large refactors are a bad idea

To create a road map, you need to have a destination and to know where you are. What do you want the end result to look like? It may not be possible to imagine everything at once because large software is really hard to wrap your head around. Instead, you can have a certain list of requirements.

Let's work on a migration example. Microsoft has two flavors of .NET in the wild. The first one is the .NET Framework, which is decades old, and the second one is just called

.NET (previously known as .NET Core), which was released in 2016. Both are still supported by Microsoft as of the writing of this book, but it's obvious that Microsoft wants to move forward with .NET and drop the .NET Framework at some point. It's very likely that you'll encounter work that needs migration from .NET Framework to .NET.

.NET Framework is dead; long live .NET!

The name *.NET* meant many things back in the 1990s, when the internet was getting big. There was even a magazine called *.net,* which was about the internet and pretty much worked as a slower version of Google. Browsing the web was commonly called "surfing the net," "traveling the information superhighway," "connecting to cyberspace," or any other combination of a misleading metaphoric verb with a made-up noun.

.NET Framework was the original software ecosystem created to make developers' lives easier in the late 1990s. It came with the runtime, standard libraries, compilers for C#, Visual Basic, and later, F# languages. The Java equivalent of .NET Framework was JDK (Java Development Kit), which had the Java runtime, a Java language compiler, the Java Virtual Machine, and probably some other things starting with *Java*.

Over time, other .NET flavors came that were not directly compatible with the .NET Framework, such as *.NET Compact Framework* and *Mono*. To allow code sharing between different frameworks, Microsoft created a common API specification that defined a common subset of the .NET functionality that was called *.NET Standard*. Java doesn't suffer from a similar problem because Oracle successfully killed all the incompatible alternatives with an army of lawyers.

Microsoft later created a new generation of .NET Framework that was cross-platform. It was initially called .NET Core and was recently renamed solely *.NET*, starting with .NET 5. It's not directly compatible with .NET Framework, but it can interoperate using a common .NET Standard subset specification.

.NET Framework is still plugged into life support, but we probably won't be seeing it around in five years. I strongly recommend anyone using .NET to start out with .NET rather than .NET Framework, and that's why I picked an example based on this migration scenario.

In addition to your destination, you need to know where you are. This reminds me of the story about a CEO who was getting a ride in a helicopter, and they got lost in the fog. They noticed the silhouette of a building and saw someone on the balcony. The CEO said, "I've got an idea. Get us closer to that person." They got closer to the person, and the CEO shouted, "Hey! Do you know where we are?" The person replied, "Yes, you're in a helicopter!" The CEO said, "Okay, then we must be at the college campus and that must be the engineering building!" The person on the balcony was surprised and asked, "How did you figure it out?" The CEO replied, "The answer you gave us was technically correct, but completely useless!" The person shouted, "Then you must be a CEO!" Now the CEO was surprised and asked, "How did you know that?" The person answered, "You got lost, have no idea where you are or where you're going, and it's still my fault!"

I can't help imagining the CEO jumping to the balcony from the helicopter and a Matrix-like fight sequence breaking out between the runaway engineer and the CEO, both wielding katanas, simply because the pilot didn't know how to read a GPS instead of practicing a precision approach maneuver to balconies.

Consider that we have our anonymous microblogging website called Blabber written in .NET Framework and ASP.NET and we'd like to move it to the new .NET platform and ASP.NET Core. Unfortunately, ASP.NET Core and ASP.NET are not binary compatible and are only slightly source compatible. The code for the platform is included in the source code of the book. I won't be listing the full code here because the ASP.NET template comes with quite a lot of boilerplate, but I'll sketch out the architectural details that will guide us in creating a refactoring road map. You don't need to know about the architecture of ASP.NET or how web apps work in general to understand our refactoring process because that's not directly relevant to refactoring work.

5.2.1   *Identify the components*

The best way to work with a large refactor is to split your code into semantically distinct components. Let's split our code into several parts for the sole purpose of a refactor. Our project is an ASP.NET MVC application with some model classes and controllers we added. We can have an approximate list of components, as in figure 5.2. It doesn't need to be accurate; it can be what you come up with initially because it will change.

After you have the list of components down, start assessing how many of them you can transfer directly to your destination, as in our example .NET 5. Note that *destination* means the destination state that symbolizes the end result. Can the

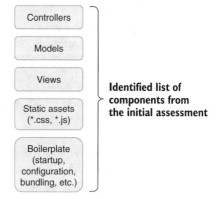

Figure 5.2   Our initial assessment of components

components be manipulated into the destination state without breaking anything? Do you think they will need some work? Assess this per component, and we will use this guesswork to prioritize. You don't really need to accurately know this because guesswork is adequate at this moment. You can have a work estimation table like the one in table 5.1.

Table 5.1   Assessing relative cost and risks of manipulating components

Component	Changes needed	Risk of conflicting with another developer
Controllers	Minimal	High
Models	None	Medium
Views	Minimal	High
Static assets	Some	Low
Boilerplate	Rewrite	Low

What's MVC?

The entire history of computer science can be summarized as fighting with entropy, also known as *spaghetti* by the believers in the Flying Spaghetti Monster, the creator of all entropy. MVC is the idea of splitting code into three parts to avoid too much interdependency, aka, spaghetti code: the part that decides how the user interface will look, the part that models your business logic, and the part that coordinates the two. They are respectively called view, model, and controller. There are many other similar attempts at splitting application code into logically separate parts like MVVM (model, view, viewmodel) or MVP (model, view, presentation), but the idea behind all of them is pretty much the same: decoupling distinct concerns from each other.

Such compartmentalization can help you in writing code, creating tests, and refactoring because the dependencies between those layers become more manageable. But as scientists David Wolpert and William Macready stated eloquently in the No Free Lunch Theorem, there is no free lunch. You usually have to write slightly more code, work with a greater number of files, have more subdirectories, and experience more moments when you curse at the screen to get the benefits of MVC. In the big picture, however, you will become faster and more efficient.

5.2.2 Estimate the work and the risk

How will you know how much work will be needed? You must have a vague idea about how both frameworks work to determine that. It's important that you know your destination before you start walking toward it. You can be wrong about some of these guesses, and that's okay, but the primary reason to follow this practice is to prioritize work to reduce your workload without breaking anything for as long as possible.

For example, I know controllers and views require minimal effort because I know their syntax hasn't changed much between frameworks. I anticipate a little work with the syntax of some HTML helpers or controller constructs, but there is a great chance that I should be moving them without any issues. Similarly, I know static assets are moved under the wwwroot/ folder in ASP.NET Core, which requires only a little work, but they definitely are not directly transferable. I also know that startup and configuration code has completely been overhauled in ASP.NET Core, which means I'll have to write them from scratch.

I assume all the other developers will be working on features, so I expect their work will involve work under controllers, views, and models. I don't expect existing `models` to change as frequently as the business logic or how the features look, so I assign `models` a medium risk while `controllers` and `views` merit a higher risk probability. Remember, other developers are working on the code while you're working on your refactoring, so you must find a way to integrate your work to their workflow as early as possible without breaking their flow. The most feasible component for that looks like `models` in table 5.1. Despite the possibility of high conflict, it requires minimal change, so resolving any conflicts should be straightforward.

It needs no change to be refactored. How do you make the existing code and the new code with the same component at the same time? You move it into a separate project. I discussed this in chapter 3 when I talked about breaking dependencies to make a project structure more open to change.

5.2.3   *The prestige*

Refactoring without disrupting your colleagues is pretty much like changing the tire of a car while driving on the highway. It resembles an illusion act that makes the old architecture disappear and replaces it with the new one without anyone noticing. Your greatest tool when you're doing that would be extracting code into shareable parts, as shown in figure 5.3.

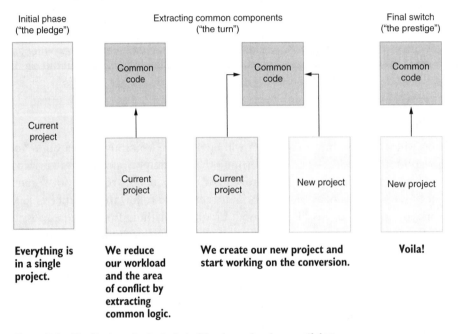

Figure 5.3   The illusion of refactoring without any developer noticing

Of course, it's impossible for developers not to notice the new project in the repository, but as long as you communicate the changes you're trying to implement with them beforehand and it's straightforward for them to adapt, you should have no problems implementing your changes as the project goes forward.

You create a separate project, as in our example, Blabber.Models, move your `models` classes to that project, and then add a reference to that project from the web project. Your code will keep running as it did before, but the new code will need to be added in the Blabber.Models project rather than Blabber, and your colleagues need to be aware of this change. You can then create your new project and reference Blabber.Models from that too. Our road map resembles that in figure 5.4.

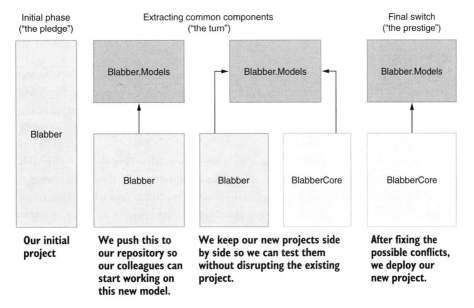

Figure 5.4 Our project's refactoring road map

The reason we are going through this is to reduce our work while staying as current as possible with the main branch. This method also lets you perform your refactoring work over a longer timeline while squeezing other, more urgent work into your schedule. It pretty much resembles checkpoint systems in video games where you can start at the same Valkyrie fight for the hundredth time in *God of War* instead of going back to the beginning of the entire game all over again. Whatever you can integrate into the main branch without breaking the build becomes a last-known good spot that you don't have to repeat. Planning your work with multiple integration steps is the most feasible way to perform a large refactor.

5.2.4 *Refactor to make refactoring easier*

When moving code across projects, you'll encounter strong dependencies that cannot be easily moved out. In our example, some of the code might depend on web components, and moving them to our shared project would be meaningless because our new project, BlabberCore, wouldn't work with the old web components.

In such cases, composition comes to our rescue. We can extract an interface that our main project can provide and pass it to the implementation instead of the actual dependency.

Our current implementation of Blabber uses an in-memory storage for the content posted on the website. That means that whenever you restart the website, all the platform content is lost. That makes sense for a post-modern art project, but users expect at least a level of persistence. Let's assume we'd like to use either Entity Framework or Entity Framework Core, based on the framework we're using, but we still would like to share the common DB access code among two projects while our migration is ongoing, so the actual work needed for the final stretch for migration will be far less.

DEPENDENCY INJECTION

You can abstract away a dependency that you don't want to deal with by creating an interface for it and receiving its implementation in a constructor. That technique is called *dependency injection.* Do not confuse it with *dependency inversion,* which is an over-hyped principle that basically states "depend on abstractions," but sounds less profound when it's put like that.

Dependency injection (DI) is also a slightly misleading term. It implies interference or disturbance, but nothing like that is going on. Perhaps it should have been called *dependency reception* because that's what it's about: receiving your dependencies during initialization such as in your constructor. DI is also called *IoC* (*inversion of control*), which sometimes is even more confusing. A typical dependency injection is a design change like that shown in figure 5.5. Without dependency injection, you instantiate your dependent classes in your code. With dependency injection, you receive the classes you depend on in a constructor.

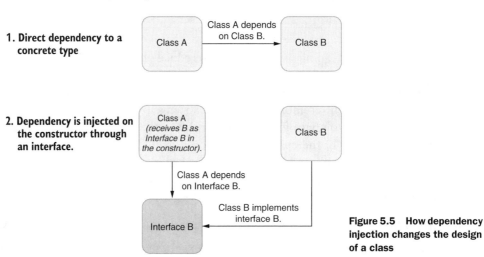

Figure 5.5   How dependency injection changes the design of a class

Let's go over how it's performed in some simple and abstract code so you can focus on the actual changes that are happening. In this example, you can see how C# 9.0 top-level program code looks, without a main method or a program class per se. You can actually type the code in the following listing in a .cs file under a project folder and run it right away, without any extra code. Note how class A initializes an instance of a class B every time the method X is called.

```
Listing 5.1   Code that uses direct dependency

using System;
                              The main code creates
var a = new A();     ←——|    an instance of A here.
a.X();

public class A {
  public void X() {
    Console.WriteLine("X got called");
    var b = new B();              ←——————|  Class A creates the
    b.Y();                                |  instance of class B.
  }
}

public class B {
  public void Y() {
    Console.WriteLine("Y got called");
  }
}
```

When you apply dependency injection, your code gets its instance of `class B` in its constructor and through an interface, so you have zero coupling between `classes A` and `B`. You can see how it shapes up in listing 5.2. However, there is a difference in conventions. Because we moved the initialization code of `class B` to a constructor, it always uses the same instance of `B` instead of creating a new one, which is how it used to work in listing 5.1. That's actually good because it reduces the load on the garbage collector, but it can create unexpected behavior if the state of the class changes over time. You might be breaking behavior. That's why having test coverage is a good idea in the first place.

What we've accomplished with the code in listing 5.2 is that we now can completely remove the code for `B` and move it to an entirely different project without breaking the code in `A`, as long as we keep the interface we've created (`IB`). More importantly, we can move everything `B` needs along with it. It gives us quite a lot of freedom to move the code around.

```
Listing 5.2   Code with dependency injection

using System;
                            The caller
var b = new B();   ←——|    initializes class B
var a = new A(b);  ←——|
a.X();                     It passes it to class
                           A as a parameter.
public interface IB {
  void Y();
}

public class A {                  The instance of
  private readonly IB b;   ←——|   B is kept here.
  public A(IB b) {
```

```
    this.b = b;
  }
  public void X() {
    Console.WriteLine("X got called");
    b.Y();                        ◁──┐
  }                                  │   The common instance
}                                    │   of B is called.

public class B : IB {
  public void Y() {
    Console.WriteLine("Y got called");
  }
}
```

Now let's apply this technique to our example in Blabber and change the code to use database storage instead of memory so our content will survive restarts. In our example, instead of depending on a specific implementation of a DB engine, in this case Entity Framework and EF Core, we can receive an interface we devise that provides required functionality to our component. This lets two projects with different technologies use the same code base, even though the common code depends on the specific DB functionality. To achieve that, we create a common interface, IBlabDb, which points to the database functionality, and use it in our common code. Our two different implementations share the same code; they let the common code use different DB access technologies. Our implementation will look like that in figure 5.6.

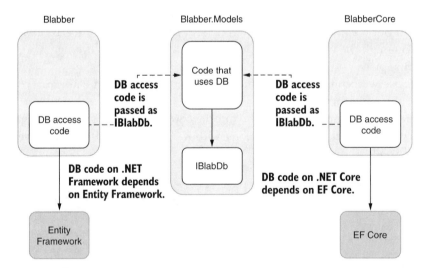

Figure 5.6   Using different technologies in common code with dependency injection

To implement that, we first change our implementation of `BlabStorage` in the Blabber .Models that we refactored, so it will defer work to an interface instead. The in-memory implementation of the `BlabStorage` class looks like that in listing 5.3. It keeps a static instance of a list that is shared between all requests, so it uses locking to ensure that things don't become inconsistent. We don't care about the consistency of our Items property because we only add items to this list, never remove them. Otherwise, it would have been a problem. Note that we use Insert instead of Add in the Add() method because it lets us keep posts in descending order by their creation date without resorting to any sorting.

Listing 5.3 Initial in-memory version of BlabStorage

```
using System.Collections.Generic;

namespace Blabber.Models {
    public class BlabStorage {
        public IList<Blab> items = new List<Blab>();         ◁─── Creating an empty list by default
        public IEnumerable<Blab> Items => items;
        public object lockObject = new object();             ◁─── We're using lock object to allow concurrency.
        public static readonly BlabStorage Default =
new BlabStorage();                                           ◁─── A default singleton instance that's used everywhere

        public BlabStorage() {
        }

        public void Add(Blab blab) {
            lock (lockObject) {                              ◁─── The most recent item goes to the top.
                items.Insert(0, blab);
            }
        }
    }
}
```

When we implement dependency injection, we remove everything related to in-memory lists and use an abstract interface for anything related to the database instead. The new version looks like listing 5.4. You can see how we remove anything related to the logic of data storage, and our BlabStorage class actually became an abstraction itself. It looks like BlabStorage doesn't do anything extra, but as we add more complicated tasks, we're able to share some logic between our two projects. For the sake of the example, this is okay.

We keep the dependency in a private and read-only field called db. It's a good habit to mark fields with the readonly keyword if they won't change after the object is created, so the compiler can catch whether you or one of your colleagues accidentally tries to modify it outside the constructor.

Listing 5.4 BlabStorage with dependency injection

```
using System.Collections.Generic;

namespace Blabber.Models {
  public interface IBlabDb {                    ◁─── The interface that abstracts away the dependency
    IEnumerable<Blab> GetAllBlabs();
    void AddBlab(Blab blab);
```

```
    }

    public class BlabStorage {
      private readonly IBlabDb db;

      public BlabStorage(IBlabDb db) {        Receiving the dependency
        this.db = db;                         in the constructor
      }

      public IEnumerable<Blab> GetAllBlabs() {
        return db.GetAllBlabs();
      }                                       Deferring work to the
                                              component that does
      public void Add(Blab blab) {            the actual work
        db.AddBlab(blab);
      }
    }
}
```

Our actual implementation is called `BlabDb`, which implements the interface `IBlabDb` and resides in the project BlabberCore, rather than Blabber.Models. It uses an SQLite (pronounced *sequel-light*) database for practical purposes because it requires no setup of third-party software, so you can start running it right away. SQLite is God's last gift to the world before he gave up on humankind. Just kidding—Richard Kipp created it before he gave up on humankind. Our BlabberCore project implements it in EF Core, as in listing 5.5.

You may not be familiar with EF Core, Entity Framework, or ORM (object-relational mapping) in general, but that's okay—you don't have to be. It's pretty straightforward, as you can see. The `AddBlab` method just creates a new database record in memory, creates a pending insertion to the Blabs table, and calls `SaveChanges` to write changes to the database. Similarly, the `GetAllBlabs` method simply gets all the records from the database, ordered by date in descending order. Notice how we need to convert our dates to UTC to make sure time zone information isn't lost because SQLite doesn't support `DateTimeOffset` types. Regardless of how many best practices you learn, you'll always encounter cases in which they just won't work. Then you'll have to improvise, adapt, and overcome.

Listing 5.5   EF Core version of `BlabDb`

```
using Blabber.Models;
using System;
using System.Collections.Generic;
using System.Linq;

namespace Blabber.DB {
  public class BlabDb : IBlabDb {
    private readonly BlabberContext db;          EF
                                                 Core DB
    public BlabDb(BlabberContext db) {           context    Receiving context through
      this.db = db;                                         dependency injection
    }
```

```
public void AddBlab(Blab blab) {
  db.Blabs.Add(new BlabEntity() {
    Content = blab.Content,
    CreatedOn = blab.CreatedOn.UtcDateTime,
  });
  db.SaveChanges();
}

public IEnumerable<Blab> GetAllBlabs() {
  return db.Blabs
    .OrderByDescending(b => b.CreatedOn)
    .Select(b => new Blab(b.Content,
      new DateTimeOffset(b.CreatedOn, TimeSpan.Zero)))
    .ToList();
}
}
}
```

Converting our DateTimeOffset to a DB-compatible type

Converting DB-time to DateTimeOffset

We managed to introduce a database storage backend to our project during our refactoring without disrupting the development workflow. We used dependency injection to avoid direct dependencies. More importantly, our content is now persisted across sessions and restarts, as figure 5.7 shows.

Figure 5.7 Screenshot of Blabber running on a SQLite database

5.2.5 *The final stretch*

You can extract as many components as can be shared between the old and the new project, but eventually, you'll hit a chunk of code that can't be shared between two web projects. For example, our controller code doesn't need to change between ASP.NET and ASP.NET Core because the syntax is the same, but it's impossible to share that piece of code between the two because they use entirely different types. ASP.NET MVC controllers are derived from `System.Web.Mvc.Controller`, while

ASP.NET Core controllers are derived from `Microsoft.AspNetCore.Mvc.Controller`. There are theoretical solutions to this, like abstracting away the controller implementation behind an interface and writing custom classes that use that interface instead of being direct descendants of the controller class, but that's just too much work. When you come up with a supposedly elegant solution to a problem, you should always ask yourself, "Is it worth it?" Elegance in engineering must always take cost into account.

That means that at some point, you'll have to risk conflicting with other developers and transfer the code to the new code base. I call that the *final stretch*, which will take a shorter time thanks to your previous preparatory work on refactoring. Because of your work, the future refactor operations will take less time because you'll end up with a compartmentalized design at the end of the process. It's a good investment.

In our example, the models component is an unusually small part of our project, therefore makes our savings negligible. However, it's expected that large projects have a significant amount of shareable code, which might reduce your work factor considerably.

In the final stretch, you need to transfer all the code and assets to your new project and then make everything work. I added a separate project to the code examples called BlabberCore, which contains the new .NET code so you can see how some constructs translate to .NET Core.

5.3 Reliable refactoring

Your IDE tries really hard so you don't break the code simply by randomly choosing menu options. If you manually edit a name, any other code that references the name will break. If you use the rename function of your IDE, all references to the name will be renamed as well. That still is not always a guarantee. There are many ways you can refer to a name without the compiler knowing. For example, it's possible to instantiate a class using a string. In our example microblogging code, Blabber, we refer to every piece of content as blabs, and we have a class that defines a content called `Blab`.

> **Listing 5.6 Class representing a content**

```
using System;

namespace Blabber
{
    public class Blab
    {
        public string Content { get; private set; }          ◁─── The constructor
        public DateTimeOffset CreatedOn { get; private set; }       ensures there are
        public Blab(string content, DateTimeOffset createdOn) {     no invalid blabs.
            if (string.IsNullOrWhiteSpace(content)) {
                throw new ArgumentException(nameof(content));
            }
            Content = content;
            CreatedOn = createdOn;
        }
    }
}
```

}We normally instantiate classes using the `new` operator, but it's also possible to instantiate the `Blab` class using reflection for certain purposes, such as when you don't know what class you're creating during compile time:

```
var blab = Activator.CreateInstance("Blabber.Models",
    "Blabber", "test content", DateTimeOffset.Now);
```

Whenever we refer to a name in a string, we risk breaking the code after a rename because the IDE cannot track the contents of strings. Hopefully, that'll stop being a problem when we start doing code reviews with our AI overlords. I don't know why in that fictional future it's still us who are doing the work and AI just grades our work. Weren't they supposed to take over our jobs? It turns out they are much more intelligent than we give them credit for.

Until the AI takeover of the world, your IDE can't guarantee a perfectly reliable refactoring. Yes, you have some wiggle room, like using constructs like `nameof()` to reference types instead of hardcoding them into strings, as I discussed in chapter 4, but that helps you only marginally.

The secret to reliable refactoring is testing. If you can make sure your code has good test coverage, you can have much more freedom in changing it. Therefore, it's usually a wise idea to start a long-term refactoring project by creating missing tests for the relevant piece of code first. If we take our architecture change example in chapter 3 as an example, a more realistic road map would involve adding missing tests to the whole architecture. We skipped that step in our example because our code base was extremely small and trivial to test manually (e.g., run the app, post a blab, and see if it appears). Figure 5.8 shows a modified version of our road map that includes the phase of adding tests to our project so it can be refactored reliably.

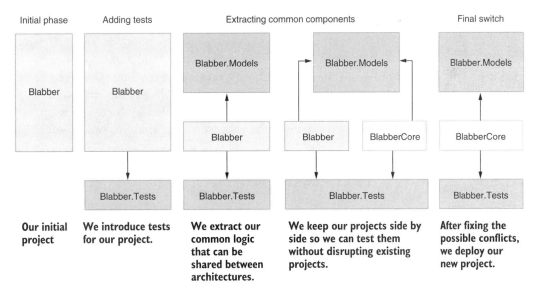

Figure 5.8   Reliable refactoring with tests

5.4   *When not to refactor*

The good thing about refactoring is that it makes you think about ways to improve code. The bad thing about refactoring is that at some point, it might become an end rather than a means, pretty much like Emacs. For the uninformed, Emacs is a text editor, a development environment, a web browser, an operating system, and a post-apocalyptic role-playing game because someone just couldn't hold their horses. The same can happen with refactoring. You start seeing every piece of code as a place for a potential improvement. It becomes such an addiction that you create excuses to make a change for the sake of making the change, but you don't consider its benefits. Not only does this waste your time, but it also wastes your team's because they need to adapt to every change you introduce.

You should essentially develop an understanding of good-enough code and worthiness when you're working in the streets. Yes, code can rust away when it's left untouched, but good-enough code can bear that burden easily. The criteria you need for good-enough code are

- Is your only reason for refactoring "This is more elegant?" That's a huge red flag because elegance is not only subjective, but also vague and therefore meaningless. Try to come up with solid arguments and solid benefits, like "This will make this component easier to use by reducing the amount of boilerplate we need to write every time we use it," "This will prepare us for migrating to the new library," "This will remove our dependency to the component X," and so forth.

- Does your target component depend on a minimal set of components? That indicates that it can be moved or refactored easily in the future. Our refactoring exercises may not benefit us for identifying rigid parts of the code. You can postpone it until you come up with a more solid improvement plan.

- Does it lack test coverage? That is an immediate red flag to avoid refactoring, especially if the component also has too many dependencies. Lack of testing for a component means you don't know what you're doing, so stop doing it.

- Is it a common dependency? That means that even with a good amount of test coverage and good justification, you might be impacting the ergonomics of your team by disrupting their workflow. You should consider postponing a refactor operation if the gains you seek aren't sufficient to compensate the cost.

If any of those criteria is met, you should consider avoiding refactoring, or at least postponing it. Prioritization work is always relative, and there are always more fish in the sea.

Summary

- Embrace refactoring because it provides more benefits than what's on the surface.
- You can perform large architectural changes in incremental steps.
- Use testing to reduce the potential problems ahead in large refactoring work.
- Estimate not only costs, but also risks.
- Always have either a mental or a written road map for incremental work when you're working on large architectural changes.
- Use dependency injection to remove roadblocks like tightly coupled dependencies when refactoring. Reduce code rigidity with the same technique.
- Consider not doing a refactor when it costs more than it yields.

Security by scrutiny

This chapter covers

- Understanding security as a whole
- Leveraging threat models
- Avoiding common security pitfalls like SQL injection, CSRF, XSS, and overflows
- Techniques to reduce attackers' capabilities
- Storing secrets correctly

Security has been a commonly misunderstood problem as early as that unfortunate incident at Troy, an ancient city in what is now western Turkey. The Trojans thought their walls were impenetrable, and they felt secure, but like modern social platforms, they underestimated the social-engineering abilities of their adversaries. The Greeks withdrew from battle and left a tall wooden horse as a gift. The Trojans loved the gesture and took the horse inside their walls to cherish it. At midnight, the Greek soldiers hidden in the hollow horse got out and opened the gates, letting the Greek armies in and causing the downfall of the city. At least, that's what we know from the postmortem blog posts of Homeros, possibly the first instance of *irresponsible disclosure* in history.

Security is both a broad and deep term, as in the story of the Trojans, which involves human psychology. That's the first perspective you need to embrace: security is never

> ## Postmortems and responsible disclosures
>
> A *postmortem blog post* is a long article usually written after a terribly embarrassing security incident to make it appear that the management is transparently providing as many details as possible while really trying to hide the fact that they have screwed up.
>
> *Responsible disclosure* is the practice of publishing a security vulnerability after providing the company, which didn't invest in identifying the problem in the first place, ample time to fix the problem. Companies invented the term to load the act with an emotional burden so the researcher would feel guilty. Security vulnerabilities themselves are always called *incidents*, never *irresponsible*. I believe that responsible disclosure should have been called something like *timed disclosure* from the get-go.

about only software or information—it's about people and the environment as well. Because of the vastness of the subject, this chapter can never make you an expert on security, but it will make you a better developer with a better understanding of it.

6.1 Beyond hackers

Software security is usually thought of in terms of vulnerabilities, exploits, attacks, and hackers. But security can be breached because of other, seemingly irrelevant factors. For example, you could be accidentally logging usernames and passwords in your web logs, which could be stored on much less secure servers than your database. It has happened to billion-dollar companies like Twitter, which learned that they were storing plaintext passwords in their internal logs,[1] and an adversary could immediately start using passwords they accessed as opposed to cracking hashed passwords.

Facebook provided an API for developers that let them browse through users' friends lists. A company used that information to generate political profiles of people to influence US elections with precision-targeted ads back in 2016. It was a feature that worked exactly as it was designed to. There was no bug, no security hole, no backdoors, and no hackers involved. Some people created it, and other people used it, but the acquired data let people be manipulated against their will, thus causing harm.

You'd be surprised to learn how many companies leave their databases accessible on the internet with no password. Database technologies like MongoDB and Redis don't authenticate users by default—you have to enable authentication manually. Obviously, many developers don't do that, which causes massive data leaks.

There is a famous motto among developers and DevOps people: "Don't deploy on Fridays." The logic is simple. If you screw something up, no one will be around to handle it during the weekend, so you should undertake high-risk activities closer to the start of the week. Otherwise, it can get really bad both for the staff and the company. The existence of weekends isn't a security vulnerability either, but it can still lead to catastrophic outcomes.

---

[1] See "Twitter says bug exposed user plaintext passwords," https://www.zdnet.com/article/twitter-says-bug-exposed-passwords-in-plaintext/.

That brings us to the relationship between security and reliability. Security, like testing, is a subset of the reliability of your services, of your data, and of your business. When you look at security from the perspective of reliability, it becomes easier to make security-related decisions because you master it along the way when you're looking at other aspects of reliability such as testing, as I've discussed in previous chapters.

Even if you have zero accountability for the security of the products you develop, taking the reliability of your code into account helps you make decisions to avoid headaches in the future. Street coders optimize their future too, not just their now. The goal is to do minimal work to achieve great success in your lifetime. Seeing security-related decisions as technical debt for reliability helps you optimize your lifetime as a whole. I recommend this for every product, regardless of potential security impacts. For example, you could be developing an internal dashboard for your access logs that will be accessed only by trusted people. I still suggest you apply best practices of secure software, like using parameterized queries for running SQL statements, which I will discuss in detail later. It might seem like slightly more work, but it helps you develop the habit, which will help you in the long run. A shortcut isn't really a shortcut if it prevents you from improving yourself.

Since we've already established that developers are humans, you need to accept that you carry the weaknesses of humans, primarily, miscalculating the probabilities. I know this as a person who used *password* as my password on almost all platforms over several years in the early 2000s. I thought nobody would think that I was that dumb. I turned out to be right; nobody noticed that I was that dumb. Luckily, I've never been hacked, at least not by having my password compromised, but I wasn't a target of many people around that time, either. That means I correctly, or randomly, hit the nail on the head with my threat model.

6.2   *Threat modeling*

A *threat model* is a clear understanding of what could possibly go wrong in the context of security. The assessment of a threat model is commonly expressed as, "Nah, it'll be fine" or "Hey, wait a second…." The goal of having a threat model is to prioritize the security measures you need to take, optimize cost, and increase effectiveness. The term itself sounds very technical because the process can be intricate, but understanding a threat model isn't.

A threat model effectively lays out what's not a security risk or what's not worth protecting against. It's similar to not worrying about a catastrophic drought in Seattle or the sudden emergence of affordable housing in San Francisco, even though these are still legitimate possibilities.

We actually develop threat models unconsciously. For example, one of the most common threat models could be "I've got nothing to hide!" against threats like hacking, government surveillance, or an ex-partner who was supposed to have become an adult a decade ago. That means we don't really care if our data is compromised and used for whatever purpose, mostly because we lack the imagination to think about how our data can be used. Privacy is like a seatbelt in that sense: you don't need it 99%

of the time, but when you need it, it can save your life. When hackers learn your SSN and apply for credit applications on your behalf and take all your money, leaving you with huge debt, you slowly start to realize that you might have one or two things to hide. When your cell phone data mistakenly matches a murder's time and coordinates, you become the greatest proponent of privacy.

Actual threat modeling is slightly more complicated. It involves analyzing actors, data flow, and trust boundaries. Formal methods have been developed to create threat models, but unless your primary role is a security researcher and you're responsible for the security of the institution you're working at, you don't need a formal approach to threat modeling, but you do need to have the basic understanding of it: prioritizing security.

First, you need to accept the rule of the land: security problems will hit your app or platform sooner or later. There is no running away from it. "But this is just an internal website," "But we're behind a VPN," "But this is just a mobile app on an encrypted device," "Nobody knows about my site anyway," and "But we use PHP" don't really help your case—especially the last one.

The inevitability of security problems also emphasizes the relativity of all things. There is no perfectly secure system. Banks, hospitals, credit-scoring companies, nuclear reactors, government institutions, cryptocurrency exchanges, and almost all other institutions have experienced a security incident with varying degrees of severity. You'd think your website about rating the best cat picture would be exempt from that, but the thing is, your website can be used as leverage for sophisticated attacks. One of the users' passwords that you store might contain the same login information as the nuclear research facility that person works at, because we're not really good at remembering passwords. You can see how that can be a problem in figure 6.1.

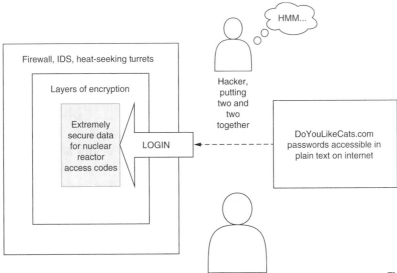

James, using the same very long and complicated password on both websites and assuming he's being secure this way. I hope you're happy now, James.

Figure 6.1 Security isn't always about software.

But mostly, hackers don't even know when they hack your website, because they don't individually walk through all the websites in the world. They use bots to do all the hard work of scanning for vulnerabilities and then just collect the data afterwards. Well, robots are taking our jobs, after all.

6.2.1 *Pocket-sized threat models*

You may not be supposed to do all the threat modeling for your application. You may not be affected by security incidents, either. But you're expected to write minimally secure code, and that's not too hard if you follow certain principles. You basically need a mini threat model for your application. It encompasses these elements:

- *The assets of your application.* Fundamentally, anything that you don't want to lose or leak is an asset, including your source code, design documents, database, private keys, API tokens, server configurations, and your Netflix watchlist.
- *The servers that assets reside on.* Every server gets accessed by some parties, and every server accesses some other servers. It's important for you to know these relationships to understand potential problems.
- *Information sensitivity.* You can assess this by asking yourself several questions: "How many people and institutions would be harmed if this information became public?," "What's the seriousness of potential harm?," and "Have I been in a Turkish prison?"
- *Access paths to resources.* Your application has access to your database. Is there any other way to access it? Who has access? How secure are they? What happens if somebody tricks them into accessing the DB? Can they delete the production database by executing a simple ████ █████████?[2] Do they only have access to source code? Thus, anyone who has access to source code also has effective access to the production DB.

You can draw a basic threat model on a piece of paper by using that information. It might look like figure 6.2 for anyone who uses your application or website. You can see in the figure that everyone has access to only the mobile app and the web servers. On the other hand, the web servers have access to most critical resources like the database and are exposed to the internet. That means your web servers are the riskiest assets that are exposed to the outside world, as shown in figure 6.2.

Besides regular users, you also have other types of users with different access privileges to your servers and the assets they contain. In figure 6.3, you can see how different types of roles can access different servers. Because the CEO loves to access and have control over every little thing, the easiest way to penetrate this server is to send the CEO an email. You'd expect other roles to have limited access to only the resources that they need access to, but that's not usually the case, as shown in figure 6.3.

---

[2] Redacted. Classified information. Therefore, our databases are secure.

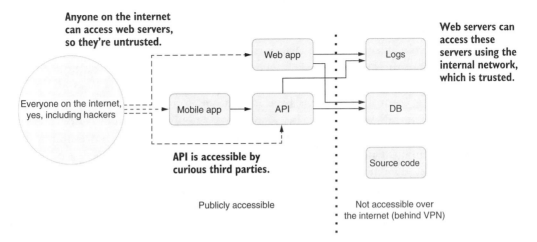

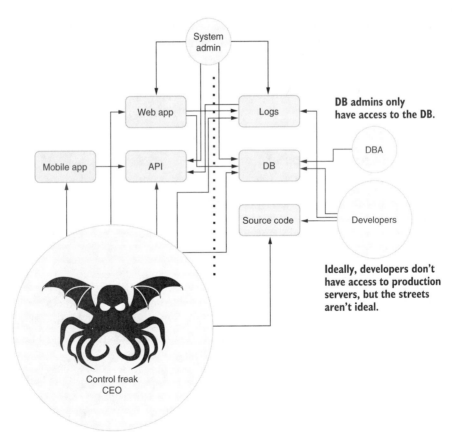

Figure 6.2   Accessibility of servers on a network

Figure 6.3   Server accessibility based on privileged user types

When you look at this model from 20,000 feet, it's obvious that sending an email to the CEO that asks them to log into the VPN to check something and then redirects them to your phishing website will give a malicious actor access to everything about a company. A threat model makes such things obvious and helps you understand the risk factors.

If your control freak CEO is the first candidate to harm your business, the code running on the web servers is the second—and not just your code, either. You could have a delayed security update on the server, causing it to be taken over. But nothing's worse than just typing some text on a form on the website to gain access or destroy all the data in the database.

After your CEO, your web application or API is one of the easiest entry points for a hacker or a bot to attain their goal. That's because your application is unique. It only exists on your servers. You're the only one who's tested it. All the third-party components on your servers have been through millions of iterations of testing, bug fixing, and security audits. Even if you had the budget to do all that, you wouldn't have the time in the short run.

The goal of a hacker or a bot can vary from simply stopping your service because it's a Rent-a-DoS (denial of service) hired by your competitor because they have no other ways to compete with you, to extracting user data to acquire some valuable resource somewhere with the same password, to just accessing private data on your servers.

When you have a list of possible threats, you can start addressing them by closing the holes. Because your web app or API is one of the popular candidates, it's important that you know how to write secure code while you are writing web applications.

6.3 Write secure web apps

Every application is unique, but you can use some really easy-to-apply practices during your coding to make your app more resilient to security problems. As street coders, we'll also ask when those practices are the best and when they are not the best. Let's examine the popular attacks on web applications that we can prevent by changing how we write and design our programs.

6.3.1 Design with security in mind

Security is hard to retrofit, mostly because of all the design decisions that led you to write insecure code in the first place. To change the security properties of an application, you might need to reassess your design. Therefore, it's important to take security into account when you're designing it. Go over these steps:

1. Review your written or mental threat model. Understand the risks, the costs of making them secure now, and the costs of making them secure later.
2. Decide where you will store your secrets (DB passwords, API keys) for your app. Make it a hard policy. Assume your source code is accessible to everyone. I will go over the best practices for storing secrets later in this chapter.

3. Design for the least privilege. A code ideally shouldn't require any more privilege than is necessary to accomplish its task. For example, don't give your app DB administrator privileges if your app doesn't need to schedule a periodic DB recovery operation. If only a few tasks need higher privileges, consider compartmentalizing them into a separate, isolated entity, such as a separate app. Run web apps under the least privileged accounts possible.

4. Apply that principle to your entire organization. Employees shouldn't have access to resources that they don't need to perform their daily tasks. CEOs shouldn't have access to the DB or to any servers at all. That's not because nobody can be trusted, but because their access can be compromised by external parties.

When you have accomplished these steps before writing a single line of code for your new app, or even your new feature, you'll be much better off in the long run.

In the next sections, some of the topics are only applicable for web/API development, and the examples are usually specific to a single library. If you're not doing anything remotely accessible, you can mostly skip to the section about storing user secrets. Otherwise, keep reading.

6.3.2 Usefulness of security by obscurity

Software security is a race against time. Despite how secure you think your software is, it comes down to how secure people are and how secure everything that surrounds your software is. Every security measure can eventually be broken. It used to be estimated that it would take longer than the lifetime of the universe to break a 4096-bit RSA key, but it turned out that it only took until the production of a quantum computer. That means the sole purpose of every security measure is to gain you time, to make attackers' work hard.

Information security experts loathe security by obscurity. As Benjamin Franklin said, "Those who try to achieve security by obscurity deserve neither security nor obscurity." Okay, he may not have said that exactly, but that's close enough. The reason for the opposition to security by obscurity is that it doesn't buy you time, or perhaps it does, but only marginally. What experts object to is the belief that obscurity is sufficient. It isn't, and it's never effective by itself. You should never prioritize it, and you should only employ it when you have available resources. But in the end, it may buy you marginal security.

That said, let's get this fact straight: marginal security isn't security. It's a temporary bandage that might keep your project up while it reaches a certain level of growth. In the first year of Eksi Sozluk, I remember keeping the administration interface behind an obscure URL with no authentication whatsoever. Let me put that into context: it was 1999, the website had 1000 users at most, and I didn't share the URL with anyone. Instead of investing a lot in an elaborate authentication and authorization mechanism, I focused on the website dynamics that were relevant to users. I definitely knew that it was only a matter of time before someone would find it out, though, so I upgraded it to an authenticated system as soon as I could.

Similarly, the web has run over HTTP protocol for a long time and used a Basic authentication scheme that didn't encrypt passwords, just encoded them in Base64.[3] It was the living testament to security by obscurity. Yes, no sane security expert recommended it, but many websites used it, whether their developers knew the risks or not. If you were on the same network with the user, like a public Wi-Fi access point, you could easily extract passwords and web traffic from the sessions of those who used them. Eventually, man-in-the-middle (MITM) attacks and password skimming applications became so prevalent that there was a huge push in the last decade to switch to HTTPS, HTTP/2, TLS 1.3, and more secure authentication protocols like OAuth2. Security by obscurity worked for decades right in front of us.

That brings us to the point: prioritize security based on your threat model, and if your model permits it, security by obscurity can work for you, just as posting a "Beware of the dog" sign on your fence can reduce the risk of robberies, even if you don't have a dog.

Perfect security isn't attainable, and you'll always encounter tradeoffs between user experience and security, like how the chat app Telegram chose a worse security model than WhatsApp did, but it provides much better usability, so people are switching to it even when they're aware of the consequences. It's really important that you have the same level of awareness of the consequences of the tradeoff decisions that you make. Simply rejecting every measure under the umbrella excuse of "Hey, security by obscurity is bad" doesn't help you.

That said, real security is getting cheaper. You had to buy $500 SSL certificates to get your website up and running with HTTPS, but now you can do it completely for free by using certificates from the Let's Encrypt initiative (Let's Encrypt: https:// letsencrypt.org). Having a secure authentication system is now only about plugging a library into your project. Make sure that you're not exaggerating the requirements of getting good security and are not just making excuses to use security by obscurity to have really bad security. Always prefer real security over security by obscurity when the difference in effort is marginal and the risks are considerable. Obscurity can't buy you real security, but it can occasionally buy you time until you sort things out.

6.3.3 *Don't implement your own security*

Security is complex. You should never write your own implementation of a security mechanism, be it hashing, encryption, or throttling. It's perfectly okay to write code as an experiment, but don't use your own security code in production. That advice is also commonly called "Don't roll your own crypto." Usually, security-related specifications expect the reader to understand the requirements of developing secure software, and a regular developer can miss critical details while implementing their own, essentially creating zero security.

---

[3] Base64 is a binary encoding method that converts unprintable characters into unreadable characters.

Take hashing, for example. Even a team of experts on cryptography has a hard time creating a cryptographically secure hash algorithm that has no weaknesses. Almost any hash algorithm before SHA2 has serious security weaknesses.

I don't expect you to become so adventurous that you'll try to write your own hashing algorithm, but would you have guessed that you shouldn't even implement your own string comparison function because it's insecure? I'll go into the details in section 6.3 about storing secrets.

You can still create defenses against vulnerability simply by changing how you do daily work without implementing anything from scratch. I'll go over these common attack vectors, but it's not an extensive list, but rather prioritized samples to show you that attaining decent security may not require a huge effort on your part. You can be as effective as you were before and write much more secure software.

6.3.4 SQL injection attacks

An SQL injection attack is a long-solved problem, but it's still a popular way to compromise a website. It should have disappeared from the face of the Earth at about the same time as George Lucas' directing career, but somehow it's persevered, unlike George Lucas.

The attack is quite simple. You have an SQL query running on your website. Let's say you want to find a user's ID from the username given to view the profile of that user, a common scenario. Say it looks like this:

```
SELECT id FROM users WHERE username='<username here>'
```

A straightforward approach to building this query with the given username as input is to embed the username into a query using string manipulation. Listing 6.1 shows a simple `GetUserId` function that takes a username as a parameter and builds the actual query by concatenating strings. This is usually the beginner's approach to building SQL queries, but it may look okay at first. The code basically creates a command, sets its query to our query after substituting the given username, and executes it. It returns the result as a nullable integer because a record may not exist at all. Also, note that we concatenate strings, but we don't do it in a loop, as I discussed in chapter 2. This technique doesn't have the redundant memory allocation overhead.

Optional return values

We specifically use a nullable return type in the `GetUserId` function in listing 6.1 instead of a pseudo identifier that denotes the absence of value, like -1 or 0. That's because the compiler can catch unchecked nullable return values in the caller's code and find programming errors. Had we used a regular integer value like 0 or -1, the compiler wouldn't know whether that's a valid value. In C# versions before 8.0, the compiler didn't have these affordances. The future is now!

Listing 6.1   Naive retrieval of a user ID from the database

```
public int? GetUserId(string username) {
  var cmd = db.CreateCommand();
  cmd.CommandText = @"
    SELECT id
      FROM users
      WHERE name='" + username + "'";
  return cmd.ExecuteScalar() as int?;
}
```

We build the actual query here. ▷

Retrieve result or null if the record doesn't exist. ◁

Let's run our function in our mind. Imagine running it with the value `placid_turn`. If we clean up the extra whitespace, the executed SQL query would look like

```
SELECT id FROM users WHERE username='placid_turn'
```

Now, consider if the value of the username contains an apostrophe, something like `hackin'`. Our query now would look like this:

```
SELECT id FROM users WHERE username='hackin''
```

Notice what happened there? We introduced a syntax error. That query would fail with a syntax error, the `SqlCommand` class would raise an `SqlException`, and the user would see an error page. That doesn't sound so scary. Our hacker would only cause an error. There'd be no impact to our service reliability or the security of our data. Now, consider a username like `' OR username='one_lame'`. This will also throw a syntax error, but it will look like this:

```
SELECT id FROM users WHERE username='' OR username='one_lame''
```

The first apostrophe closed the quote, and we could continue our query with additional expressions. It's getting scarier. You see, we can manipulate the query to see the records we're not supposed to see by simply eliminating the syntax error by adding double dashes at the end of the username:

```
SELECT id FROM users WHERE username='' OR username='one_lame' --'
```

The double dashes mean an inline comment, which assumes the rest of the line is a comment in SQL. It's similar to doubles slashes (//) in all C-style languages, except C—well, early versions of it, at least. That means the query runs perfectly and returns the information for `one_lame` instead of `placid_turn`.

We're not limited to a single SQL statement, either. We can run multiple SQL statements by separating them with a semicolon in most SQL dialects. With a long enough username, you can do this:

```
SELECT id FROM users WHERE username='';DROP TABLE users --'
```

That query would delete the table users along with all the records in the table immediately unless there's a lock contention or an active transaction causing a timeout. Think about it—you can do this to a web application remotely by simply typing a specially crafted username and clicking a button. You can leak or lose your data. You might be able to recover the lost data from a backup, depending on how good you are at it, but you can't put the leaked data back into the bottle.

Backups and the 3-2-1 backup rule

Remember that I discussed that regressions are the worst type of bugs that lose us time, like destroying a perfectly built building only to build it from scratch, in earlier chapters? Having no backups may be worse than that. A regression makes you fix a bug again, while lost data makes you *create* the data from scratch. If it's not your data, your users will never bother creating it again. That's one of the first lessons I've learned in my development career. I was a very risk-taking (aka, dumb) person in my early career. Back in 1992, I wrote a compression tool and tried it on its own source code, replacing the original. The tool converted my whole source code into a single byte, and its contents were 255. I'm still confident that there'll be an algorithm in the future to extract those densely packed bits, but I was careless. Version control systems weren't a thing in personal development back then, either. I learned about the importance of having backups right then.

I learned my second lesson about backups in early 2000. A year had passed since I had created Eksi Sozluk, luckily without having any Y2K issues. I was convinced of the importance of backups, but I used to get my hourly backups on the same server and only copied those to a remote server once a week. One day, the disks on the server burned—quite literally, they spontaneously combusted, and the data on them was completely unrecoverable. That was when I understood the importance of backups on separate servers. Later in my career, I learned that there was an unspoken rule called the "3-2-1 backup rule" in the wild that states, "Have three separate backups, two on separate media, and one at a separate location." Obviously, developing a sane backup strategy requires more thinking than that, and it might never be your job, but that's the minimum you might consider embracing.

WRONG SOLUTION TO SQL INJECTION

How would you consider fixing an SQL injection vulnerability in your app? The first thing that comes to mind is escaping: replacing every single apostrophe character (') with double apostrophes (''), so a hacker can't close the quote that your SQL query opens because double apostrophes are considered regular characters rather than syntactic elements.

The problem with this approach is that there isn't a single apostrophe in the Unicode alphabet. The one you escape has the Unicode point value of U+0027 (APOSTROPHE) while, for example, U+02BC (MODIFIED LETTER APOSTROPHE) also represents an apostrophe symbol, albeit for a different purpose, and it's possible that the DB technology you're using might treat it as a regular apostrophe or translate all the other apostrophe look-alikes to a character DB accepts. Thus, the problem comes down to the fact that you can't know the underlying technology well enough to do the escaping on behalf of it correctly.

IDEAL SOLUTION TO SQL INJECTION

The safest way to solve an SQL injection problem is to use *parameterized queries*. Instead of modifying the query string itself, you pass down an additional list of parameters, and the underlying DB provider handles it all. The code in listing 6.1 looks like that in listing 6.2 when applied with a parameterized query. Instead of putting the string as a parameter in the query, we specify a parameter with @parameterName syntax and specify the value of this parameter in a separate Parameters object associated with that command.

> **Listing 6.2   Using parameterized queries**

```
public int? GetUserId(string username) {
  var cmd = db.CreateCommand();
  cmd.CommandText = @"
    SELECT id
      FROM users
      WHERE username=@username";          ⟵———  Name of the parameter
  cmd.Parameters.AddWithValue("username", username);    ⟵⎤  We pass the actual
  return cmd.ExecuteScalar() as int?;                     ⎦  value here.
}
```

Voila! You can send whatever character you want in the username, but there's no way you can change the query. There isn't even any escaping happening anymore because the query and the value of the parameters are sent in separate data structures.

Another advantage of using parameterized queries is to reduce *query plan cache* pollution. Query plans are execution strategies DBs develop when running a query for the first time. The DB keeps this plan in the cache, and if you run the same query again, it reuses the existing query. It uses a dictionary-like structure, so lookups are O(1), really fast. But, like everything in the universe, a query plan cache has limited capacity. If you send these queries to the DB, they'll all have different query plan entries in the cache:

```
SELECT id FROM users WHERE username='oracle'
SELECT id FROM users WHERE username='neo'
SELECT id FROM users WHERE username='trinity'
SELECT id FROM users WHERE username='morpheus'
SELECT id FROM users WHERE username='apoc'
SELECT id FROM users WHERE username='cypher'
SELECT id FROM users WHERE username='tank'
SELECT id FROM users WHERE username='dozer'
SELECT id FROM users WHERE username='mouse'
```

Because the size of the query plan cache is limited, if you run this query with enough different username values, other useful query plan entries will be evicted from the cache and it will get filled up with these possibly useless entries. That's query plan cache pollution.

When you use parameterized queries instead, your executed queries will all look the same:

```
SELECT id FROM users WHERE username=@username
SELECT id FROM users WHERE username=@username
SELECT id FROM users WHERE username=@username
SELECT id FROM users WHERE username=@username
SELECT id FROM users WHERE username=@username
SELECT id FROM users WHERE username=@username
SELECT id FROM users WHERE username=@username
SELECT id FROM users WHERE username=@username
SELECT id FROM users WHERE username=@username
SELECT id FROM users WHERE username=@username
```

Since all queries have the same text, the DB will be using only a single query plan cache entry for all the queries you run this way. Your other queries will have a better chance of finding their spot in this place, and you will get better overall performance with your queries in addition to being perfectly safe from SQL injections. And this is all free!

Like every recommendation in this book, you'll still have to keep in mind that a parameterized query isn't a silver bullet. You might be tempted to say, "Hey, if it's that good, I'll make everything parameterized!" But you shouldn't unnecessarily parameterize, say, constant values because the query plan optimizer can find better query plans for certain values. For example, you might want to write this query, although you always use `active` as the value for `status`:

```
SELECT id FROM users WHERE username=@username AND status=@status
```

The query plan optimizer will think that you can send any value as `status` and will pick a plan that works well enough for all possible values of `@status`. That might mean using the wrong index for `active` and getting a worse-performing query. Hmm, maybe a chapter about databases is in order?

WHEN YOU CAN'T USE PARAMETERIZED QUERIES

Parameterized queries are very versatile. You can even use a variable number of parameters by naming them `@p0`, `@p1`, and `@p2` in code and add parameter values in a loop. Still, there might be cases when you can't really use parameterized queries, or you don't want to, such as to avoid polluting the query plan cache again; or you might need certain SQL syntax like pattern matching (think of `LIKE` operators and characters like `%` and `_`) that may not be supported by parameterized queries. What you can do in this case is aggressively sanitize the text, rather than escaping.

If the parameter is a number, parse it into a correct numeric type (`int`, `float`, `double`, `decimal`, etc.) and use that in the query instead of placing it in the string directly, even if that means unnecessarily converting between an integer and a string more than once.

If it's a string but you don't need any special characters or you only need a subset of special characters, remove everything except the valid characters from the string. This is nowadays called *allow-listing*, as in having a list of allowed elements instead of a list of denied elements. This helps you avoid accidentally sneaking a malicious character into your SQL queries.

Some DB abstractions may not seem to support parameterized queries in the common way. Those can have alternative ways to pass parameterized queries. For example, Entity Framework Core uses a `FormattableString` interface to perform the same operation. A query similar to that in listing 6.2 would look like listing 6.3 in EF Core. The `FromSqlInterpolated` function does a clever thing by using `FormattableString` and C#'s string interpolation syntax together. This way, the library can use the string template, replace arguments with parameters, and build a parameterized query behind the scenes without you knowing it.

Interpolate me, complicate me, elevate me (courtesy of the band Rush)

In the beginning, there was `String.Format()`. You could substitute strings with it without dealing with the messy syntax of string concatenation. For example, instead of `a.ToString() + "+" + b.ToString() + "=" + c.ToString()`, you could just write `String.Format("{0}+{1}={2}" a, b, a + b)`. It's easier to understand what the resulting string will look like using `String.Format`, but which parameter corresponds to which expression is not really straightforward. Then came string interpolation syntax with C# 6.0, which let you write the same expression as `$"{a}+{b}={a+b}"`. It's brilliant: it lets you understand what the resulting string will look like, and yet it's clear which variable corresponds where in the template.

The thing is that `$."..."` is pretty much syntactic sugar for `String.Format(..., ...)` syntax, which processes the string before calling the function. If we needed the interpolation arguments in our function itself, we had to write new function signatures similar to `String.Format`'s and call formatting ourselves, which complicates our work.

Luckily, the new string interpolation syntax also allows automatic casting to the `FormattableString` class that holds both the string template and its arguments. Your function can receive the string and arguments separately if you change the type of the string parameter to `FormattableString`. This leads to interesting uses like delaying the text processing in logging libraries, or, like the example in listing 6.3, to parameterized queries without processing the string. `FormattableString` is pretty much the same in JavaScript's template literals, which serve the same purpose.

Listing 6.3 Parameterized query with EF Core

```
public int? GetUserId(string username) {
  return dataContext.Users
    .FromSqlInterpolated(
```
Uses string interpolation to
create a parameterized query

```
    $@"SELECT * FROM users WHERE username={username}")   ←── Cast to
  .Select(u => (int?)u.Id)   ←──                              FormattableString
  .FirstOrDefault();   ←──     Makes our default value null    when passed to
}                              instead of zero for integers    FromSqlInterpolated
     Returns the first value from    by typecasting to nullable
         the query, if there is any
```

SUMMARY

Don't use parameterized queries too much, mostly for user input. Parameterization is powerful; it's perfect for keeping your app secure and the query plan cache a decent size simultaneously. Still, understand the gotchas of parameterization, like poor query optimization, and avoid using it for constant values.

6.3.5 *Cross-site scripting*

I think cross-site scripting (I prefer XSS as a shorthand because the other alternative, CSS, is also a popular styling language on the web) should have been called *JavaScript injection* for dramatic effect. Cross-site scripting actually sounds like a competitive sports category in programming, like cross-country skiing. If I didn't know what it was, I could easily be sold on the concept. "Wow, cross-site scripting. That sounds nice. I'd love for my scripting to work across sites."

XSS is a two-phase attack. The first one is the ability to insert JavaScript code in the page, and the second is to load a larger JavaScript code over the network and execute it on your web page. The advantages of this are multiple. You can capture a user's actions, information, and even their session by stealing session cookies from another session, which is called session hijacking.

SORRY, I CAN'T INJECT THAT, DAVE

XSS mainly stems from poorly encoded HTML. It resembles SQL injection in that sense. Instead of providing an apostrophe in the user input, we can provide angled brackets to manipulate HTML code. If we can modify the HTML code, we can manipulate it to have `<script>` tags and provide JavaScript code inside.

A simple example is the search feature of websites. When you search for something, the results are listed on the resulting page, but if no results are found, there is usually an error message that says, "Your search query for 'flux capacitors for sale' didn't return any results." So what happens if we search for "`<script>alert('hello!');</script>`"? If the output isn't properly encoded, there's a chance that you can see something like figure 6.4.

Figure 6.4 Your code runs on someone else's website, so what can go wrong?

If you can inject a simple `alert` command, you can certainly inject more. You can read the cookies and send them to another web page. You can even load whole JavaScript code from a remote URL and run it on the page. That's where the term "cross-site" comes in. Allowing JavaScript code to send requests to third-party websites is regarded as a cross-site request.

PREVENTING XSS

The easiest way to defend against XSS is to encode text so that special HTML characters are escaped. That way, they are represented with an equivalent HTML entity instead of their own character, as table 6.1 shows. Normally, you shouldn't need these tables and can perform any encoding using existing, well-tested functions. This table is just for your reference to recognize these entities when you see them in your HTML. When escaped with HTML entities, user input won't be regarded as HTML and will be shown as plain text, as figure 6.5 shows.

Table 6.1   **HTML entity equivalents of special characters**

Character	Escaped HTML entity	Alternative
&	&	&
<	<	<
>	>	>
"	"	"
'	'	'

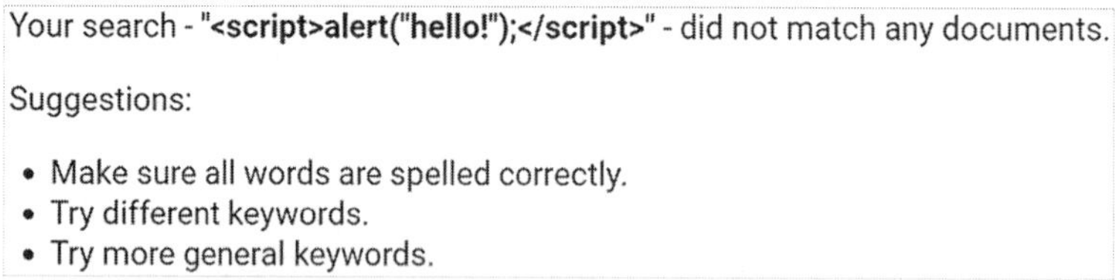

Your search - **"<script>alert("hello!");</script>"** - did not match any documents.

Suggestions:

- Make sure all words are spelled correctly.
- Try different keywords.
- Try more general keywords.

Figure 6.5   **When properly escaped, HTML can be quite harmless.**

Many modern frameworks actually encode HTML for regular text by default. Consider the Razor template code in our own search engine, Fooble, in the following listing. As you can see, we're using @ syntax to directly include a value in our resulting HTML page without performing any encoding at all.

Listing 6.4   **An excerpt from our search engine results page**

```
<p>
  Your search for <em>"@Model.Query"</em>     ◁─┐  We use no extra
  didn't return any results.                    │  code for encoding.
</p>
```

Even though we directly output the query string, there is no XSS error, as figure 6.6 shows. If you view the source code of the generated web page, you'll see that it's quoted perfectly, as it is in the following listing.

Welcome to Fooble

Fooble is the ultimate useless search engine that returns nothing.

Your search for "*<script>alert("hello!");</script>*" didn't return any results.

| Enter your search query | Search! | I'm feeling a little peculiar |

Figure 6.6 We perfectly avoid an XSS attack here.

Listing 6.5 Actual HTML source generated

```
<p>
    Your search for
➥   <em>"&lt;script&gt;alert(&quot;hello!&quot;);&lt;/script&gt;"</em>   ◁─┐
    didn't return any results.          Perfectly escaped, as all things should be
</p>
```

Then why do we need to care about XSS at all? That's because, again, programmers are human. Despite the emergence of elegant templating technologies, there are cases when you might still think that using raw HTML output can be good.

COMMON XSS PITFALLS

One popular pitfall is ignorance about the separation of concerns, such as keeping HTML in your model. You might be tempted to return a string with some HTML embedded in it because it's easier to integrate logic into your page code. For example, you might want to return a plain text or a link in your get method, depending on whether the text is clickable. With ASP.NET MVC, it might feel easier to type this

```
return View(isUserActive
    ? $"<a href='/profile/{username}'>{username}</a>"
    : username);
```

and then this in the view

```
@Html.Raw(Model)
```

instead of creating a new class to hold `active` and `username` together, like this

```
public class UserViewModel {
    public bool IsActive { get; set; }
    public string Username { get; set; }
}
```

and then creating that model in the controller

```
return View(new UserViewModel()
{
    IsActive = isUserActive,
    Username = username,
});
```

and creating conditional logic in the template to render the username properly:

```
@model UserViewModel
. . . other code here
@if (Model.IsActive) {
    <a href="/profile/@Model.IsActive">
        @Model.Username
    </a>
} else {
    @Model.Username
}
```

It might seem like a lot of work do things the right way when the only objective you have is about writing less code. There are ways to avoid a lot of overhead, though. You can even make your job much easier by switching to Razor Pages from ASP.NET MVC, but if that's not possible, you can do a lot on existing code as well. For example, you can eliminate a separate model by using a tuple instead:

```
return View((Active: isUserActive, Username:  username));
```

This way, you can keep the template code as is. That will save you from creating a new class, although there are benefits to that, like reuse. You can get the same benefit from new C# records by declaring a view model with a single line of code as immutable too!

```
public record UserViewModel(bool IsActive, string Username);
```

A Razor Pages application already helps you shorten your code because you don't need a separate model class anymore. Controller logic is encapsulated in the View-Model class created in the page.

   If including HTML code in your MVC Controller or Razor Pages ViewModel can't be avoided, consider using `HtmlString` or `IHtmlContent` types instead, which let you define well-encoded HTML strings with explicit declarations. If you had to create the same scenario with `HtmlString`, it would look like listing 6.6. Since ASP.NET doesn't encode `HtmlStrings`, you wouldn't even need to wrap it with the `Html.Raw` statement.

   In listing 6.6, you can see how we implement XSS-safe HTML output. We define `Username` as `IHtmlContent` instead of a `string`. This way, Razor will directly use the content of the string without encoding. The encoding is handled by `HtmlContent-Builder` only for the parts you explicitly specified.

Listing 6.6 Using XSS-safe constructs for HTML encoding

```
public class UserModel : PageModel {
  public IHtmlContent? Username { get; set; }

  public void OnGet(string username) {
    bool isActive = isUserActive(username);
    var content = new HtmlContentBuilder();
    if (isActive) {
      content.AppendFormat("<a href='/user/{0}'>", username);      This HTML-
    }                                                              encodes the
    content.Append(username);      This also encodes the username. username only.
    if (isActive) {
      content.AppendHtml("</a>");      No encoding is
    }                                  applied here at all.
    Username = content;
  }
}
```

CONTENT SECURITY POLICY (CSP)

CSP is another weapon in the battle against XSS attacks. It's an HTTP header that limits the resources that can be requested from third-party servers. I find CSP hard to use because the modern web involves many external resources on a website, whether it's fonts, script files, analytics code, or CDN content, for example. All those resources and trusted domains are subject to change at any time. It's hard to maintain a trusted list of domains and keep it up to date. It's hard to tackle its slightly cryptic syntax. It's hard to verify its correctness, too. Is your CSP correct if your website keeps working without warnings, or is your policy too flexible? It can be a powerful ally, but I won't risk confusing you and herding you over a cliff by only skimming the subject. Whether you use CSP or not, you should always take care of encoding your HTML output properly.

SUMMARY

XSS is easily avoided by not trying to cut corners like injecting HTML and bypassing encoding completely. If you have to inject HTML, be extra careful about encoding the values properly. If you think being XSS-conscious increases your code size, there are ways to reduce the code overhead.

6.3.6 Cross-site request forgery

There is a reason why operations that modify the content on the web are performed with the POST verb instead of GET in the HTTP protocol. You cannot produce a clickable link to a POST address. It can only be posted once. If it fails, your browser warns you if you need to submit it again. Consequently, posting to a forum, logging in, and making a meaningful change are usually denoted with a POST. There are also DELETE and PUT with a similar purpose, but they aren't as commonly used, and they can't be triggered from an HTML form.

This nature of POST makes us trust it more than we ought to. The weakness of POST arises because the original form doesn't have to reside on the same domain as the one the POST request is made from. It can be on any web page on the internet. That lets attackers make POST submissions by tricking you into clicking a link on their web page. Let's just assume that Twitter's delete operation works like a POST operation at a URL like https://twitter.com/delete/{tweet_id}.

What happens if I put a website on my domain, streetcoder.org/about, and put a form like that in the following listing without even using a single line of JavaScript?

Listing 6.7   A completely innocent web form, really

```
<h1>Welcome to the super secret website!</h1>
<p>Please click on the button to continue</p>
<form method="POST"
      action="https://twitter.com/i/api/1.1/statuses/destroy.json">
   <input type="hidden" name="id" value="123" />
   <button type="submit">Continue</button>
</form>
```

Luckily, there is no tweet with the ID of 123, but if there was, and Twitter was just a simple startup that didn't know how to protect against CSRF, we would be able to delete someone else's tweet just by asking them to visit our shady website. If you can use JavaScript, you can even send POST requests without requiring any click to any web form element.

The way to avoid this kind of problem is to use a randomly generated number for every form generated that is replicated on both the form itself and on the website response headers. Since the shady website can't know those numbers and can't manipulate the web server response headers, it can't really make its request pretend that it came from the user. The good thing is that usually the framework you use covers for you, so you just need to enable generation of tokens and verification of them on the client side. ASP.NET Core 2.0 automatically includes them into forms, so you don't need to perform any action, but you need to make sure that those tokens are verified in case you're creating forms in a different way, such as in your own HTML helper. In that case, you need to explicitly produce request forgery tokens in your template using a helper like this:

```
<form method="post">
    @Html.AntiForgeryToken()
    ...
</form>
```

You need to make sure that it's validated on the server side too. Again, this is normally automatic, but in case you have it disabled globally, you can selectively enable it on certain controller actions or Razor Pages using the ValidateAntiForgeryToken attribute:

```
[ValidateAntiForgeryToken]
public class LoginModel: PageModel {
    ...
}
```

Since CSRF mitigation is already automatic in modern frameworks like ASP.NET Core, you only need to know the basics to understand the benefits. But in case you need to implement it yourself, it's important that you know how and why it works.

6.4 Draw the first flood

Denial of service (DoS) is the common name for making your service not work. It can simply be something that causes your server to stop, hang, or crash, or something that can spike the CPU usage or saturate the available bandwidth. Sometimes the latter type of attacks is called a *flood*. We'll specifically look at floods and how we can resist them.

There isn't a complete solution for floods because regular users in greater numbers can also bring down a website. It's hard to distinguish a legitimate user from an attacker. There are ways to mitigate DoS attacks so the attacker's capabilities are reduced. A popular one is captcha.

6.4.1 Don't use captcha

Captcha is the bane of the web. It's a popular way to separate the wheat from the chaff, but it's a great friction for humans. The idea is basically asking a mathematically complex problem that a human can solve easily, but that automated software used in attacks will have a hard time tackling, such as "What shall we have for lunch?"

The problem with captcha is that it's hard for humans, too. Consider "Mark all the squares with traffic lights." Do I just mark the squares that show the light bulb itself, or do I also mark the enclosure of the traffic light? Do I trace the light pole too? How about that graffiti-like art we're supposed to read easily? Are those letters rn or just m? Is 5 a letter? Why do you make me suffer? This experience is illustrated in figure 6.7.

Write the letters you see below:

Figure 6.7   Am I human?

Captcha is useful but harmful at the same time as a denial-of-service measure. You don't want UX friction during your application's growth phase. When I first released Eksi Sozluk in 1999, there wasn't even a login. Anyone could write anything on the website immediately using whatever nickname they wanted. That caused problems shortly because people started to write using each other's nicknames, but that was after people started really loving it. Don't make your users suffer until you get popular enough. That's when bots will discover your website and attack, but your users will tolerate slightly more pain because they already love your app.

That point applies to all kinds of solutions that involve UX friction for a technical problem. Cloudflare's "Please wait for five seconds while we determine if you're an attacker or not" web page is similar. Fifty-three percent of visitors leave a web page when they have to wait three seconds for it to load. You're effectively losing users on the mere chance that someone might find your website lucrative enough to attack and saturate. Do you want to lose 53% of your visitors all the time, or lose all your visitors for an hour once a month?

6.4.2 *Captcha alternatives*

Write performant code, cache aggressively, and use throttling when necessary. I've already discussed the performance benefits of certain programming techniques, and we have an entire chapter ahead of us that's solely about performance optimization.

There is a gotcha to all this. If you throttled based on an IP address, you'd be throttling everyone from the same IP address, such as a business or a company. When you grow beyond a certain extent, that might hinder your ability to serve requests quickly enough to a significant portion of your users.

There is an alternative to throttling: proof of work. You might have heard about proof of work from cryptocurrencies. To make a request, your computer or your device is required to solve a really hard problem that is guaranteed to take a certain amount of time. One of the methods is integer factorization. Another proven method is asking the computer the meaning of life, the universe, and everything. It's known to take some time.

Proof of work consumes client resources extensively, which might impact battery life and performance on slower devices. That might also impact user experience badly, even worse than captcha.

You can present more user-friendly challenges, such as a requirement of login after your website passes the barrier of popularity. Checking authentication is cheap, but registering to your website and confirming an email address definitely takes time. Again, that's a user friction. If you ask your users to do something before they can access the content on your website, such as registering or installing the mobile app, there is a high chance that the user will just swear and leave your website. When you're deciding about reducing an attacker's capability, you need to consider those pros and cons.

6.4.3 *Don't implement a cache*

A dictionary is possibly the most popular structure used in web frameworks. HTTP request and response headers, cookies, and cache entries are all kept in dictionaries. That's because, as I discussed in chapter 2, dictionaries are blazingly fast because they have O(1) complexity. Lookups are instantaneous.

The problem with dictionaries is that they're so practical that we might decide to just fire one up to keep a cache of something. There is even a `ConcurrentDictionary` in .NET that is thread-safe, making it an attractive candidate for a hand-rolled cache.

Regular dictionaries included in a framework aren't usually designed for keys based on user input. If an attacker knows which runtime you use, they can cause a hash collision attack. They can send requests with many different keys that correspond to the same hash code, causing collisions, as I've discussed in chapter 2, which causes lookups to get closer to O(N) instead of O(1) and brings the application to its knees.

Custom dictionaries developed for web-facing components, such as SipHash, usually use a different hash code algorithm with better distribution properties and therefore less collision probability. Such algorithms can be slightly slower than regular hash functions on average, but because of their resistance to collision attacks, they perform better in worst cases.

Dictionaries also don't have an eviction mechanism by default. They grow indefinitely. That might look okay when you test it locally, but it can fail spectacularly in production. Ideally, a cache data structure should be able to evict older entries to keep memory usage in check.

Because of all these factors, consider leveraging an existing cache infrastructure, preferably one provided by the framework, whenever you think, "Hey, I know, I'll just cache these in a dictionary."

6.5 Storing secrets

Secrets (passwords, private keys, and API tokens) are the keys to your kingdom. They are small pieces of data, yet they provide a disproportional amount of access. You've got the password to the production DB? Then you've got access to everything. You've got an API token? You can do whatever that API permits you to do. That's why secrets have to be part of your threat model.

Compartmentalization is one of the best mitigations against security threats. Storing secrets safely is one way to achieve it.

6.5.1 Keeping secrets in source code

Programmers are great at finding the shortest path to a solution. That includes taking shortcuts and cutting corners. That's why putting a password in the source code is our default tendency. We love rapid prototyping because we hate anything that causes friction to our flow.

You might think that keeping secrets in source code is okay, because nobody other than you has access to the code or because developers already have access to the production DB passwords, and therefore keeping the secret in source code wouldn't hurt. The problem is that you don't take the time dimension into account. In the long run, all source code gets hosted on GitHub. Source code doesn't get treated with the same level of sensitivity as your production DB, but rather, it contains the keys to it. Your customers can request the source code for contractual purposes. Your developers can keep local copies of source code to review it, and their computers can get compromised. Developers can't keep production DB the same way because it's usually too big to handle and they associate a higher level of sensitivity with it.

RIGHT STORAGE

If you don't have your secrets in your source code, how would the source code know the secret? You can keep it in the DB itself, but that creates a paradox. Where do you store the password to the DB, then? It's also a bad idea because it unnecessarily puts all protected resources in the same trust group with the DB. If you have the password to the database, you have everything. Let's say you're running the Pentagon's IT and you keep nuclear launch codes in the employee database, because that database is well protected. That creates an awkward situation when an accountant accidentally opens the wrong table in the database. Similarly, your app might have API access to more valuable resources than your database. You need to consider that disparity in your threat model.

The ideal way is to store secrets in a separate storage that's designed for that purpose, such as a password manager as cold storage and a cloud key vault (Azure Key Vault, AWS KMS). If your web servers and DB are in the same trust boundary in your threat model, you can simply add those secrets into environment variables on your server. Cloud services let you set up environment variables through their administration interface.

Modern web frameworks support various storage options for secrets, backed by the operating system's or the cloud provider's secure storage facilities in addition to environment variables that can directly map into your configuration. Let's say you have this configuration for your application:

```
{
    "Logging": {
        "LogLevel": {
            "Default": "Information"
        }
    },
    "MyAPIKey": "somesecretvalue"
}
```

You don't want to keep `MyAPIKey` in your configuration because anyone with source access would have access to the API key. So you go ahead and remove the key there and pass it as an environment variable in the production environment. On a developer machine, instead of using the environment variable, you can use user secrets instead. Using .NET, you can initialize and set up user secrets by running the `dotnet` command:

```
dotnet user-secrets init -id myproject
```

That initializes the project to use the `myproject id` as an access identifier to relevant user secrets. You can then add user secrets for your developer account by running this command:

```
dotnet user-secrets set MyAPIkey somesecretvalue
```

Now, when you set up user secrets to be loaded in your configuration, the secrets will be loaded from the user secrets file and will override the configuration. You can access your secret API key the same way you access the configuration:

```
string apiKey = Configuration["MyAPIKey"];
```

Cloud services like Azure or AWS let you configure the same secrets through their environment variables or key vault configurations.

DATA SHALL BE LEAKED

The popular website Have I Been Pwned? (https://haveibeenpwned.com) is a notification service for leaked passwords associated with email addresses. As of this writing, I seem to have been *pwned*[4] 16 times in different data leaks. Data leaks. Data has leaked, and data shall leak. You should always assume the risk of data going public and design against it.

DON'T COLLECT DATA YOU DON'T NEED

Your data can't be leaked if it doesn't exist in the first place. Be aggressive about saying no to collecting data except for data you don't think your service could function without. There are side benefits like less storage requirements, higher performance, less data management work, and less friction for the user. For example, many websites require first name and last name when registering. Do you really need that data?

You may not be able to do without some data, like passwords. However, the responsibility of having someone's password is great because people tend to use the same password across multiple services. That means if your password data leaks, the user's bank accounts might get compromised too. You might think that's on the user for not using a password manager, but you're dealing with humans here. There are simple things that you can do that prevent this from happening.

THE RIGHT WAY OF PASSWORD HASHING

The most common way to prevent passwords from being leaked is to use a hashing algorithm. Instead of storing passwords, you store a cryptographically secure hash of the password. We can't use just any hashing algorithm, like `GetHashCode()` from chapter 2, because regular hash algorithms are easy to break or cause collisions with. Cryptographically secure hash algorithms are deliberately slow and resistant to several other forms of attacks.

---

[4] *Pwned* is a modified form of *owned*, as in being dominated by a hacker. It's slang for having your ass handed to you. Example: "I got pwned because I chose my birth date as my PIN."

Cryptographically secure hash algorithms vary in their characteristics. For password hashing, the preferred method is to use an algorithm that uses multiple iterations of the same algorithm many times to slow down the execution. Similarly, modern algorithms may also require a lot of memory relative to the work they're doing to prevent attacks by custom manufactured chips specifically designed to crack a certain algorithm.

Never use single iteration hash functions, even if they are cryptographically secure, such as SHA2, SHA3, and, God forbid, never MD5 or SHA1 because they have long been broken. Cryptographic security property only ensures that the algorithm has exceptionally low collision probability; it doesn't ensure that they are resistant to brute-force attacks. To get brute-force resistance, you need to ensure that the algorithm will work really slowly.

A common hash function that is designed to work slowly is PBKDF2, which sounds like a Russian secret service subdivision, but stands for *Password-Based Key Derivation Function Two*. It can work with any hash function because it only runs them in a loop and combines the results. It uses a variant of the SHA1 hash algorithm, which is now considered a weak algorithm and shouldn't be used in any application anymore because it's getting easier to create a collision with SHA1 every day.

Unfortunately, PBKDF2 can be cracked relatively quickly because it can be processed in parallel on GPU, and there are specialized ASIC (custom chip) and FPGA (programmable chip) designs for cracking it. You don't want an attacker to try combinations too quickly when they're trying to crack your data that just leaked. There are newer hash algorithms like bcrypt, scrypt, and Argon2 that are also resistant to GPU or ASIC-based attacks.

All modern brute-force resistant hash algorithms take either a difficulty coefficient as a parameter or a number of iterations. You should make sure that your difficulty settings aren't so high that it becomes a DoS attack to attempt to log in on the website. You probably shouldn't aim for any difficulty that takes more than 100 ms on your production server. I strongly recommend benchmarking your password hashing difficulty to make sure it doesn't hurt you because changing hash algorithms on the road is difficult.

Modern frameworks like ASP.NET Core provide password hashing functionality out of the box, and you don't really even need to know how it works, but its current implementation relies on PBKDF2, which is a bit behind in security, as I've discussed. It's important to make conscious decisions about proper hashing.

When picking an algorithm, I recommend favoring one that's supported by the framework that you use. If that's not available, then you should go for the most tested one. Newer algorithms usually aren't tested and verified as much as the older ones.

COMPARE STRINGS SECURELY

So you've picked an algorithm, and you store hashes of the passwords instead of the passwords themselves. Now all you need to do is to read the password from the user, hash it, and compare it with the password on the DB. Sounds simple, right? That could easily be a simple loop comparison, as in listing 6.8. You can see that we implement a straightforward array comparison. We first check the lengths, and then we iterate in a loop to see if every element is equal. If we find a mismatch, we return immediately, so we don't bother to check the rest of the values.

Listing 6.8 A naive comparison function for two hash values

```
private static bool compareBytes(byte[] a, byte[] b) {
  if (a.Length != b.Length) {
    return false;              ⊲──── Length mismatch check, just in case
  }
  for (int n = 0; n < a.Length; n++) {
    if (a[n] != b[n]) {
      return false;     ⊲──── Value mismatch
    }
  }
  return true;       ⊲──── Success!
}
```

How can that code be not secure? The problem comes from our mini-optimization of bailing out early when we find mismatched values. That means we can find out how long the match is by measuring how quickly the function returns, as in figure 6.8, and we can find the correct hash if we know the hash algorithm by producing passwords that correspond to a certain first value of the hash, then the first two values, and so on. Yes, the timing differences will be small, milliseconds, maybe nanoseconds, but they can still be measured against a baseline. If they can't be measured, measurements can be repeated to get more accurate results. It's way faster than trying every possible combination.

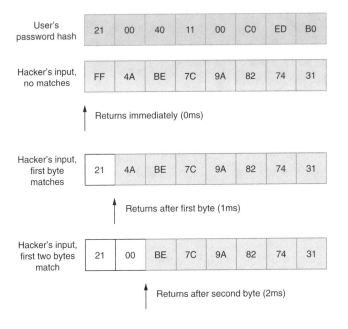

Figure 6.8 How fast comparison can help attackers figure out your hash

To solve this, you need a comparison function that takes a constant time, as in listing 6.9. Instead of returning early, we keep a result value and keep comparisons going even if the comparison fails. Thus, all our comparisons take a constant value, avoiding leaking the hash values of users.

> **Listing 6.9   Secure hash comparison**

```
private static bool compareBytesSafe(byte[] a, byte[] b) {
  if (a.Length != b.Length) {
    return false;              ◁┐  This is an exceptional case. It will
  }                            │   never be hit ideally, so we keep it.
  bool success = true;
  for (int n = 0; n < a.Length; n++) {
    success = success && (a[n] == b[n]);   ◁┐  We constantly update our result
  }                                        │   variable without finishing early.
  return success;   ◁┐
}                   └─ We return the final result.
```

DON'T USE FIXED SALTS

Salts are additional values introduced into password-hashing algorithms to make values deviate even though they are for the same hash values. The reason is that you don't want the attacker to figure out all the same passwords by guessing only the hash value of one. This way, even if every user's password is hunter2, all users will have different hash values, making an attacker's life harder.

Developers can find using well-known values for hash salts—like a hash of a user's name, or a user's identifier—that are secure enough because they're usually easier to generate than an array of random values, but that's a completely unnecessary shortcut for way less security. You should always use random values for salts, but not just regular pseudorandom values, either. You need values generated by a CSPRNG (cryptographically secure pseudorandom number generator).

OH RANDOM, OH CHANCE!

Regular random values are generated with simple and predictable algorithms. Their goal isn't to create real unpredictability, but just an imitation of it. They're okay if you're writing an unpredictable enemy in your game, and they're okay for picking today's featured post on your website. They're fast, but they aren't secure. They can either be predicted, or the search space for valid random values can be narrowed down because they tend to repeat themselves in relatively shorter intervals. People managed to figure out the random value generator algorithms of slot machines in casinos in Las Vegas in the old days when the designers of those machines didn't know any better.

You need cryptographically secure pseudorandom numbers because they're extremely hard to predict, as they use multiple strong entropy sources, like a machine's hardware components, and more complex algorithms. As a result, they're naturally slower, so they should usually only be used in the context of security.

Many cryptographically secure hash libraries provide a hash generation function that only receives the length of the salt, not the salt itself. The library takes care of generating that random salt for you, and you can retrieve it from the results, as in listing 6.10, which uses PBKDF2 as an example. We create an implementation of the RFC2898 key derivation function. It's a PBKDF2 with an HMAC-SHA1 algorithm. We use the using statement because security primitives can use an operating system's unmanaged resources, and it's good to have them cleaned up when they leave the scope. We leverage a simple record to return both the hash and the newly generated salt in a single package.

> **Listing 6.10 Generating cryptographically secure random values**

```
public record PasswordHash(byte[] Hash, byte[] Salt);           ◁── Our record that holds
                                                                      hash and salt values
private PasswordHash hashPassword(string password) {
  using var pbkdf2 = new Rfc2898DeriveBytes(password,
    saltSizeInBytes, iterations);              ◁──── Creating an instance
  var hash = pbkdf2.GetBytes(keySizeInBytes);  ◁──── of a hash generator
  return new PasswordHash(hash, pbkdf2.Salt);
}                                               We generate the hash value here.
```

UUIDs AREN'T RANDOM

Universally unique identifiers (UUIDs), or *globally unique identifiers* (GUIDs), as they're called in the Microsoft universe, are random-looking numbers like 14e87830-bf4c-4bf3-8dc3-57b97488ed0a. They used to be generated based on obscure data like a network adapter's MAC address or system date/time. Nowadays, they're mostly random, but they're designed to be unique, not necessarily secure. They can still be predicted because there is no guarantee that they'd be created using a *cryptographically secure pseudorandom number generator* (CSPRNG). You shouldn't rely on the randomness of GUIDs, for, let's say, generating an activation token when you're sending out a confirmation email to your newly registered users. Always use CSPRNGs for generating security-sensitive tokens. UUIDs may not be perfectly random, but they're more secure as identifiers than simple monotonic (incrementing one by one) integers. There's a possibility that an attacker can guess previous order numbers or how many orders a store has received so far by looking at that number. That's not possible with a fully random UUID.

On the other hand, fully random UUIDs have bad index scattering. Even if you insert two consecutive records, they'd be placed at completely irrelevant spots in the database index, causing slow sequential reads. To avoid that, new UUID standards, namely, UUIDv6, UUIDv7, and UUIDv8, have emerged. Those UUIDs still have some randomness, but they also contain timestamps that create much more uniform index distribution.

Summary

- Use either mental or paper threat models to prioritize security measures and identify weaknesses.
- Design with security in mind first because retrofitting security can be hard.
- Security by obscurity isn't real security, but it can be a real detriment. Prioritize it as such.
- Don't implement your own security primitives, even when it comes to comparing two hash values. Trust well-tested and well-implemented solutions.
- User input is evil.
- Use parameterized queries against SQL injection attacks. If you can't use parameterized queries for any reason, validate and sanitize user input aggressively.
- Make sure user input is properly HTML encoded when it's included in the page to avoid XSS vulnerabilities.
- Avoid captcha, especially in your growth phase, to deter DoS attacks. Try other methods like throttling and aggressive caching first.
- Store secrets in separate secret stores rather than in the source code.
- Store password hashes in your database with strong algorithms that are designed for the purpose.
- Use cryptographically secure pseudorandom numbers in security-related contexts, never GUIDs.

Opinionated optimization

7

This chapter covers

- Embracing premature optimization
- Taking a top-down approach to performance problems
- Optimizing CPU and I/O bottlenecks
- Making safe code faster and unsafe code safer

Programming literature on optimization always starts with a well-known quote by the famous computer scientist Donald Knuth: "Premature optimization is the root of all evil." Not only is the statement wrong, but it's also always misquoted. First, it's wrong because everybody knows that the root of all evil is object-oriented programming since it leads to bad parenting and class struggles. Second, it's wrong because the actual quote is more nuanced. This is almost another case of lorem ipsum, which is gibberish because it is quoted from the middle of an otherwise meaningful Latin text. Knuth's actual statement is, "We should forget about small efficiencies, say about 97% of the time: premature optimization is the root of all evil. Yet we should not pass up our opportunities in that critical 3%."[1]

---

[1] Donald Knuth let me know that his quote in the original article had been revised and reprinted in his book *Literate Programming*. Getting a personal response from him was one of the greatest highlights of my writing process.

171

I claim that premature optimization is the root of all learning. Don't hold yourself back from something you are so passionate about. Optimization is problem solving, and premature optimization creates nonexistent, hypothetical problems to solve, just like how chess players set up pieces to challenge themselves. It's a good exercise. You can always throw away your work, as I've discussed in chapter 3, and keep the wisdom you gained. Exploratory programming is a legitimate way to improve your skills as long as you're in control of the risks and the time. Don't deprive yourself of learning opportunities.

That said, people try to discourage you from premature optimization for a reason. Optimization can bring rigidness to the code, making it harder to maintain. Optimization is an investment, and its return heavily depends on how long you can keep it. If specifications change, the optimizations you've performed may have you dug into a hole that is painful to get out of. More importantly, you could be trying to optimize for a problem that doesn't exist in the first place, and making your code less reliable.

For example, you could have a file-copying routine, and you might know that the larger the buffer sizes you read and write at once, the faster the whole operation becomes. You might be tempted to just read everything in memory and write it to get the maximum possible buffer size. That might make your app consume unreasonable amounts of memory or cause it to crash when it tries to read an exceptionally large file. You need to understand the tradeoffs you're making when you're optimizing, which means you must correctly identify the problem you need to solve.

7.1 Solve the right problem

Slow performance can be fixed in many ways, and depending on the exact nature of the problem, the solution's effectiveness and how much time you spend implementing it can vary drastically. The first step to understanding the true nature of a performance problem is to determine if there is a performance problem in the first place.

7.1.1 Simple benchmarking

Benchmarking is the act of comparing performance metrics. It may not help you identify the root cause of a performance problem, but it can help you identify its existence. Libraries like BenchmarkDotNet (https://github.com/dotnet/BenchmarkDotNet) make it extremely easy to implement benchmarks with safety measures to avoid statistical errors. But even if you don't use any library, you can use a timer just to understand the execution time of the pieces of your code.

Something I have always wondered about is how much faster the `Math.DivRem()` function can be than a regular division-and-remainder operation. It's been recommended that you use `DivRem` if you're going to need the result of the division and the remainder at the same time, but I've never had the chance to test whether the claim holds up until now:

```
int division = a / b;
int remainder = a % b;
```

That code looks very primitive, and therefore it's easy to assume that the compiler can optimize it just fine, while the `Math.DivRem()` version looks like an elaborate function call:

```
int division = Math.DivRem(a, b, out int remainder);
```

> **TIP** You might be tempted to call the % operator the modulus operator, but it's not. It's the remainder operator in C or C#. There is no difference between the two for positive values, but negative values produce different results. For example, –7 % 3 is –1 in C#, while it's 2 in Python.

You can create a benchmark suite right away with BenchmarkDotNet, and it's great for microbenchmarking, a type of benchmarking in which you measure small and fast functions because either you're out of options or your boss is on vacation. BenchmarkDotNet can eliminate the measurement errors related to fluctuations or the function call overhead. In listing 7.1, you can see the code that uses BenchmarkDotNet to test the speed of `DivRem` versus manual division/remainder operations. We basically create a new class that describes the benchmark suite with benchmarked operations marked with `[Benchmark]` attributes. BenchmarkDotNet itself figures out how many times it needs to call those functions to get accurate results because a one-time measurement or running only a few iterations of benchmarks is susceptible to errors. We use multitasking operating systems, and other tasks running in the background can impact the performance of the code we're benchmarking on these systems. We mark the variables used in calculation with the `[Params]` attribute to prevent the compiler from eliminating the operations it deems unnecessary. Compilers are easily distracted, but they're smart.

Listing 7.1   Example BenchmarkDotNet code

```
public class SampleBenchmarkSuite {
    [Params(1000)]            ⊲⎯⎯⎯⎯⎯⎯⎯⎯⎯⎯⎯    We're avoiding compiler
    public int A;                              optimizations.

    [Params(35)]              ⊲⎯⎯⎯⎯⎯⎯⎯⎯⎯⎯⎯
    public int B;

    [Benchmark]               ⊲⎯⎯⎯⎯⎯⎯⎯⎯⎯⎯⎯    Attributes mark the
    public int Manual() {                      operations to be
        int division = A / B;                  benchmarked.
        int remainder = A % B;
        return division + remainder;                              ⊲⎯⎯⎯⎯⎯⎯⎯⎯⎯⎯⎯
    }                                                                              We return values,
                                                                                   so the compiler
    [Benchmark]               ⊲⎯⎯⎯⎯⎯⎯⎯⎯⎯⎯⎯                                          doesn't throw away
    public int DivRem() {                                                          computation steps.
        int division = Math.DivRem(A, B, out int remainder);
        return division + remainder;                              ⊲⎯⎯⎯⎯⎯⎯⎯⎯⎯⎯⎯
    }
}
```

You can run these benchmarks simply by creating a console application and adding a using line and Run call in your Main method:

```
using System;
using System.Diagnostics;
using BenchmarkDotNet.Running;

namespace SimpleBenchmarkRunner {
  public class Program {
    public static void Main(string[] args) {
      BenchmarkRunner.Run<SampleBenchmarkSuite>();
    }
  }
}
```

If you run your application, the Benchmark results will be shown after a minute of running:

```
| Method | a    | b   | Mean     | Error      | StdDev     |
|--------|------|-----|---------:|-----------:|-----------:|
| Manual | 1000 | 35  | 2.575 ns | 0.0353 ns  | 0.0330 ns  |
| DivRem | 1000 | 35  | 1.163 ns | 0.0105 ns  | 0.0093 ns  |
```

It turns out Math.DivRem() is twice as fast as performing division and remainder operations separately. Don't be alarmed by the Error column because it's only a statistical property to help the reader assess accuracy when BenchmarkDotNet doesn't have enough confidence in the results. It's not the standard error, but rather, half of the 99.9% confidence interval.

Although BenchmarkDotNet is dead simple and comes with features to reduce statistical errors, you may not want to deal with an external library for simple benchmarking. In that case, you can just go ahead and write your own benchmark runner using a Stopwatch, as in listing 7.2. You can simply iterate in a loop long enough to get a vague idea about the relative differences in the performance of different functions. We're reusing the same suite class we created for BenchmarkDotNet, but we're using our own loops and measurements for the results.

Listing 7.2   Homemade benchmarking

```
private const int iterations = 1_000_000_000;

private static void runBenchmarks() {
  var suite = new SampleBenchmarkSuite {
    A = 1000,
    B = 35
  };

  long manualTime = runBenchmark(() => suite.Manual());
  long divRemTime = runBenchmark(() => suite.DivRem());
```

```
    reportResult("Manual", manualTime);
    reportResult("DivRem", divRemTime);
}

private static long runBenchmark(Func<int> action) {
    var watch = Stopwatch.StartNew();
    for (int n = 0; n < iterations; n++) {
        action();                          ⟵——————————   We call the benchmarked
    }                                                     code here.
    watch.Stop();
    return watch.ElapsedMilliseconds;
}

private static void reportResult(string name, long milliseconds) {
    double nanoseconds = milliseconds * 1_000_000;
    Console.WriteLine("{0} = {1}ns / operation",
        name,
        nanoseconds / iterations);
}
```

When we run it, the result is relatively the same:

```
Manual = 4.611ns / operation
DivRem = 2.896ns / operation
```

Note that our benchmarks don't try to eliminate function call overhead or the overhead of the for loop itself, so they seem to be taking longer, but we successfully observe that DivRem is still twice as fast as manual division-and-remainder operations.

7.1.2 *Performance vs. responsiveness*

Benchmarks can only report relative numbers. They can't tell you if your code is fast or slow, but they can tell you if it's slower or faster than some other code. A general principle about slowness from a user's point of view is that any action that takes more than 100 ms feels delayed, and any action that takes more than 300 ms is considered sluggish. Don't even think about taking a full second. Most users will leave a web page or an app if they have to wait for more than three seconds. If a user's action takes more than five seconds to respond, it might as well take the lifetime of the universe—it doesn't matter at that point. Figure 7.1 illustrates this.

Obviously, performance isn't always about responsiveness. In fact, being a responsive app might require performing an operation more slowly. For example, you might have an app that replaces faces in a video with your face using machine learning. Because such a task is computationally intensive, the fastest way to calculate it is to do nothing else until the job's done. But that would mean a frozen UI, which would make the user think something's wrong and persuade them to quit the app. So instead of doing the computation as fast as you can, you instead spare some of the computational cycles to show a progress bar, perhaps to calculate estimated time remaining and to show a nice animation that can entertain users while they're waiting. In the end, you have slower code, but a more successful outcome.

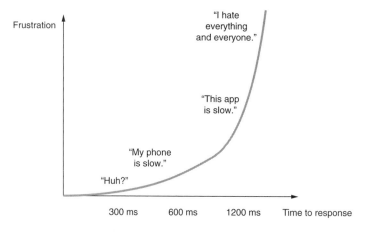

Figure 7.1   Response delays vs. frustration

That means that even if benchmarks are relative, you can still have some understanding of slowness. Peter Norvig came up with the idea in his blog[2] of listing latency numbers to have a context of how things can be slower by orders of magnitude in different contexts. I create a similar table with my own back-of-the-envelope calculations in table 7.1. You can come up with your own numbers by looking at this.

Table 7.1   Latency numbers in various contexts

Read a byte from	Time
A CPU register	1 ns
CPU's L1 cache	2 ns
RAM	50 ns
NVMe disk	250,000 ns
Local network	1,000,000 ns
Server on the other side of the world	150,000,000 ns

Latency affects performance too, not just user experience. Your database resides on a disk, and your database server resides on a network. That means that even if you write the fastest SQL queries and define the fastest indexes on your database, you're still bound by the laws of physics, and you can't get any result faster than a millisecond. Every millisecond you spend eats into your total budget, which is ideally less than 300 ms.

---

[2]   "Teach Yourself Programming in Ten Years," Peter Norvig, http://norvig.com/21-days.html#answers.

7.2   *Anatomy of sluggishness*

To understand how to improve performance, you must first understand how performance fails. As we've seen, not all performance problems are about speed—some are about responsiveness. The speed part, though, is related to how computers work in general, so it's a good idea to acquaint yourself with some low-level concepts. This will help you understand the optimization techniques I'll discuss later in the chapter.

CPUs are chips that process instructions they read from RAM and perform them repetitively in a never-ending loop. You can imagine it like a wheel turning, and every rotation of the wheel typically performs another instruction, as depicted in figure 7.2. Some operations can take multiple turns, but the basic unit is a single turn, popularly known as a *clock cycle*, or a *cycle* for short.

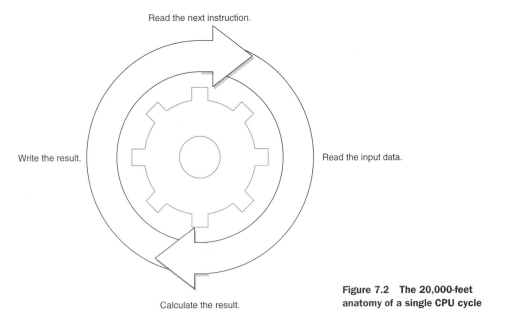

Figure 7.2   **The 20,000-feet anatomy of a single CPU cycle**

The speed of a CPU, typically expressed in hertz, indicates how many clock cycles it can process in a second. The first electronic computer, ENIAC, could process 100,000 cycles a second, shortened to 100 KHz. The antique 4 MHz Z80 CPU in my 8-bit home computer back in the 1980s could only process 4 million cycles per second. A modern 3.4 GHz AMD Ryzen 5950X CPU can process 3.4 *billion* cycles in a second on each of its cores. That doesn't mean CPUs can process that many instructions, because first, some instructions take more than one clock cycle to complete, and second, modern CPUs can process multiple instructions in parallel on a single core. Thus, sometimes CPUs can even run more instructions than what their clock speed allows.

Some CPU instructions can also take an arbitrary amount of time depending on their arguments, such as block memory copy instructions. Those take O(N) time based on how large the block is.

Basically, every performance problem related to code speed comes down to how many instructions are executed and for how many times. When you optimize code, what you're trying to do is either reduce the number of instructions executed or use a faster version of an instruction. The `DivRem` function runs faster than division and remainder because it gets converted into instructions that take fewer cycles.

7.3   *Start from the top*

The second-best way to reduce the number of instructions executed is to choose a faster algorithm. The best way obviously is to delete the code entirely. I'm serious: delete the code you don't need. Don't keep unneeded code in the codebase. Even if it doesn't degrade the performance of the code, it degrades the performance of developers, which eventually degrades the performance of the code. Don't even keep commented-out code. Use the history features of your favorite source control system like Git or Mercurial to restore old code. If you need the feature occasionally, put it behind configuration instead of commenting it out. This way, you won't be surprised when you finally blow the dust off the code and it won't compile at all because everything's changed. It'll remain current and working.

As I pointed out in chapter 2, a faster algorithm can make a tremendous difference, even if it's implemented in a poorly optimized way. So first ask yourself, "Is this the best way to do this?" There are ways to make badly implemented code faster, but nothing beats solving the problem at the *top*, as in the broadest scope, the scenario itself, and delve deeper until you figure out the actual location of the problem. This way is usually faster, and the result ends up being way more easily maintained.

Consider an example in which users complain that viewing their profile on the app is slow, and you can reproduce the problem yourself. The performance problem can come from either the client or the server. So you start from the top: you first identify which major layer the problem appears in by eliminating one of the two layers the problem can possibly be in. If a direct API call doesn't have the same problem, the problem must be in the client, or, otherwise, in the server. You continue on this path until you identify the actual problem. In a sense, you're doing a binary search, as shown in figure 7.3.

When you follow a top-down approach, you're guaranteed to find the root cause of the problem in an efficient way, instead of guessing. Since you do a binary search manually here, you're now using algorithms in real life to make your life easier, so, good job! When you determine where the problem happens, check any red flags for obvious code complexity. You can identify patterns that might be causing more complex code to execute when a simple one could suffice. Let's go over some of them.

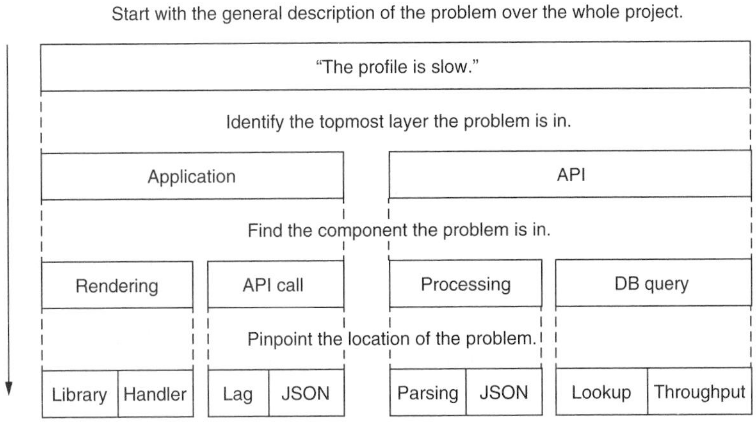

Start with the general description of the problem over the whole project.

Figure 7.3   A top-down approach for identifying the root cause

7.3.1   *Nested loops*

One of the easiest ways to slow down code is to put it inside another loop. When writing code in nested loops, we underestimate the effects of multiplication. Nested loops aren't always visible, either. To expand on our example about the slow user profile, suppose you found the problem in the backend code that generates the profile data. There is a function that returns the badges a user has and shows them on their profile. Some sample code might look like this:

```
public IEnumerable<string> GetBadgeNames() {
  var badges = db.GetBadges();
  foreach (var badge in badges) {
    if (badge.IsVisible) {
      yield return badge.Name;
    }
  }
}
```

There are no apparent nested loops here. As a matter of fact, it's possible to write the same function with LINQ without any loops at all, but with the same slowness problem:

```
public IEnumerable<string> GetBadgesNames() {
  var badges = db.GetBadges();
  return badges
    .Where(b => b.IsVisible)
    .Select(b => b.Name);
}
```

Where is the inner loop? That's something you'll have to ask yourself over the course of your programming career. The culprit is the `IsVisible` property because we just don't know what it's doing underneath.

Properties in C# were invented because the developers of the language were tired of writing get in front of every function name regardless of how simple it might be. As a matter of fact, property code is converted to functions when compiled, with get_ and set_ prefixes added to their name. The upside of using properties is that they allow you to change how a field-looking member in a class functions without breaking compatibility. The downside of properties is that they conceal potential complexity. They look like simple fields, basic memory access operations, which might make you assume that calling a property may not be expensive at all. Ideally, you should never put computationally intensive code inside properties, but it's impossible for you to know whether someone else has done it, at least not without looking.

When we look at the source of the IsVisible property of the Badge class, we can see it's more expensive than it looks:

```
public bool IsVisible {
  get {
    var visibleBadgeNames = db.GetVisibleBadgeNames();
    foreach (var name in visibleBadgeNames) {
      if (this.Name == name) {
        return true;
      }
    }
    return false;
  }
}
```

This property, without any shame, dares to call the database to retrieve the list of visible badge names and compares them in a loop to see if our supposed badge is one of the visible ones. There are too many sins in that code to explain, but your first lesson is to beware of properties. They contain logic, and their logic may not always be simple.

There are many optimization opportunities in the IsVisible property, but the first and foremost one is to not retrieve the list of visible badge names every time the property is called. You could keep them in a static list that's retrieved only once, assuming the list rarely changes and you can afford a restart when it happens. You can also do caching, but I'll get to that later. That way, you could reduce the property code to this:

```
private static List<string> visibleBadgeNames = getVisibleBadgeNames();

public bool IsVisible {
  get {
    foreach (var name in visibleBadgeNames) {
      if (this.Name == name) {
        return true;
      }
    }
    return false;
  }
}
```

The good thing about keeping a list is that it already has a Contains method so you can eliminate the loop in IsVisible:

```
public bool IsVisible {
  get => visibleBadgeNames.Contains(this.Name);
}
```

The inner loop has finally disappeared, but we still haven't destroyed its spirit. We need to salt and burn its bones. Lists in C# are essentially arrays, and they have O(N) lookup complexity. That means our loop hasn't gone away, but has only moved inside another function, in this case, List<T>.Contains(). We can't reduce complexity by eliminating the loop—we have to change our lookup algorithm too.

We can sort the list and do a binary search to reduce lookup performance to O(logN), but luckily, we've read chapter 2, and we know how the HashSet<T> data structure can provide a much better O(1) lookup performance, thanks to looking up an item's location using its hash. Our property code has finally started to look sane:

```
private static HashSet<string> visibleBadgeNames = getVisibleBadgeNames();

public bool IsVisible {
  get => visibleBadgeNames.Contains(this.Name);
}
```

We haven't done any benchmarking on this code, but looking at computational complexity pain points can provide you good insight, as you can see in this example. You should still always test whether your fix performs better because code will always contain surprises and dark corners that might ambush you.

The story of the GetBadgeNames() method doesn't end here. There are other questions to ask, like why the developer keeps a separate list of visible badge names instead of a single bit flag in the Badge record on the database or why they don't simply keep them in a separate table and join them while querying the database. But as far as nested loops are concerned, it has probably become orders of magnitude faster now.

7.3.2 *String-oriented programming*

Strings are extremely practical. They are readable, they can hold any kind of text, and they can be manipulated easily. I have already discussed how using the right type can give better performance than using a string, but there are subtle ways that strings can seep into your code.

One of the common ways that strings can be used unnecessarily is to assume every collection is a string collection. For example, if you want to keep a flag in an HttpContext .Items or ViewData container, it's common to find someone writing something like

```
HttpContext.Items["Bozo"] = "true";
```

You find them later checking the same flag like this:

```
if ((string)HttpContext.Items["Bozo"] == "true") {
.  .  .
}
```

The typecast to string is usually added after the compiler warns you, "Hey, are you sure you want to do this? This isn't a string collection." But the whole picture that the collection is actually an object collection is usually missed. You could, in fact, fix the code by simply using a Boolean variable instead:

```
HttpContext.Items["Bozo"] = true;
```

Check the value with

```
if ((bool?)HttpContext.Items["Bozo"] == true) {
...
}
```

This way, you avoid storage overhead, parsing overhead, and even occasional typos like typing True instead of true.

The actual overhead of these simple mistakes is minuscule, but when they become habits, it can accumulate significantly. It's impossible to fix the nails on a leaking ship, but nailing them the right way when you build it can help you stay afloat.

7.3.3 *Evaluating 2b || !2b*

Boolean expressions in if statements are evaluated in the order they're written. The C# compiler generates smart code for evaluation to avoid unnecessarily evaluating cases altogether. For example, remember our awfully expensive IsVisible property? Consider this check:

```
if (badge.IsVisible && credits > 150_000) {
```

An expensive property gets evaluated before a simple value check. If you're calling this function mostly with values of x less than 150,000, IsVisible wouldn't be called most of the time. You can simply swap the places of expressions:

```
if (credits > 150_000 && badge.IsVisible) {
```

This way, you wouldn't be running an expensive operation unnecessarily. You can also apply this with logical OR operations (||). In that case, the first expression that returns true would prevent the rest of the expression from being evaluated. Obviously, in real life, having that kind of expensive property is rare, but I recommend sorting expressions based on operand types:

1. Variables
2. Fields
3. Properties
4. Method calls

Not every Boolean expression can be safely moved around the operators. Consider this:

```
if (badge.IsVisible && credits > 150_000 || isAdmin) {
```

You can't simply move isAdmin to the beginning because it would change the evaluation. Make sure you don't accidentally break the logic in the if statement while you're optimizing Boolean evaluation.

7.4 Breaking the bottle at the neck

There are three types of delays in software: CPU, I/O, and human. You can optimize each category by finding a faster alternative, parallelizing the tasks, or removing them from the equation.

When you're sure you're using an algorithm or a method that's suitable for the job, it finally comes down to how you can optimize the code itself. To evaluate your options for optimizations, you need to be aware of the luxuries that CPUs provide you.

7.4.1 Don't pack data

Reading from a memory address, say, 1023, can take more time than reading from memory address 1024 because CPUs can incur a penalty when reading from unaligned memory addresses. Alignment in that sense means a memory location on the multiples of 4, 8, 16, and so forth, at least the *word size* of the CPU, as seen in figure 7.4. On some older processors, the penalty for accessing unaligned memory is death by a thousand small electrical shocks. Seriously, some CPUs don't let you access unaligned memory at all, such as the Motorola 68000 that is used in Amiga and some ARM-based processors.

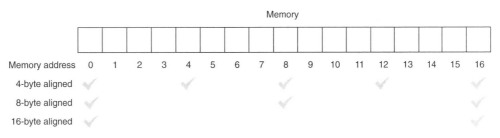

Figure 7.4 Memory address alignment

CPU word size

Word size is typically defined by how many bits of data the CPU can process at a time. The concept is closely related to how a CPU is called a 32-bit or 64-bit. Word size mostly reflects the size of a CPU's accumulator register. Registers are like CPU-level variables, and the accumulator is the most commonly used register. Take the Z80 CPU, for example. It has 16-bit registers, and it can address 16-bit memory, but it's considered an 8-bit processor because it has an 8-bit accumulator register.

Thankfully, we have compilers, and they usually take care of the alignment stuff. But it's possible to override the behavior of the compiler, and it still may not feel that something's wrong: you're storing more stuff in a small space, there is less memory to read, so it should be faster. Consider the data structure in listing 7.4. Because it's a struct, C# will apply alignment only based on some heuristics, and that can mean no alignment at all. You might be tempted to keep the values in bytes so it becomes a small packet to pass around.

Listing 7.3   A packed data structure

```
struct UserPreferences {
  public byte ItemsPerPage;
  public byte NumberOfItemsOnTheHomepage;
  public byte NumberOfAdClicksICanStomach;
  public byte MaxNumberOfTrollsInADay;
  public byte NumberOfCookiesIAmWillingToAccept;
  public byte NumberOfSpamEmailILoveToGetPerDay;
}
```

But, since memory accesses to unaligned boundaries are slower, your storage savings are offset by the access penalty to each member in the struct. If you change the data types in the struct from `byte` to `int` and create a benchmark to test the difference, you can see that byte access is almost twice as slow, even though it occupies a quarter of the memory, as shown in table 7.2.

Table 7.2   Difference between aligned and unaligned member access

Method	Mean
ByteMemberAccess	0.2475 ns
IntMemberAccess	0.1359 ns

The moral of the story is to avoid optimizing memory storage unnecessarily. There are benefits to doing it in certain cases: for example, when you want to create an array of a billion numbers, the difference between `byte` and `int` can become three gigabytes. Smaller sizes can also be preferable for I/O, but, otherwise, trust the memory alignment. The immutable law of benchmarking is, "Measure twice, cut once, then measure again, and you know what, let's go easy on the cutting for a while."

7.4.2 *Shop local*

Caching is about keeping frequently used data at a location that can be accessed faster than where it usually resides. CPUs have their own cache memories with different speeds, but all are faster than RAM itself. I won't go into the technical details of how cache is structured, but basically, CPUs can read memory in their cache much faster than regular memory in RAM. That means, for example, that sequential reads are faster than random reads around the memory. For example, reading an array sequentially can be faster than reading a linked list sequentially, although both take O(N) time to read end to end, and arrays can perform better than linked lists. The reason is that there is a higher chance of the next element being in the cached area of the memory. The elements of linked lists, on the other hand, are scattered around in the memory because they are separately allocated.

Suppose you have a CPU with a 16-byte cache, and you have both an array of three integers and a linked list of three integers. In figure 7.5, you can see that reading the first element of the array would also trigger loading the rest of the elements into the CPU cache, while traversing the linked list would cause a cache miss and force the new region to be loaded into the cache.

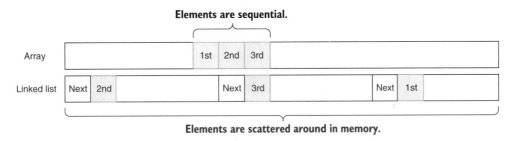

Figure 7.5 Array vs. linked list cache locality

CPUs usually bet that you're reading data sequentially. That doesn't mean linked lists don't have their uses. They have excellent insert/delete performance and less memory overhead when they are growing. Array-based lists need to reallocate and copy buffers when they're growing, which is terribly slow, so they allocate more than they need, which can cause disproportionate memory use in large lists. In most cases, though, a list would serve you fine, and it might well be faster for reading.

7.4.3 *Keep dependent works separated*

A single CPU instruction is processed by discrete units on the processor. For example, one unit is responsible for decoding the instruction, while another is responsible for memory access. But since a decoder unit needs to wait for an instruction to complete, it can do other decoding work for the next instruction while memory access is running.

That technique is called *pipelining*, and it means the CPU can execute multiple instructions in parallel on a single core as long as the next instruction doesn't depend on the result of the previous one.

Consider an example: you need to calculate a checksum in which you simply add the values of a byte array to get a result, as in listing 7.4. Normally, checksums are used for error detection, and adding numbers can be the worst implementation, but we'll assume that it was a government contract. When you look at the code, it constantly updates the value of the `result`. Therefore, every calculation depends on i and `result`. That means the CPU cannot parallelize any work, because it depends on an operation.

Listing 7.4   A simple checksum

```
public int CalculateChecksum(byte[] array) {
  int result = 0;
  for (int i = 0; i < array.Length; i++) {
    result = result + array[i];        ◁         Depends on both i and the
  }                                                previous value of the result
  return result;
}
```

There are ways to reduce dependencies or at least reduce the blocking impact of the instruction flow. One is to reorder instructions to increase the gap between dependent code so an instruction doesn't block the following one in the pipeline due to the dependency on the result of the first operation.

Since addition can be done in any order, we can split the addition into four parts in the same code and let the CPU parallelize the work. We can implement the task as I have in the following listing. This code contains more instructions, but four different result accumulators can now complete the checksum separately and later be summed. We then sum the remaining bytes in a separate loop.

Listing 7.5   Parallelizing work on a single core

```
public static int CalculateChecksumParallel(byte[] array) {
  int r0 = 0, r1 = 0, r2 = 0, r3 = 0;    ◁         The four accumulators!
  int len = array.Length;
  int i = 0;
  for (; i < len - 4; i += 4) {
    r0 += array[i + 0];
    r1 += array[i + 1];             These calculations
    r2 += array[i + 2];             are independent of
    r3 += array[i + 3];             each other.
  }
  int remainingSum = 0;
  for (; i < len; i++) {
    remainingSum += i;          ◁         Calculate the sum of
  }                                       the remaining bytes.
  return r0 + r1 + r2 + r3 + remainingSum;    ◁
}                                               Bring everything together.
```

We're doing a lot more work than in the simpler code in listing 7.4, and yet, this process turns out be 15% faster on my machine. Don't expect magic from such a micro-optimization, but you'll love it when it helps you tackle CPU-intensive code. The main takeaway is that reordering code—and even removing dependencies in code—can improve your code's speed because dependent code can clog up the pipeline.

7.4.4 *Be predictable*

The most upvoted, the most popular question in the history of Stack Overflow is, "Why is processing a sorted array faster than processing an unsorted array?"[3] To optimize execution time, CPUs try to act preemptively ahead of the running code to make preparations before there is a need. One technique CPUs employ is called *branch prediction*. Such code is just a sugarcoated version of comparisons and branches:

```
if (x == 5) {
  Console.WriteLine("X is five!");
} else {
  Console.WriteLine("X is something else");
}
```

The if statement and curly braces are the elements of structured programming. They are a sugarcoated version of what the CPU processes. Behind the scenes, the code gets converted into a low-level code like this during the compilation phase:

```
  compare x with 5
  branch to ELSE if not equal
  write "X is five"
  branch to SKIP_ELSE
ELSE:
  write "X is something else"
SKIP_ELSE:
```

I'm just paraphrasing here because the actual machine code is more cryptic, but this isn't entirely inaccurate. Regardless of how elegant the design you create with your code is, it eventually becomes a bunch of comparison, addition, and branch operations. Listing 7.6 shows the actual assembly output for x86 architecture for the same code. It might feel more familiar after you've seen the pseudocode. There is an excellent online tool at sharplab.io that lets you see the assembly output of your C# program. I hope it will outlive this book.

---

3   The Stack Overflow question can be found at http://mng.bz/Exxd.

Listing 7.6   Actual assembly code for our comparison

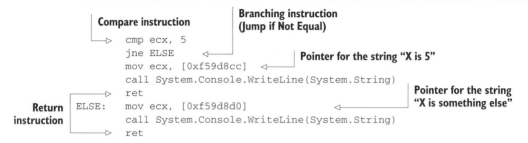

```
            cmp ecx, 5
            jne ELSE
            mov ecx, [0xf59d8cc]
            call System.Console.WriteLine(System.String)
            ret
ELSE:       mov ecx, [0xf59d8d0]
            call System.Console.WriteLine(System.String)
            ret
```

Compare instruction

Branching instruction
(Jump if Not Equal)

Pointer for the string "X is 5"

Pointer for the string
"X is something else"

Return
instruction

Stop worrying, and learn to love assembly

Machine code, the native language of a CPU, is just a series of numbers. Assembly is a human-readable syntax for machine code. Assembly syntax differs among CPU architectures, so I recommend you become familiar with at least one. It's a humbling experience, and it will reduce your fear about what's going on under the hood. It may seem complicated, but it's simpler than the languages we write programs in, even primitive, if you will. An assembly listing is a series of labels and instructions like

```
    let a, 42
some_label:
    decrement a
    compare a, 0
    jump_if_not_equal some_label
```

That's a basic decrementing loop counting from 42 to 0 and written in a pseudo-assembly syntax. In real assembly, instructions are shorter to make them easier to write and excruciating to read. For example, the same loop would be written like this on an x86 CPU:

```
    mov al, 42
some_label:
    dec al
    cmp al, 0
    jne some_label
```

On an ARM processor architecture, it can look like this instead:

```
    mov r0, #42
some_label:
    sub r0, r0, #1
    cmp r0, #0
    bne some_label
```

This can be written more briefly with different instructions, but as long as you're familiar with the structure of an assembly, you can take a peek at what kind of machine code a JIT compiler generates and understand its actual behavior. It especially does wonders when you need to understand CPU-intensive tasks.

A CPU can't know if a comparison will be successful before it's executed, but thanks to branch prediction, it can make a strong guess based on what it observes. Based on its guesses, the CPU makes a bet and starts processing instructions from that branch it predicted, and if it's successful in its prediction, everything is already in place, boosting the performance.

That's why processing an array with random values can be slower if it involves comparisons of values: branch prediction fails spectacularly in that case. A sorted array performs better because the CPU can predict the ordering properly and predict the branches correctly.

Keep that in mind when you're processing data. The fewer surprises you give the CPU, the better it will perform.

7.4.5 SIMD

CPUs also support specialized instructions that can perform computations on multiple data at the same time with a single instruction. That technique is called *single instruction, multiple data* (SIMD). If you want to perform the same calculation on multiple variables, SIMD can boost its performance significantly on supported architectures.

SIMD works pretty much like multiple pens taped together. You can draw whatever you want, but the pens will all perform the same operation on different coordinates of the paper. An SIMD instruction will perform an arithmetic computation on multiple values, but the operation will remain constant.

C# provides SIMD functionality via Vector types in the System.Numerics namespace. Since every CPU's SIMD support is different, and some CPUs don't support SIMD at all, you first must check whether it's available on the CPU:

```
if (!Vector.IsHardwareAccelerated) {
    . . . non-vector implementation here . . .
}
```

Then you need to figure out how many of a given type the CPU can process at the same time. That changes from processor to processor, so you have to query it first:

```
int chunkSize = Vector<int>.Count;
```

In this case, we're looking to process int values. The number of items the CPU can process can change based on the data type. When you know the number of elements you can process at a time, you can go ahead and process the buffer in chunks.

Consider that we'd like to multiply values in an array. Multiplication of a series of values is a common problem in data processing, whether it's changing the volume of a sound recording or adjusting the brightness of an image. For example, if you multiply pixel values in an image by 2, it becomes twice as bright. Similarly, if you multiply voice data by 2, it becomes twice as loud. A naive implementation would look like that in the following listing. We simply iterate over the items and replace the value in place with the result of the multiplication.

Listing 7.7   Classic in-place multiplication

```
public static void MultiplyEachClassic(int[] buffer, int value) {
  for (int n = 0; n < buffer.Length; n++) {
    buffer[n] *= value;
  }
}
```

When we use the Vector type to make these calculations instead, our code becomes more complicated, and it looks slower, to be honest. You can see the code in listing 7.8. We basically check for SIMD support and query the chunk size for integer values. We later go over the buffer at the given chunk size and copy the values into vector registers by creating instances of Vector<T>. That type supports standard arithmetic operators, so we simply multiply the vector type with the number given. It will automatically multiply all of the elements in the chunk in a single go. Notice that we declare the variable n outside the for loop because we're starting from its last value in the second loop.

Listing 7.8   "We're not in Kansas anymore" multiplication

**Call the classic implementation
if SIMDs are not supported.**

```
public static void MultiplyEachSIMD(int[] buffer, int value) {
  if (!Vector.IsHardwareAccelerated) {
    MultiplyEachClassic(buffer, value);
  }
  int chunkSize = Vector<int>.Count;          ⟵ Query how many values
                                                  SIMD can process at once.
  int n = 0;
  for (; n < buffer.Length - chunkSize; n += chunkSize) {
    var vector = new Vector<int>(buffer, n);  ⟵
    vector *= value;                             Copy the array segment
    vector.CopyTo(buffer, n);    ⟵               into SIMD registers.
  }                              Replace the
                                 results.
  for (; n < buffer.Length; n++) {
    buffer[n] *= value;          Process the remaining
  }                              bytes the classic way.
}
```

**Multiply
all values
at once.**

It looks like too much work, doesn't it? Yet, the benchmarks are impressive, as shown in table 7.3. In this case, our SIMD-based code is twice as fast as the regular code. Based on the data types you process and operations you perform on the data, it can be much higher.

Table 7.3   The SIMD difference

Method	Mean
MultiplyEachClassic	5.641 ms
MultiplyEachSIMD	2.648 ms

You can consider SIMD when you have a computationally intensive task and you need to perform the same operation on multiple elements at the same time.

7.5 *1s and 0s of I/O*

I/O encompasses everything a CPU communicates with the peripheral hardware, be it disk, network adapter, or even GPU. I/O is usually the slowest link on the performance chain. Think about it: a hard drive is actually a rotating disk with a spindle seeking over the data. It's basically a robotic arm constantly moving around. A network packet can travel at the speed of light, and yet, it would still take it more than 100 milliseconds to rotate the earth. Printers are especially designed to be slow, inefficient, and anger inducing.

You can't make I/O itself faster most of the time because its slowness arises from physics, but the hardware can run independently of the CPU, so it can work while the CPU is doing other stuff. That means you can overlap the CPU and I/O work and complete an overall operation in a smaller timeframe.

7.5.1 *Make I/O faster*

Yes, I/O is slow due to the inherent limitations of hardware, but it can be made faster. For example, every read from a disk incurs an operating system call overhead. Consider file-copy code like that in the following listing. It's pretty much straightforward. It copies every byte read from the source file and writes those bytes to the destination file.

Listing 7.9 Simple file copy

```
public static void Copy(string sourceFileName,
  string destinationFileName) {

  using var inputStream = File.OpenRead(sourceFileName);
  using var outputStream = File.Create(destinationFileName);
  while (true) {
    int b = inputStream.ReadByte();     <——— Read the byte.
    if (b < 0) {
      break;
    }
    outputStream.WriteByte((byte)b);    <——— Write the byte.
  }
}
```

The problem is that every system call implies an elaborate ceremony. The `ReadByte()` function here calls the operating system's read function. The operating system calls the switch-to-kernel mode. That means the CPU changes its execution mode. The operating system routine looks up the file handle and necessary data structures. It checks whether the I/O result is already in cache. If it's not, it calls the relevant device drivers to perform the actual I/O operation on the disk. The read portion of the memory gets copied to a buffer in the process's address space. These operations happen lightning fast, and it can become significant when you just read one byte.

Many I/O devices read/write in blocks called *block devices*. Network and storage devices are usually block devices. The keyboard is a character device because it sends one character at a time. Block devices can't read less than the size of a block, so it doesn't make sense to read anything less than a typical block size. For example, a hard drive can have a sector size of 512 bytes, making it a typical block size for disks. Modern disks can have larger block sizes, but let's see how much performance can be improved simply by reading 512 bytes. The following listing shows the same copy operation that takes a buffer size as a parameter and reads and writes using that chunk size.

Listing 7.10   File copy using larger buffers

```
public static void CopyBuffered(string sourceFileName,
  string destinationFileName, int bufferSize) {

  using var inputStream = File.OpenRead(sourceFileName);
  using var outputStream = File.Create(destinationFileName);
  var buffer = new byte[bufferSize];
  while (true) {
    int readBytes = inputStream.Read(buffer, 0, bufferSize);   ⟵  Read bufferSize
    if (readBytes == 0) {                                           bytes at once.
      break;
    }
    outputStream.Write(buffer, 0, readBytes);   ⟵  Write bufferSize
  }                                                  bytes at once.
}
```

If we write a quick benchmark that tests against the byte-based copy function and the buffered variant with different buffer sizes, we can see the difference that reading large chunks at a time makes. You can see the results in table 7.4.

Table 7.4   Effect of buffer size on I/O performance

Method	Buffer size	Mean
Copy	1	1,351.27 ms
CopyBuffered	512	217.80 ms
CopyBuffered	1024	214.93 ms
CopyBuffered	16384	84.53 ms
CopyBuffered	262144	45.56 ms
CopyBuffered	1048576	43.81 ms
CopyBuffered	2097152	44.10 ms

Even using a 512-byte buffer makes a tremendous difference—the copy operation becomes six times faster. Yet, increasing it to 256 KB makes the most difference, and making it anything larger yields only marginal improvement. I ran these benchmarks on a Windows machine, and Windows I/O uses 256 KB as the default buffer size for its I/O operations and cache management. That's why the returns suddenly become marginal after 256 KB. In the same way as food package labels say "actual contents may vary," your actual experience on your operating system may vary. Consider finding the ideal buffer size when you're working with I/O, and avoid allocating more memory than you need.

7.5.2 *Make I/O non-blocking*

One of the most misunderstood concepts in programming is asynchronous I/O. It's often confused with multithreading, which is a parallelization model to make any kind of operation faster by letting a task run on separate cores. Asynchronous I/O (or async I/O for short) is a parallelization model for I/O-heavy operations only, and it can work on a single core. Multithreading and async I/O can also be used together because they address different use cases.

I/O is naturally asynchronous because the external hardware is almost always slower than the CPU, and the CPU doesn't like waiting and doing nothing. Mechanisms like interrupts and direct memory access (DMA) were invented to allow hardware to signal the CPU when an I/O operation is complete, so the CPU can transfer the results. That means that when an I/O operation is issued to the hardware, the CPU can continue executing other stuff while the hardware is doing its work, and the CPU can check back when the I/O operation is complete. This mechanism is the foundation of async I/O.

Figure 7.6 gives an idea of how both types of parallelization work. In both illustrations, the second computational code (CPU Op #2) is dependent on the result of the first I/O code (I/O Op #1). Because computational code can't be parallelized on the same thread, they execute in tandem and therefore take longer than multithreading on a four-core machine. On the other hand, you still gain significant parallelization benefits without consuming threads or occupying cores.

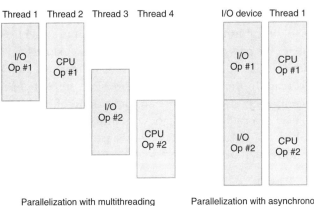

Parallelization with multithreading   Parallelization with asynchronous I/O

Figure 7.6   The difference between multithreading and async I/O

The performance benefit of async I/O comes from its providing natural paralleliza-tion to the code without you doing any extra work. You don't even need to create an extra thread. It's possible to run multiple I/O operations in parallel and collect the results without suffering through the problems multithreading brings, like race condi-tions. It's practical and scalable.

Asynchronous code can also help with responsiveness in event-driven mechanisms, especially user interfaces, without consuming threads. It might seem like UI has noth-ing to do with I/O, but user input also comes from I/O devices like a touchscreen, a keyboard, or a mouse, and user interfaces are triggered by those events. They consti-tute perfect candidates for async I/O and asynchronous programming in general. Even timer-based animations are hardware driven because of how a timer on a device operates, so they are therefore ideal candidates for async I/O.

7.5.3 *The archaic ways*

Until the early 2010s, async I/O was managed with callback functions. Async operat-ing system functions required you to pass them a callback function, and OS would then execute your callback function when the I/O operation was completed. Mean-while, you could perform other tasks. If we wrote our file-copy operation in old asyn-chronous semantics, it would look pretty much like that in listing 7.11. Mind you, this is a very cryptic and ugly code, and it's probably why boomers don't like async I/O very much. Actually, I had so much trouble writing this code myself that I had to resort to some modern constructs like `Task` to finish it. I'm just showing you this so that you'll love and appreciate the modern constructs and how much time they save us.

The most interesting thing about this ancient code is that it returns immediately, which is magical. That means I/O is working in the background, the operation con-tinues, and you can do other work while it's being processed. You're still on the same thread, too. No multithreading is involved. In fact, that's one of the greatest advan-tages of async I/O, because it conserves OS threads, so it becomes more scalable, which I will discuss in chapter 8. If you don't have anything else to do, you can always wait for it to complete, but that's just a preference.

In listing 7.11, we define two handler functions. One is an asynchronous `Task` called `onComplete()`, which we want to run when the whole execution finishes, but not right away. Another is a local function called `onRead()` that is called every time a read operation is complete. We pass this handler to the `stream`'s `BeginRead` function, so it initiates an asynchronous I/O operation and registers `onRead` as a callback to be called when the block is read. In the `onRead` handler, we start the write operation of the buffer we just read completely and make sure another round of read is called with the same `onRead` handler set as a callback. This goes on until the code reaches the end of the file, and that's when the `onComplete` `Task` gets started. It's a very convoluted way to express asynchronous operations.

> **Listing 7.11 Old-style file-copy code using async I/O**

```
public static Task CopyAsyncOld(string sourceFilename,
  string destinationFilename, int bufferSize) {

  var inputStream = File.OpenRead(sourceFilename);
  var outputStream = File.Create(destinationFilename);

  var buffer = new byte[bufferSize];
  var onComplete = new Task(() => {              ◁──┘ Called when the
    inputStream.Dispose();                             function finishes
    outputStream.Dispose();
  });
                                                    Called whenever a read
                                                    operation is complete
  void onRead(IAsyncResult readResult) {    ◁──┘
    int bytesRead = inputStream.EndRead(readResult);  ◁──┐ Get the number
    if (bytesRead == 0) {                                │ of bytes read.
      onComplete.Start();    ◁──── Start the final Task.
      return;
    }                                               Start the write
    outputStream.BeginWrite(buffer, 0, bytesRead,   ◁──┘ operation.
      writeResult => {
        outputStream.EndWrite(writeResult);
        inputStream.BeginRead(buffer, 0, bufferSize, onRead,  ◁──┐
          null);                                                 │ Start the next
      }, null);                                                  │ read operation.
  }

  var result = inputStream.BeginRead(buffer, 0, bufferSize,  ◁──┐
    onRead, null);                                               │ Start the first
  return Task.WhenAll(onComplete);  ◁──┐                         │ read operation.
}                                      Return a waitable
                                       Task for onComplete.
```

Acknowledge completion of the write. ──▷ `outputStream.EndWrite(writeResult);`

The problem with this approach is that the more async operations you start, the easier it is to lose track of the operations. Things could easily turn into *callback hell*, a term coined by Node.js developers.

7.5.4 Modern async/await

Luckily, the brilliant designers at Microsoft found a great way to write async I/O code using async/await semantics. The mechanism, first introduced in C#, became so popular and proved itself so practical that it got adopted by many other popular programming languages such as C++, Rust, JavaScript, and Python.

You can see the async/await version of the same code in listing 7.12. What a breath of fresh air! We declare the function with the `async` keyword so we can use `await` in the function. Await statements define an anchor, but they don't really wait for the expression following them to be executed. They just signify the points of return when the awaited I/O operation completes in the future, so we don't have to define a new callback for every continuation. We can write code like regular synchronous code. Because of that, the function still returns immediately, as in listing 7.11. Both `ReadAsync` and `WriteAsync` functions are functions that return a `Task` object like `CopyAsync` itself. By the way, the

Stream class already has a CopyToAsync function to make copying scenarios easier, but we're keeping read and write operations separate here to align the source with the original code.

Listing 7.12   Modern async I/O file-copy code

```
public async static Task CopyAsync(string sourceFilename,
    string destinationFilename, int bufferSize) {

  using var inputStream = File.OpenRead(sourceFilename);
  using var outputStream = File.Create(destinationFilename);
  var buffer = new byte[bufferSize];
  while (true) {
    int readBytes = await inputStream.ReadAsync(
buffer, 0, bufferSize);
    if (readBytes == 0) {
      break;
    }
    await outputStream.WriteAsync(buffer, 0, readBytes);
  }
}
```

The function is declared with the async keyword, and it returns Task.

Any operation following await is converted to a callback behind the scenes.

When you write code with async/await keywords, the code behind the scenes gets converted to something similar to that in listing 7.11 during compilation, with callbacks and everything. Async/await saves you a lot of legwork.

7.5.5   *Gotchas of async I/O*

Programming languages don't require you to use async mechanisms just for I/O. You can declare an async function without calling any I/O-related operations at all and perform only CPU work on them. In that case, you'd have created an unnecessary level of complexity without any gains. The compiler usually warns you of that situation, but I've seen many examples of compiler warnings being ignored in a corporate setting because nobody wants to deal with the fallout from any problems a fix would cause. The performance issues would pile up, and then you'd get tasked with fixing all those problems at once, thus dealing with greater fallout. Bring this up in code reviews, and make your voice heard.

One rule of thumb you need to keep in mind with async/await is that await doesn't wait. Yes, await makes sure that the next line is run after it completes executing, but it does that without waiting or blocking, thanks to asynchronous callbacks behind the scenes. If your async code waits for something to complete, you're doing it wrong.

7.6   *If all else fails, cache*

Caching is one of the most robust ways to improve performance immediately. Cache invalidation might be a hard problem, but it's not a problem if you only cache things you don't worry about invalidating. You don't need an elaborate caching layer residing on a separate server like Redis or Memcached, either. You can use an in-memory cache like the one Microsoft provides in the `MemoryCache` class in the `System.Runtime` `.Caching` package. True, it cannot scale beyond a certain point, but scaling may not be something you'd be looking for at the beginning of a project. Ekşi Sözlük serves 10 million requests per day on a single DB server and on four web servers, but it still uses in-memory cache.

Avoid using data structures that are not designed for caching. They usually don't have any eviction or expiration mechanism, thus becoming the source of memory leaks and, eventually, crashes. Use things that are designed for caching. Your database can also be a great persistent cache.

Don't be afraid of infinite expiration in cache, because either a cache eviction or an application restart will arrive before the end of the universe.

Summary

- Use premature optimizations as exercises, and learn from them.
- Avoid painting yourself into a corner with unnecessary optimizations.
- Always validate your optimizations with benchmarking.
- Keep optimization and responsiveness in balance.
- Make a habit of identifying problematic code like nested loops, string-heavy code, and inefficient Boolean expressions.
- When building data structures, consider the benefits of memory alignment to get better performance.
- When you need micro-optimizations, know how a CPU behaves, and have cache locality, pipelining, and SIMD in your toolbelt.
- Increase I/O performance by using correct buffering mechanisms.
- Use asynchronous programming to run code and I/O operations in parallel without wasting threads.
- In case of emergency, break the cache.

Palatable scalability

This chapter covers

- Scalability vs. performance
- Progressive scalability
- Breaking database rules
- Smoother parallelization
- The truth in monolith

> *"It was the best of times, it was the worst of times, it was the age of wisdom, it was the age of foolishness."*
>
> —Charles Dickens on scalability

I've had my share of experience with scalability because of the technical decisions I made for Ekşi Sözlük back in 1999. The whole database for the website was a single text file at first. The writes held locks on the text file, causing everything to freeze for all visitors. The reads weren't very efficient, either—retrieving a single record would be in O(N) time, which required scanning the whole database. It was the worst of the worst possible technical designs.

It wasn't because the server's hardware was so slow that the code froze. The data structures and the parallelization decisions all contributed to the sluggishness. That's the gist of scalability itself. Performance alone can't make a system scalable. You need all aspects of your design to cater to an increasing number of users.

More importantly, that terrible design wasn't more important than how quickly I released the website, which took place in mere hours. Initial technical decisions didn't matter in the long run because I was able to pay most of the technical debt along the way. I changed the database technology as soon as it started causing too many problems. I wrote the code from scratch when the technology I used didn't work out anymore. A Turkish proverb states, "A caravan is prepared on the road," which means, "Make it up as you go."

I have also recommended measuring twice and cutting once at several places in this book, which seemingly is in conflict with the "Que será, será"[1] motto. That's because there's no single prescription for all our problems. We need to keep all these methods in our tool belts and apply the right one for the problem at hand.

From a systems perspective, scalability means the ability to make a system faster by throwing more hardware at it. From a programming perspective, a scalable code can keep its responsiveness constant in the face of increasing demand. There is obviously an upper limit of how some code can keep up with the load, and the goal of writing scalable code is to push that upper limit as far as possible.

Like refactoring, scalability is best addressed progressively in tangible, smaller steps toward a bigger goal. It's possible to design a system to be fully scalable from scratch, but the amount of effort and time required to achieve that and the returns you get are overshadowed by the importance of getting a product released as soon as possible.

Some things don't scale at all. As Fred Brooks eloquently said in his marvelous book *The Mythical Man Month,* "The bearing of a child takes nine months, no matter how many women are assigned." Brooks was talking about how assigning more people to an already delayed project might only add to the delays, but it's also applicable to certain factors of scalability. For example, you can't make a CPU core run more instructions in a second than its clock frequency. Yes, I've said that we can surpass it slightly by appealing to SIMD, branch prediction, and so forth, but there is still an upper limit to the performance you can achieve on a single CPU core.

The first step to achieving scalable code is to remove the bad code that prevents it from scaling. Such code can create bottlenecks, causing the code to remain slow even after you've added more hardware resources. Removing some of such code may even seem counterintuitive to you. Let's go over these potential bottlenecks and how we can remove them.

8.1 Don't use locks

In programming, locking is a feature that lets you write thread-safe code. *Thread-safe* means that a piece of code can work consistently even when it's called by two or more threads simultaneously. Consider a class that's responsible for generating unique identifiers for entities created in your application, and let's assume that it needs to

---

[1] A popular song from the 1950s by Doris Day, my father's favorite singer, "Que Será, Será" means "Whatever will be, will be" in Italian. It's the official mantra for code deploys on Fridays, usually followed by the 4 Non Blondes hit "What's Up?" on Saturday, which ends with Aimee Mann's "Calling It Quits" on Monday.

generate sequential numeric identifiers. That's usually not a good idea, as I discussed in chapter 6, because incremental identifiers can leak information about your application. You may not want to expose how many orders you receive in a day, how many users you have, and so forth. Let's assume that there's a legitimate business reason for having consecutive identifiers, say, to ensure there are no missing items. A simple implementation would look like this:

```
class UniqueIdGenerator {
  private int value;
  public int GetNextValue() => ++value;
}
```

When you have multiple threads using the same instance of this class, it's possible for two threads to receive the same value, or values that are out of order. That's because the expression ++value translates to multiple operations on the CPU: one that reads value, one that increments it, one that stores the incremented value back in the field, and finally one that returns the result, as can be seen clearly in the x86 assembly output of the JIT compiler:[2]

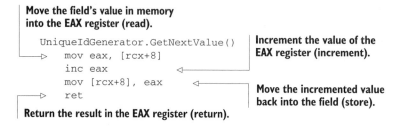

Move the field's value in memory into the EAX register (read).

```
UniqueIdGenerator.GetNextValue()
    mov eax, [rcx+8]
    inc eax
    mov [rcx+8], eax
    ret
```

Increment the value of the EAX register (increment).

Move the incremented value back into the field (store).

Return the result in the EAX register (return).

Every line is an instruction that a CPU runs, one after the other. When you try to visualize multiple CPU cores running the same instructions at the same time, it's easier to see how that can cause conflicts in the class, as figure 8.1 shows. There you can see that three threads return the same value, 1, even though the function was called three times.

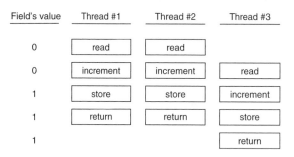

Field's value	Thread #1	Thread #2	Thread #3
0	read	read	
0	increment	increment	read
1	store	store	increment
1	return	return	store
1			return

Figure 8.1 **Multiple threads running simultaneously, causing state to break**

---

[2] A JIT (just in time) compiler converts either source code or the intermediate code (called bytecode, IL, IR, etc.) to the native instruction set of the CPU architecture it's running on to make it faster.

The previous code that uses the EAX register isn't thread-safe. The way all threads try to manipulate the data themselves without respecting other threads is called a *race condition*. CPUs, programming languages, and operating systems provide a variety of features that can help you deal with that problem. They usually all come down to blocking other CPU cores from reading from or writing to the same memory region at the same time, and that, folks, is called locking.

In the next example, the most optimized way is to use an atomic increment operation that increments the value in the memory location directly and prevents other CPU cores from accessing the same memory region while doing that, so no thread reads the same value or incorrectly skips values. It would look like this:

```
using System.Threading;
class UniqueIdGeneratorAtomic {
  private int value;
  public int GetNextValue() => Interlocked.Increment(ref value);
}
```

In this case, the locking is implemented by the CPU itself, and it would behave as is shown in figure 8.2 when it's executed. The CPU's lock instruction only holds the execution on parallel cores at that location during the lifetime of the instruction that immediately follows it, so the lock automatically gets released when each atomic in-memory add operation is executed. Notice that the return instructions don't return the field's current value, but the result of a memory add operation instead. The field's value stays sequential regardless.

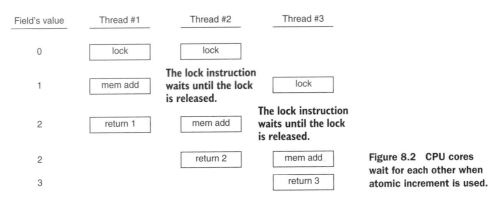

Figure 8.2 CPU cores wait for each other when atomic increment is used.

There will be many cases when a simple atomic increment operation isn't enough to make your code thread-safe. For example, what if you needed to update two different counters in sync? In cases when you can't ensure consistency with atomic operations, you can use C#'s `lock` statement, as shown in listing 8.1. For simplicity, we stick to our original counter example, but locks can be used to serialize any state change on the same process. We allocate a new dummy object to use as a lock because .NET uses an object's header to keep lock information.

Listing 8.1   A thread-safe counter with C#'s `lock` statement

```
class UniqueIdGeneratorLock {
  private int value;
  private object valueLock = new object();          Our lock object, specific
  public int GetNextValue() {                       for our purpose
    lock (valueLock) {          Other threads wait
      return ++value;           until we're done.
    }
  }                   Exiting the scope automatically
}                     releases the lock.
}
```

Why do we allocate a new object? Couldn't we just use this so our own instance would also act like a lock? That would save us some typing. The problem is that your instance can also be locked by some code outside of your control. That can cause unnecessary delays or even *deadlocks* because your code might be waiting on that other code.

Deadlocks go brrr

A deadlock occurs when two threads wait on the resources acquired by the other. It's quite easy to hit: thread 1 acquires resource A and waits for resource B to be released, while thread 2 acquires resource B and waits for resource A to be released, as shown in the following figure.

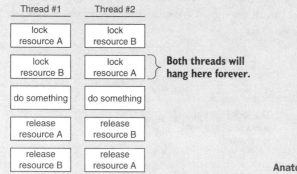

Anatomy of a deadlock

The result is like an infinite loop, waiting for a condition that will never be satisfied. That's why it's important to be explicit about which lock we use for what purpose in the code. Having a separate object for our locks is always a good idea so you can trace the code that uses certain locks and make sure they're not shared by other code. That's not possible with `lock(this)`.

Some of the application hangs you encounter are results of a deadlock, and contrary to popular belief, they can't be fixed by hitting your table with your mouse, screaming at the monitor, or rage quitting.

There is no magical solution to deadlocks other than a clear understanding of the locking mechanisms in your code, but a good rule of thumb is always to release the most recently acquired lock first and release locks as soon as possible. Some programming constructs may make it easier to avoid using locks, like channels in the Go programming language, but it's still possible to have deadlocks with those too, just less likely.

Our own implemented locking code would behave like that in figure 8.3. As you can see, it's not as efficient as an atomic increment operation, but it's still perfectly thread-safe.

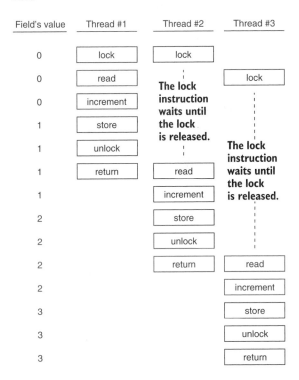

Figure 8.3   Using C#'s `lock` statement to avoid race conditions

As you can see, locks can make other threads stop and wait for a certain condition. While providing consistency, this can be one of the greatest challenges against scalability. There's nothing worse than wasting valuable CPU time waiting. You should strive to wait as little as possible. How do you achieve that?

First, make sure that you really need locks. I've seen code written by smart programmers that can be fine without acquiring any locks at all, but that unnecessarily waits for a certain condition to be met. If an object instance won't be manipulated by other threads, that means you may not need locks at all. I don't say you won't because it's hard to assess the side effects of code. Even a locally scoped object can use shared objects and therefore might require locks. You need to be clear about your intent and the side effects of your code. Don't use locks because they magically make the code they surround thread-safe. Understand how locks work, and be explicit about what you're doing.

Second, find out if the shared data structure you use has a *lock-free* alternative. Lock-free data structures can be directly accessed by multiple threads without requiring any locks. That said, the implementation of lock-free structures can be complicated. They can even be slower than their locked counterparts, but they can be more scalable. A common scenario in which a lock-free structure can be beneficial is shared dictionaries, or, as they're called in some platforms, maps. You might need a dictionary of something shared by all threads, like certain keys and values, and the usual way to handle that is to use locks.

Consider an example in which you need to keep API tokens in memory so you don't have to query the database for their validity every time they're accessed. A correct data structure for this purpose would be a cache, and cache data structures can have lock-free implementations too, but developers tend to use the tool that's closest when they try to solve a problem, in this case, a dictionary:

```
public Dictionary<string, Token> Tokens { get; } = new();
```

Notice the cool new() syntax in C# 9.0? Finally, the dark days of writing the same type twice when declaring class members are over. The compiler can now assume its type based on its declaration.

Anyway, we know that dictionaries aren't thread-safe, but thread-safety is only a concern when there will be multiple threads modifying a given data structure. That's an important point: if you have a data structure that you initialize at the start of your application and you never change it, you don't need it to be locked or thread-safe by other means because all read-only structures without *side effects* are thread-safe.

Side effects

What does code having side effects mean, apart from the occasional headache and nausea you get in a code review session? The term comes from the domain of functional programming. If a function changes anything outside its scope, that's considered a side effect—not just variables or fields, but anything. For example, if a function writes a log message, it causes an irreversible change in the log output, which is considered a side effect, too. A function without any side effects can be run any number of times, and nothing in the environment will change. Functions without side effects are called *pure functions*. A function that calculates the area of a circle and returns the result is a pure function:

```
class Circle {
  public static double Area(double radius) => Math.PI * Math.Pow(radius, 2);
}
```

> That's a pure function not just because it has no side effects, but because the members and functions it accesses are also pure. Otherwise, those could cause side effects too, and that would also render our function impure. One benefit of pure functions is that they are guaranteed to be thread-safe, so they can be run in parallel with other pure functions without any problems.

Because we need to manipulate the data structure in the example, we need to have a wrapper interface to provide locking, as shown in listing 8.2. You can see in the get method that if the token can't be found in the dictionary, it's rebuilt by reading related data from the database. Reading from the database can be time consuming, and that means all requests would be put on hold until that read operation finished.

Listing 8.2 Lock-based thread-safe dictionary

```
class ApiTokens {
  private Dictionary<string, Token> tokens { get; } = new();   ← This is the shared
                                                                  instance of the
  public void Set(string key, Token value) {                    dictionary.
    lock (tokens) {
      tokens[key] = value;   ← A lock is still needed here because
    }                          it's a multistep operation.
  }

  public Token Get(string key) {
    lock (tokens) {
      if (!tokens.TryGetValue(key, out Token value)) {
        value = getTokenFromDb(key);   ← This call can take a long time,
        tokens[key] = value;             thereby blocking all other callers.
        return tokens[key];
      }
      return value;
    }
  }

  private Token getTokenFromDb(string key) {
    . . . a time-consuming task . . .
  }
}
```

That's not scalable at all, and a lock-free alternative would be great here. .NET provides two different sets of thread-safe data structures. The names of one start with Concurrent*, in which short-lived locks are used. They're not all lock-free. They still use locks, but they're optimized to hold them for brief periods of time, making them quite fast and possibly simpler than a true lock-free alternative. The other set of alternatives is Immutable*, in which the original data is never changed, but every modify operation creates a new copy of the data with the modifications. It's as slow as it sounds, but there are cases when they might be preferable to Concurrent flavors.

If we use a `ConcurrentDictionary` instead, our code suddenly becomes way more scalable, as shown in the following listing. You can now see that `lock` statements aren't needed anymore, so the time-consuming query can run better in parallel with other requests and will block as little as possible.

Listing 8.3   Lock-free thread-safe dictionary

```
class ApiTokensLockFree {
  private ConcurrentDictionary<string, Token> tokens { get; } = new();

  public void Set(string key, Token value) {
    tokens[key] = value;
  }

  public Token Get(string key) {
    if (!tokens.TryGetValue(key, out Token value)) {
      value = getTokenFromDb(key);          ◁─┐  This will run in
      tokens[key] = value;                    │  parallel now!
      return tokens[key];
    }
    return value;
  }

  private Token getTokenFromDb(string key) {
    . . . a time-consuming task . . .
  }
}
```

A minor downside of this change is that multiple requests can run an expensive operation such as `getTokenFromDb` for the same token in parallel because no locks are preventing that from happening anymore. In the worst case, you'd be running the same time-consuming operation in parallel for the same token unnecessarily, but even so, you wouldn't be blocking any other requests, so it's likely to beat the alternate scenario. Not using locks might be worth it.

8.1.1   *Double-checked locking*

Another simple technique lets you avoid using locks for certain scenarios. For example, ensuring that only a single instance of an object is created when multiple threads are requesting it can be hard. What if two threads make the same request at once? For example, let's say we have a cache object. If we accidentally provide two different instances, different parts of the code would have a different cache, causing inconsistencies or waste. To avoid this, you protect your initialization code inside a lock to make sure, as shown in the following listing. The static `Instance` property would hold a lock before creating an object, so it makes sure that no other instances will create the same instance twice.

Listing 8.4 Ensuring only one instance is created

```
class Cache {
    private static object instanceLock = new object();    ⟵—— The object used for locking
    private static Cache instance;    ⟵————┐
    public static Cache Instance {          │ The cached instance value
      get {
        lock(instanceLock) {    ⟵————┐
          if (instance is null) {       │ All other callers wait here
            instance = new Cache();      │ if there is another thread
          }                              │ running in this block.
          return instance;
        }
      }
    }
}
```

The object gets created, and only once, too!

The code works okay, but every access to the `Instance` property will cause a lock to be held. That can create unnecessary waits. Our goal is to reduce locking. You can add a secondary check for the value of an instance: return its value before acquiring the lock if it's already initialized, and acquire the lock only if it hasn't been, as shown in listing 8.5. It's a simple addition, but it eliminates 99.9% of lock contentions in your code, making it more scalable. We still need the secondary check inside the `lock` statement because there's a small possibility that another thread may have already initialized the value and released the lock just before we acquired it.

Listing 8.5 Double-checked locking

```
public static Cache Instance {
  get {                                        Notice the pattern-matching-based
    if (instance is not null) {    ⟵———        "not null" check in C# 9.0.
      return instance;    ⟵————┐
    }                            │ Return the instance
    lock (instanceLock) {        │ without locking anything.
      if (instance is null) {
        instance = new Cache();
      }
      return instance;
    }
  }
}
```

Double-checked locking may not be possible with all data structures. For example, you can't do it for members of a dictionary because it's impossible to read from a dictionary in a thread-safe manner outside of a lock while it's being manipulated.

C# has come a long way and made safe singleton initializations much easier with helper classes like `LazyInitializer`. You can write the same property code in a simpler way. It already performs double-checked locking behind the scenes, saving you extra work.

Listing 8.6   Safe initialization with `LazyInitializer`

```
public static Cache Instance {
  get {
    return LazyInitializer.EnsureInitialized(ref instance);
  }
}
```

There are other cases in which double-checked locking might be beneficial. For example, if you want to make sure a list only contains a certain number of items at most, you can safely check its Count property because you're not accessing any of the list items during the check. Count is usually just a simple field access and is mostly thread-safe unless you use the number you read for iterating through the items. An example would look like the following listing, and it would be fully thread-safe.

Listing 8.7   Alternative double-checked locking scenarios

```
class LimitedList<T> {
  private List<T> items = new();

  public LimitedList(int limit) {
    Limit = limit;
  }

  public bool Add(T item) {
    if (items.Count >= Limit) {    ◁──── First check outside the lock
      return false;
    }
    lock (items) {
      if (items.Count >= Limit) {   ◁──── Second check inside the lock
        return false;
      }
      items.Add(item);
      return true;
    }
  }

  public bool Remove(T item) {
    lock (items) {
      return items.Remove(item);
    }
  }

  public int Count => items.Count;
  public int Limit { get; }
}
```

You might have noticed that the code in listing 8.7 doesn't contain an indexer property to access list items with their index. That's because it's impossible to provide thread-safe enumeration on direct index access without fully locking the list before enumerating. Our class is only useful for counting items, not accessing them. But accessing the counter property itself is quite safe, so we can employ it in our double-checked locking to get better scalability.

8.2 *Embrace inconsistency*

Databases provide a vast number of features to avoid inconsistencies: locks, transactions, atomic counters, transaction logs, page checksums, snapshots, and so forth. That's because they're designed for systems in which you can't afford to retrieve the wrong data, like banks, nuclear reactors, and matchmaking apps.

Reliability isn't a black-and-white concept. There are levels of unreliability that you can survive with significant gains in performance and scalability. NoSQL is a philosophy that foregoes certain consistency affordances of traditional relational database systems, like foreign keys and transactions, while gaining performance, scalability, and obscurity in return.

You don't need to go full NoSQL to get the benefits of such an approach. You can achieve similar gains on a traditional database like MySQL or SQL Server.

8.2.1 *The dreaded NOLOCK*

As a query hint, NOLOCK dictates that the SQL engine that reads it can be inconsistent and can contain data from not-yet-committed transactions. That might sound scary, but is it really? Think about it. Let's consider Blabber, the microblogging platform we discussed in chapter 4. When you post every time, another table that contains post counts would be updated, too. If a post isn't posted, the counter shouldn't get incremented, either. Sample code would look like that in the following listing. You can see in the code that we wrap everything in a transaction, so if the operation fails at any point, we don't get inconsistent numbers in post counts.

> **Listing 8.8 A tale of two tables**

```
public void AddPost(PostContent content) {        Encapsulate everything
    using (var transaction = db.BeginTransaction()) {  in a transaction.
        db.InsertPost(content);
        int postCount = db.GetPostCount(userId);    Insert the post into its own table.
        postCount++;
        db.UpdatePostCount(userId, postCount);      Update the incremented
    }                                                post count.
}
```

Retrieve the post count.

The code might remind you of our unique ID generator example in the previous section; remember how threads worked in parallel with steps like read, increment, and store, and we had to use a lock to ensure that we kept consistent values? The same thing's happening here. Because of that, we sacrifice scalability. But do we need this kind of consistency? Can I entertain you with the idea of eventual consistency?

Eventual consistency means you ensure certain consistency guarantees, but only after a delay. In this example, you can update the incorrect post counts at certain time intervals. The best thing about that is that such an operation doesn't need to hold any locks. Users will rarely see their post counts not reflecting the actual post count until it gets fixed by the system. You gain scalability because the fewer locks you hold, the more parallel requests can be run on the database.

A periodic query that updates a table would still hold locks on that table, but they would be more granular locks, probably on a certain row, or in the worst case, on a single page on the disk. You can alleviate that problem with double-checked locking: you can first run a read-only query that just queries which rows need to be updated, and you can run just your update query thereafter. That would make sure that the database doesn't get nervous about locking stuff because you simply executed an update statement on the database. A similar query would look like that in listing 8.9. First, we execute a SELECT query to identify mismatched counts, which doesn't hold locks. We then update post counts based on our mismatched records. We can also batch these updates, but running them individually would hold more granular locks, possibly at the row level, so it would allow more queries to be run on the same table without holding a lock any longer than necessary. The drawback is that updating every individual row will take longer, but it will end eventually.

> **Listing 8.9   Code running periodically to achieve eventual consistency**

```
public void UpdateAllPostCounts() {
  var inconsistentCounts = db.GetMismatchedPostCounts();      // No locks are held while
  foreach (var entry in inconsistentCounts) {                //  running this query.
    db.UpdatePostCount(entry.UserId, entry.ActualCount);     // A lock is held only
  }                                                          //  for a single row
}                                                            //  when running this.
```

A SELECT query in SQL doesn't hold locks on the table, but it can still be delayed by another transaction. That's where NOLOCK as a query hint comes into the picture. A NOLOCK query hint lets a query read *dirty data*, but in return, it doesn't need to respect locks held by other queries or transactions. It's easy for you, too. For example, in SQL Server, instead of SELECT * FROM customers, you use SELECT * FROM customers (NOLOCK), which applies NOLOCK to the customers table.

What is dirty data? If a transaction starts to write some records to the database but isn't finished yet, those records are regarded as dirty at that moment. That means a query with a NOLOCK hint can return rows that may not exist on the database yet or that will never exist. In many scenarios, that can be a level of inconsistency your app can live with. For example, don't use NOLOCK when authenticating a user because that might be a security issue, but there shouldn't be a problem with using it on, say, showing posts. At worst, you'll see a post that seemingly exists only a brief period, and it will go away in the next refresh anyway. You might have experienced this already with the social platforms you're using. Users delete their content, but those posts keep showing up in your feed, although you usually get an error if you try to interact with them.

That's because the platform is okay with some level of inconsistency for the sake of scalability.

You can apply NOLOCK to everything in an SQL connection by running an SQL statement first that sounds unnecessarily profound: SET TRANSACTION ISOLATION LEVEL READ_UNCOMMITTED. I think Pink Floyd released a song with a similar title. Anyway, the statement makes more sense and conveys your intent better, too.

Don't be afraid of inconsistencies if you're aware of the consequences. If you can see the impact of the tradeoff clearly, you can prefer intentional inconsistency to allow space for more scalability.

8.3 Don't cache database connections

It's a rather common malpractice to open a single connection to a database and share it in the code. The idea is sane on paper: it avoids the overhead of connection and authentication for every query, so they become faster. It's also a bit cumbersome to write open and close commands everywhere. But the truth is, when you only have a single connection to a database, you can't run parallel queries against the database. You can effectively only run one query at a time. That's a huge scalability blocker, as can be seen in figure 8.4.

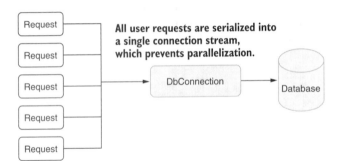

Figure 8.4 A bottleneck created by sharing a single connection in the application

Having a single connection isn't a good idea for other reasons, too. Queries might require different transaction scopes when they're running, and they may conflict when you try to reuse a single connection for multiple queries at once.

I must agree that part of the problem comes from naming these things connections when, in fact, they're not. You see, most client-side database connectivity libraries don't really open a connection when you create a connection object. They instead maintain a certain number of already open connections and just retrieve one for you. When you think you're opening a connection, you're in fact retrieving an already open connection from what's famously called *the connection pool*. When you close the connection, the actual connection isn't closed, either. It's put back into the pool, and its state gets reset, so any leftover work from a previously running query wouldn't affect the new queries.

I can hear you saying, "I know what to do! I'll just keep a connection for every request and close the connection when the request ends!" That would allow parallel requests to run without blocking each other, as shown in figure 8.5. You can see that every request gets a separate connection, and thanks to that, they can run in parallel.

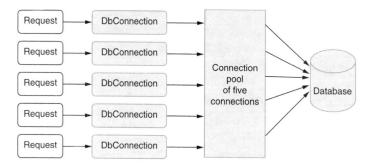

Figure 8.5   Keeping a single connection per HTTP request

The problem with that approach is that when there are more than five requests, the connection pool must make the client wait until it can serve an available connection to them. Those requests wait in the queue, killing the ability to scale more requests, even though the request may not be in use at the time, because the connection pool has no way of knowing if the connection requested is in use unless it's closed explicitly. This situation is depicted in figure 8.6.

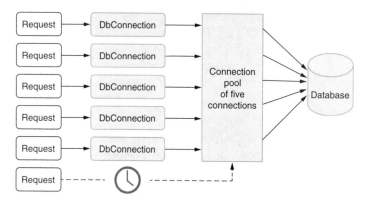

Figure 8.6   Per-request connection objects blocking additional requests

What if I told you that there is an even better approach that's completely counterintuitive but that will make the code as scalable as possible? The secret solution is to maintain connections only for the lifetime of the queries. This would return a connection to the pool as soon as possible, allowing other requests to grab the available connection and leading to maximum scalability. Figure 8.7 shows how it works. You can see how the connection pool serves no more than three queries at once, leaving room for another request or two.

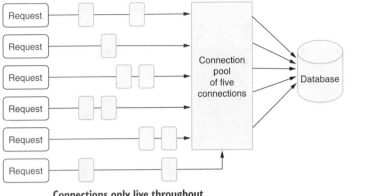

Connections only live throughout the lifetime of queries, leaving them available for other requests when they're not in use.

Figure 8.7 Per-query connections to the database

The reason that works is because a request is never just about running a query. Some processing is usually going on besides the queries themselves. That means that the time you hold a connection object while something irrelevant is running is wasted. By keeping connections open as briefly as possible, you leave a maximum number of connections available for other requests.

The problem is that it's more work. Consider an example in which you need to update the preferences of a customer based on their name. Normally, a query execution is pretty much like that in the following listing. You run the queries right away, without considering connection lifetime.

Listing 8.10 A typical query execution with a shared connection instance

```
public void UpdateCustomerPreferences(string name, string prefs) {
    int? result = MySqlHelper.ExecuteScalar(customerConnection,     ◄─┐
        "SELECT id FROM customers WHERE name=@name",                  │
        new MySqlParameter("name", name)) as int?;                    │  Using a shared
    if (result.HasValue) {                                            │  connection
        MySqlHelper.ExecuteNonQuery(customerConnection,              ◄─┘
            "UPDATE customer_prefs SET pref=@prefs",
            new MySqlParameter("prefs", prefs));
    }
}
```

That's because you have an open connection that you can reuse. Had you added the connection open-and-close code, it would have become a little bit more involved, like that in listing 8.11. You might think we should close and open the connection between two queries so the connection can be returned to the connection pool for other requests, but that's completely unnecessary for such a brief period. You'd even be adding more overhead. Also note that we don't explicitly close the connection at the end of the function. The reason is that the using statement at the beginning ensures that all resources regarding the connection object are freed immediately upon exiting the function, forcing the connection to be closed in turn.

```
public void UpdateCustomerPreferences(string name, string prefs) {
  using var connection = new MySqlConnection(connectionString);
  connection.Open();
  int? result = MySqlHelper.ExecuteScalar(customerConnection,
    "SELECT id FROM customers WHERE name=@name",
    new MySqlParameter("name", name)) as int?;
  //connection.Close();
  //connection.Open();
  if (result.HasValue) {
    MySqlHelper.ExecuteNonQuery(customerConnection,
      "UPDATE customer_prefs SET pref=@prefs",
      new MySqlParameter("prefs", prefs));
  }
}
```

> The ceremony to open a connection to database

> This is just silly.

You can wrap the connection-open ceremony in a helper function and avoid writing it everywhere like this:

```
using var connection = ConnectionHelper.Open();
```

That saves you some keystrokes, but it's prone to mistakes. You might forget to put the `using` statement before the call, and the compiler might forget to remind you about it. You can forget closing connections this way.

8.3.1   *In the form of an ORM*

Luckily, modern object relational mapping (ORM) tools are libraries that hide the intricacies of a database by providing an entirely different set of intricate abstractions, like Entity Framework, that do this automatically for you, so you don't need to care about when the connection would be opened or closed. It opens the connection when necessary and closes it when it's done with it. You can use a single, shared instance of a `DbContext` with Entity Framework throughout the lifetime of a request. You may not want to use a single instance of it for the whole app, though, because `DbContext` isn't thread-safe.

A query similar to listing 8.11 can be written like that in listing 8.12 with Entity Framework. You can write the same queries using LINQ's syntax, but I find this functional syntax easier to read and more composable.

```
public void UpdateCustomerPreferences(string name, string prefs) {
  int? result = context.Customers
    .Where(c => c.Name == name)
    .Select(c => c.Id)
    .Cast<int?>()
```

```
      .SingleOrDefault();
  if (result.HasValue) {
    var pref = context.CustomerPrefs
      .Where(p => p.CustomerId == result)
      .Single();
    pref.Prefs = prefs;
    context.SaveChanges();
  }
}
```

The connection will be opened before and closed automatically after each of these lines.

You can have more space to scale your application over when you are aware of the lifetime semantics of the `Connection` classes, connection pools, and actual network connections established to the database.

8.4 Don't use threads

Scalability isn't only about more parallelization—it's also about conserving resources. You can't scale beyond a full memory, nor can you scale beyond 100% of CPU usage. ASP.NET Core uses a thread pool structure to keep a certain number of threads to serve web requests in parallel. The idea is quite similar to a connection pool: having a set of already initialized threads lets you avoid the overhead of creating them every time. Thread pools usually have more threads than the number of CPU cores on the system because threads frequently wait for something to complete, mostly I/O. This way, other threads can be scheduled on the same CPU core while certain threads are waiting for I/O to complete. You can see how more threads than the number of CPU cores can help utilize CPU cores better in figure 8.8. The CPU can use the time a thread is waiting for something to complete to run another thread on the same core by serving more threads than the number of available CPU cores.

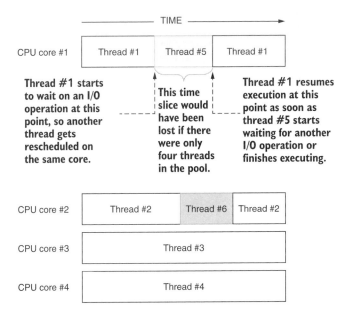

Figure 8.8 Optimizing CPU usage by having more threads than the number of CPU cores

This is better than having the same number of threads as CPU cores, but it's not precise enough to make the best use of your precious CPU time. The operating system gives threads a short amount of time to execute and then relinquishes the CPU core to other threads to make sure every thread gets a chance to run in a reasonable time. That technique is called *preemption,* and it's how multitasking used to work with single-core CPUs. The operating system juggled all the threads on the same core, creating the illusion of multitasking. Luckily, since most threads wait for I/O, users wouldn't notice that threads took turns to run on the single CPU they have unless they ran a CPU-intensive application. Then they'd feel its effects.

Because of how operating systems schedule threads, having a greater number of threads in the thread pool than the number of CPU cores is just a ballpark way of getting more utilization, but as a matter of fact, it can even harm scalability. If you have too many threads, they all start to get a smaller slice of CPU time, so they take longer to run, bringing your website or API to a crawl.

A more precise way to leverage time spent waiting for I/O is to use asynchronous I/O, as I discussed in chapter 7. Asynchronous I/O is explicit: wherever you have an `await` keyword, that means the thread will wait for a result of a callback, so the same thread can be used by other requests while the hardware is working on the I/O request itself. You can serve multiple requests on the same thread in parallel this way, as you can see in figure 8.9.

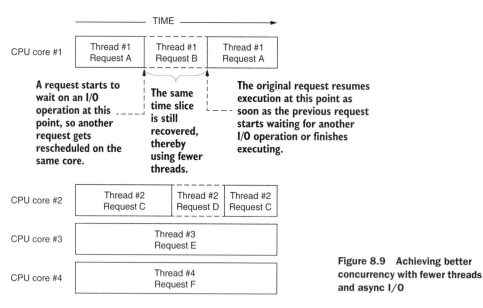

Figure 8.9   Achieving better concurrency with fewer threads and async I/O

Asynchronous I/O is very promising. Upgrading an existing code to asynchronous I/O is straightforward, too, as long as you have a framework that supports async calls at the root. For example, on ASP.NET Core, controller actions or Razor Page handlers can be written either as regular methods or as asynchronous methods because the framework builds the necessary scaffolding around them. All you need to do is to rewrite the function using asynchronous calls and mark the method as async. Yes, you still need to make sure that your code works properly and passes your tests, but it's still a straightforward process.

Let's revise the example in listing 8.6 and convert it to async in listing 8.13. You don't need to go back and see the original code because the differences are highlighted in the listing in bold. Take a look at the differences, and I'll break them down afterward.

> **Listing 8.13 Converting blocking code to async code**

```
public async Task UpdateCustomerPreferencesAsync(string name,
  string prefs) {
  int? result = await MySqlHelper.ExecuteScalarAsync(
    customerConnection,
    "SELECT id FROM customers WHERE name=@name",
    new MySqlParameter("name", name)) as int?;
  if (result.HasValue) {
    await MySqlHelper.ExecuteNonQueryAsync(customerConnection,
        "UPDATE customer_prefs SET pref=@prefs",
        new MySqlParameter("prefs", prefs));
  }
}
```

It's important that you know what all these are for, so you can use them consciously and correctly.

- Async functions don't actually need to be named with the suffix Async, but the convention helps you see that it's something you need to await. You might think, "But the async keyword is right there!" but the keyword only affects the implementation and isn't part of the function signature. You must navigate the source code to find out if an async function is really async. If you don't await an async function, it returns immediately while you may incorrectly assume it has finished running. Try to stick to convention unless you can't afford it when you need specific names for your functions, such as the names of controller actions because they can designate the URL routes as well. It also helps if you want to have two overloads of the same function with the same name because return types aren't considered a differentiator for overloads. That's why almost all async methods are named with an Async suffix in .NET.

- The async keyword at the beginning of the function declaration just means you can use await in the function. Behind the scenes, the compiler takes those async statements, generates the necessary handling code, and converts them into a series of callbacks.

- All async functions must return a Task or Task<T>. An async function without a return value could also have a void return type, but that's known to cause problems. For example, exception-handling semantics change, and you lose composability. Composability in async functions lets you define an action that will happen when a function finishes in a programmatical way using `Task` methods like `ContinueWith`. Because of all that, async functions that don't have a return value should always use `Task` instead. When you decorate a function with the `async` keyword, values after `return` statements are automatically wrapped with a `Task<T>`, so you don't need to deal with creating a `Task<T>` yourself.

- The `await` keyword ensures that the next line will only be executed after the expression that precedes it has finished running. If you don't put `await` in front of multiple async calls, they will start running in parallel, and that can be desirable at times, but you need to make sure that you wait for them to finish because, otherwise, the tasks may be interrupted. On the other hand, parallel operations are prone to bugs; for example, you can't run multiple queries in parallel by using the same `DbContext` in Entity Framework Core because `DbContext` itself isn't thread-safe. However, you can parallelize other I/O this way, like reading a file. Think of an example in which you want to make two web requests at once. You may not want them to wait for each other. You can make two web requests concurrently and wait for both of them to finish, as is shown in listing 8.14. We define a function that receives a list of URLs and starts a download task for each URL without waiting for the previous one to complete so that the downloads run in parallel on a single thread. We can use a single instance of the `HttpClient` object because it's thread-safe. The function waits for all tasks to complete and builds a final response out of the results of all tasks.

Listing 8.14   Downloading multiple web pages in parallel on a single thread

```
using System;
using System.Collections.Generic;
using System.Linq;
using System.Net.Http;
using System.Threading.Tasks;

namespace Connections {
  public static class ParallelWeb {                              Temporary
    public static async Task<Dictionary<Uri, string>>            storage to keep
    DownloadAll(IEnumerable<Uri> uris) {                         track of running
      var runningTasks = new Dictionary<Uri, Task<string>>();    tasks
      var client = new HttpClient();
      foreach (var uri in uris) {         A single instance is enough.
        var task = client.GetStringAsync(uri);
        runningTasks.Add(uri, task);      Start the task, but
      }                                   don't await it.
      await Task.WhenAll(runningTasks.Values);
      return runningTasks.ToDictionary(kp => kp.Key,
        kp => kp.Value.Result);           Wait until all tasks
    }                                     are complete.
  }
}
```

The resulting type → `public static async Task<Dictionary<Uri, string>>`

Store the task somewhere. → `runningTasks.Add(uri, task);`

Build a new result Dictionary out of the results of the completed Tasks.

8.4.1 The gotchas of async code

You need to keep certain things in mind when you're converting your code to async. It's easy to think "Make everything async!" and make everything worse in the process. Let's go over some of those pitfalls.

NO I/O MEANS NO ASYNC

If a function doesn't call an async function, it doesn't need to be async. Asynchronous programming only helps with scalability when you use it with I/O-bound operations. Using async on a CPU-bound operation won't help scalability because those operations will need separate threads to run on, unlike I/O operations, which can run in parallel on a single thread. The compiler might also warn you when you try to use an async keyword on a function that doesn't run other async operations. If you choose to ignore those warnings, you'll just get unnecessarily bloated and perhaps slower code due to the async-related scaffolding added to the function. Here's an example of unnecessary use of an async keyword:

```
public async Task<int> Sum(int a, int b) {
  return a + b;
}
```

I know this happens because I've seen it in the wild, where people just decorated their functions as async for no good reason. Always be explicit and clear about why you want to make a function async.

DON'T MIX SYNC AND ASYNC

It's extremely hard to call an async function in a synchronous context safely. People will say, "Hey, just call Task.Wait(), or call Task.Result, and you'll be fine." No, you won't. That code will haunt your dreams, it will cause problems at the most unexpected times, and eventually, you'll wish you could get some sleep instead of having nightmares.

The greatest problem with waiting for async functions in synchronous code is that it can cause a deadlock due to other functions in the async function that depend on the caller code to complete. Exception handling can also be counterintuitive because it would be wrapped inside a separate AggregateException.

Try not to mix asynchronous code inside a synchronous context. It's a complicated setup, which is why only frameworks do it, usually. C# 7.1 added support for async Main functions, which means you can start running async code right away, but you can't call an async function from your synchronous web action. The opposite is fine, though. You can, and you will, have synchronous code in your async functions because not every function is suitable for async.

8.4.2 Multithreading with async

Asynchronous I/O provides better scalability characteristics than multithreading on I/O heavy code because it consumes less resources. But multithreading and async are not mutually exclusive. You can have both. You can even use asynchronous programming constructs to write multithreaded code. For example, you can handle long-running CPU work in an async fashion like this:

```
await Task.Run(() => computeMeaningOfLifeUniverseAndEverything());
```

It will still run the code in a separate thread, but the await mechanism simplifies the synchronization of work completion. If you wrote the same code using traditional threads, it would look a little bit more involved. You need to have a synchronization primitive such as an event:

```
ManualResetEvent completionEvent = new(initialState: false);
```

> ### Notice the new?
>
> For a long time, programmers had to write `SomeLongTypeName something = new SomeLongTypeName();` to initialize an object. Typing the same type had always been a chore, even with the help of the IDE. That problem was remediated a bit after the introduction of the `var` keyword in the language, but it doesn't work with class member declarations.
>
> C# 9.0 brought a great improvement to quality of life: you don't have to write the type of class after `new` if the type is declared before. You can go ahead and just write `SomeLongTypeName something = new();`. This is brought to you by the awesome C# design team!

The event object you declare also needs to be accessible from the point of synchronization, which creates additional complexity. The actual code becomes more involved too:

```
ThreadPool.QueueUserWorkItem(state => {
  computeMeaningOfLifeUniverseAndEverything();
  completionEvent.Set();
});
```

Thus, async programming can make some multithreaded work easier to write, but it's neither a complete replacement for multithreading nor does it help scalability. Multithreaded code written in async syntax is still regular multithreaded code; it doesn't conserve resources like async code

8.5   *Respect the monolith*

There should be a note stuck to your monitor that you'll only remove when you become rich from your vested startup stocks. It should say, "No microservices."

The idea behind microservices is simple: if we split our code into separate self-hosted projects, it will be easier in the future to deploy those projects to separate servers, so, free scaling! The problem here, like many of the issues in software development I've discussed, is added complexity. Do you split all the shared code? Do the projects really not share anything? What about their dependencies? How many projects will you need to update when you just change the database? How do you share context, like authentication and authorization? How do you ensure security? There'll be added round trip delays caused by the millisecond-level delays between servers. How do you preserve compatibility? What if you deploy one first, and another one breaks because of the new change? Do you have the capacity to handle this level of complexity?

I use the term *monolith* as the opposite of microservices, where the components of your software reside in a single project, or at least in tightly coupled multiple projects deployed together to the same server. Because the components are interdependent, how do you move some of them to another server to make your app scale?

In this chapter, we've seen how we can achieve better scalability even on a single CPU core, let alone on a single server. A monolith can scale. It can work fine for a long time until you find yourself in a situation where you must split your app. At that point, the startup you're working for is already rich enough to hire more developers to do the work. Don't complicate a new project with microservices when authentication, coordination, and synchronization can become troublesome at such an early stage in the lifetime of the product. Ekşi Sözlük, more than 20 years later, is still serving 40 million users every month on a monolithic architecture. A monolith is the natural next step to switch to from your local prototype, too. Go with the flow and consider adopting a microservice architecture only when its benefits outweigh its drawbacks.

Summary

- Approach scalability as a multistep diet program. Small improvements can eventually lead you to a better, scalable system.
- One of the greatest blocks of scalability is locks. You can't live with them, and you can't live without them. Understand that they're sometimes dispensable.
- Prefer lock-free or concurrent data structures over acquiring locks yourself manually to make your code more scalable.
- Use double-checked locking whenever it's safe.
- Learn to live with inconsistencies for better scalability. Choose which types of inconsistencies your business would be okay with, and use the opportunity to create more scalable code.
- ORMs, while usually seen as a chore, can also help you create more scalable apps by employing optimizations that you may not think of.
- Use asynchronous I/O in all the I/O-bound code that needs to be highly scalable to conserve available threads and optimize CPU usage.
- Use multithreading for parallelizing CPU-bound work, but don't expect the scalability benefits of asynchronous I/O, even when you use multithreading with async programming constructs.
- A monolith architecture will complete a full tour around the world before the design discussion over a microservice architecture is finished.

Living with bugs

9

The most profound work of literature on bugs is *Metamorphosis* by Franz Kafka. It tells the story of Gregor Samsa, a software developer, who wakes up one day to find out that he is actually the only bug. Well, he isn't actually a software developer in the story because the entire practice of programming in 1915 only consisted of a couple of pages of code Ada Lovelace wrote 70 years before Kafka wrote his book. But Gregor Samsa's profession was the next best thing to a software developer: he was a traveling salesperson.

Bugs are basic units of metrics for determining software quality. Because software developers consider every bug a stain on the quality of their craftsmanship, they usually either aim for zero bugs or actively deny their existence by claiming that it works on their computer or that it's a feature, not a bug.

The traveling salesperson problem

The traveling salesperson problem is a cornerstone subject in computer science because calculating the optimal route for a traveling salesperson is *NP-complete*, an entirely counterintuitive acronym for *mondeterministic polynomial-time complete*. Because many words are missing in this acronym, I believed for a long time that it stood for *non-polynomial complete*, and I was very confused about it.

Polynomial-time (P) problems can be solved faster than by trying all possible combinations that otherwise have factorial complexity, the second-worst complexity of all complexities. NP is the superset of P (polynomial) problems that can only be solved with brute force. Polynomial problems, compared to NP, are always welcome. NP, non-deterministic polynomial-time problems, don't have a known polynomial algorithm to solve them, but their solution can be verified in polynomial time. In that sense, NP-complete means, "We're terrible at solving this, but we can verify a suggested solution quite quickly."

Software development is immensely complex because of the inherent unpredictability of a program. That's the nature of a *Turing machine*, a theoretical construct that all computers and most programming languages are based on, thanks to the works of Alan Turing. A programming language based on a Turing machine is called *Turing complete*. Turing machines allow the infinite levels of creativity we have with software, but it's just impossible to verify their correctness without executing them. Some languages depend on a non-Turing complete machine, such as HTML, XML, or regular expressions that are way less capable than Turing complete languages. Because of the nature of a Turing machine, bugs are inevitable. It's impossible to have a bug-free program. Accepting this fact before you set out to develop software will make your job easier.

9.1 Don't fix bugs

A development team must have a triaging process for deciding which bugs to fix for any sizable project. The term *triaging* originated during World War I, when medics had to decide which patients to treat and which to leave unattended to allocate their limited resources for those who still had a chance of surviving. It's the only way to effectively utilize a scarce resource. Triaging helps you decide what you need to fix first or whether you should fix it at all.

How do you prioritize a bug? Unless you're just a single person driving all the business decisions, your team needs to have shared criteria to determine the priority of a given bug. On the Windows team at Microsoft, we had a complicated set of criteria to decide which bugs to fix as assessed by multiple engineering authorities. Consequently, we had daily meetings to prioritize bugs and debated, in a place called the War Room, whether a bug was worth fixing. That's understandable for a product with such an immense scale like Windows, but it may be unnecessary for most software projects. I had to ask for prioritization of a bug because an automated system at an official marriage center in Istanbul was broken after an update and all marriage ceremonies had to stop. I had to make my case by breaking down being unable to marry into tangible metrics like *applicability, impact,* and *severity.* "How many couples get married in a day in Istanbul?" suddenly sounded like a meaningful interview question.

A simpler way to assess priority could be by using a tangential second dimension called *severity.* Although the goal is essentially to have a single priority, having a secondary dimension can make assessment easier when two different issues seemingly have the same priority. I find priority/severity dimensions handy and a good balance between business-oriented and technology-oriented. *Priority* is the business impact of a bug, while *severity* is the impact on the customer. For example, if a web page on your platform isn't working, it's a high severity issue because the customer can't use it. But its priority might be entirely different depending on whether it's on the home page or an obscure page only a few customers visit. Similarly, if your business logo on your home page goes missing, it might have no severity at all, yet it can have the topmost business priority. The severity dimension takes some load off business prioritization because it's impossible to come up with accurate metrics to prioritize bugs.

Couldn't we achieve the same level of granularity with a single priority dimension? For example, instead of having three priority and severity levels, wouldn't just six priority levels do the same job? The problem is that the more levels you have, the more difficult it becomes to differentiate between them. Usually, a secondary dimension helps you come up with a more accurate assessment of the importance of an issue.

You should have a threshold for priority and severity so that any bugs that rank below it are categorized as *won't fix.* For example, any bug that has both low priority and low severity can be considered a won't fix and can be taken off your radar. Table 9.1 shows the actual meanings of priority and severity levels.

Table 9.1   Actual meanings of priority and severity

Priority	Severity	Actual meaning
High	High	Fix immediately.
High	Low	The boss wants this fixed.
Low	High	Let the intern fix it.
Low	Low	Won't fix. Never fix these unless there's nothing else to do at the office. In that case, let the intern fix it.

Tracking bugs incurs costs, too. At Microsoft, it took our team at least an hour a day just to assess the priority of bugs. It's imperative for your team to avoid revisiting bugs that aren't ever likely to be fixed. Try to decide on that earlier in the process. It gains you time, and it still ensures you maintain decent product quality.

9.2   *The error terror*

Not every bug is caused by an error in your code, and not every error implies the existence of a bug in your code. This relationship between bugs and errors is most evident when you see a pop-up dialogue that says, *unknown error.* If it's an unknown error, how can you be so sure that it's an error in the first place? Maybe it's an unknown success!

Such situations are rooted in the primitive association between errors and bugs. Developers instinctively treat all errors as bugs and try to eliminate them consistently and insistently. That kind of reasoning usually leads to an unknown error situation because something has gone wrong, and the developer just doesn't care to understand whether it's an error. This understanding makes developers treat all kinds of errors the same way, usually either by reporting every error regardless of whether the user needs to see them or by hiding them all and burying them inside a log file on a server that no one will ever bother to read.

The solution to that kind of obsession with treating all errors the same way is to consider them part of your state. Perhaps it was a mistake to call them *errors*. We should have just called them *uncommon and unexpected state changes* or *exceptions*. Oh wait, we already have those!

9.2.1 *The bare truth of exceptions*

Exceptions may be the most misunderstood construct in the history of programming. I can't even count the times I've seen someone simply put their failing code inside a `try` block followed with an empty `catch` block and call it good. It's like closing the door to a room that's on fire and assuming the problem will sort itself out eventually. It's not a wrong assumption, but it can be quite costly.

Listing 9.1 The solution to all of life's problems

```
try {
  doSomethingMysterious();
}
catch {
  // this is fine
}
```

I don't blame programmers for that, either. As Abraham Maslow said in 1966, "If the only tool you have is a hammer, you tend to see every problem as a nail." I'm sure when the hammer was first invented, it was the next big thing, and everybody tried to adopt it in their solution process. Neolithic people probably published blog posts using hand markings on cave walls about how revolutionary the hammer was and how it could make problems go away, without knowing that better tools would emerge in the future for spreading butter on bread.

I've seen instances where the developer added a generic exception handler for the whole application that actually ignores all exceptions, preventing all crashes. Then why do we keep getting bugs? We would have solved the bug problem a long time ago if adding an empty handler was the cure.

Exceptions are a novel solution to the undefined state problem. In the days when error handling was only done with return values, it was possible to omit handling the error, assume success, and continue running. That would put the application in a state the programmer never anticipated. The problem with an unknown state is that it's impossible to know the effects of that state or how serious they can be. That's pretty much the sole reason behind operating system fatal error screens, like the kernel panic on UNIX systems or the infamous Blue Screen of Death on Windows. They halt the system to prevent potential further damage. *Unknown state* means that you can't predict what will happen next anymore. Yes, the CPU might just freak out and enter an infinite loop, or the hard disk drive might decide to write zeros on every sector, or your Twitter account might decide to publish random political opinions in all caps.

Error codes are different from exceptions in that it's possible to detect if exceptions aren't handled during runtime—not so with error codes. The usual recourse for unhandled exceptions is to terminate the application because the given state isn't anticipated. Operating systems do the same thing: they terminate the application if it fails to handle an exception. They can't do the same for device drivers or kernel-level components because they don't run in isolated memory spaces, unlike user mode processes. That's why they must halt the system completely. That's less of a problem with microkernel-based operating systems because the number of kernel-level components is minimal and even device drivers run in user space, but that has a slight performance penalty that we haven't come to terms with yet.

The greatest nuance we're missing about exceptions is the fact that they're exceptional. They're not for generic flow control; you have result values and flow control constructs for that. Exceptions are for cases when something happens outside a function's contract and it can't fulfill its contract anymore. A function like (a,b) => a/b guarantees performing a division operation, but it can't do that when b's value is 0. It's an unexpected and undefined case.

Suppose you download software updates for your desktop app, store the downloaded copy on disk, and switch your app with the newly downloaded one when the user starts your app next time. That's a common technique for self-updating apps outside a package management ecosystem. An update operation would look like figure 9.1. This is a bit naive because it doesn't take half-finished updates into account, but that's the whole point.

If any exception is raised at any point during the self-update, you'd get an incomplete app2 folder that would cause the app files to be replaced with a broken version, causing a catastrophic state that's impossible to recover from.

At every step, you can encounter an exception, and that might cause everything to fall apart if it's not handled, or if it's handled incorrectly.

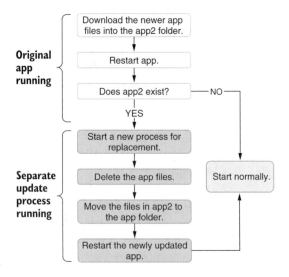

Figure 9.1 Some primitive logic for a self-updating app

The figure also shows the importance of how your process design should be resilient against exceptions. Any failure at any step could leave your app in a corrupt state, never to be recovered. You shouldn't leave the app in a dirty state even when an exception occurs.

9.2.2 *Don't catch exceptions*

`Try/catch` blocks are considered quick and easy patches for code that crashes because of an exception. Ignoring an exception makes the crash disappear, but it doesn't make the root cause go away.

Exceptions are supposed to cause crashes because that's the easiest way to identify the problem without causing further problems. Don't be afraid of crashes. Be afraid of bugs that don't cause clean crashes along with a convenient stack trace that helps you pinpoint the exact place where it happened. Be afraid of problems that are hidden by empty `catch` statements, lurking in the code and disguised as a mostly correct-looking state, slightly accumulating a bad state over a long time, and finally causing either a noticeable slowdown or a completely irrelevant-looking crash, like an `OutOfMemoryException`. Unnecessary `catch` blocks can prevent some crashes, but they might cost you hours in reading logs. Exceptions are great because they let you catch a problem before it becomes a hard-to-catch issue.

The first rule of exception handling is, you don't catch an exception. The second rule of exception handling is `IndexOutOfRangeException` at *Street Coder* chapter 9.

See what happens when you have only one rule? Don't catch an exception because it causes a crash. If it's caused by an incorrect behavior, fix the bug that causes it. If it's caused by a known possibility, put explicit handling statements in the code for that specific case.

Whenever there is a possibility of getting an exception at some point in the code, ask yourself, "Do I have a specific recourse planned for this exception, or do I just want to prevent a crash?" If it's the latter, handling that exception may not be necessary and may be even harmful because blindly handling an exception can hide a deeper, more serious problem with your code.

Consider the self-updating application I mentioned in section 9. 2.1. It could have a function that downloads a series of application files into a folder, as shown in listing 9.2. We need to download two files from our update server, assuming they are the latest versions. Obviously, there are many problematic issues with that approach, like not using a central registry to identify the latest version and downloading that specific version. What happens if I start downloading an update while the developers are in the middle of updating remote files? I'd get half of the files from the previous version and half from the next version, causing a corrupt installation. For the sake of our example, let's assume the developers shut down the web server before an update, update the files, and turn it back on after it's complete, preventing such a screw-up.

Listing 9.2   Code for downloading multiple files

```
private const string updateServerUriPrefix =
  "https://streetcoder.org/selfupdate/";

private static readonly string[] updateFiles =
  new[] { "Exceptions.exe", "Exceptions.app.config" };          The list of files to
                                                                be downloaded

private static bool downloadFiles(string directory,
  IEnumerable<string> files) {
  foreach (var filename in updateFiles) {
    string path = Path.Combine(directory, filename);
    var uri = new Uri(updateServerUriPrefix + filename);
    if (!downloadFile(uri, path)) {
      return false;          We detect a problem with
    }                        download and signal cleanup.
  }
  return true;
}

private static bool downloadFile(Uri uri, string path) {
  using var client = new WebClient();
  client.DownloadFile(uri, path);          Download an
  return true;                             individual file.
}
```

We know that `DownloadFile` can throw exceptions for various reasons. Actually, Microsoft has great documentation for the behavior of .NET functions, including which exceptions they can throw. There are three exceptions that `WebClient`'s `DownloadFile` method can throw:

- `ArgumentNullException` when a given argument is null
- `WebException` when something unexpected happens during a download, like a loss of internet connection
- `NotSupportedException` when the same `WebClient` instance is called from multiple threads to signify that the class itself isn't thread-safe

To prevent an unpleasant crash, a developer might choose to wrap the call to `DownloadFile` in a `try` / `catch`, so the downloads would continue. Because many developers wouldn't care about which types of exceptions to catch, they just do it with an untyped `catch` block. We introduce a result code so we can detect whether an error has occurred.

Listing 9.3   Preventing crashes by creating more bugs

```
private static bool downloadFile(Uri uri, string path) {
  using var client = new WebClient();
  try {
    client.DownloadFile(uri, path);
    return true;
  }
  catch {
    return false;
  }
}
```

The problem with that approach is that you catch all three possible exceptions, two of which actually point to a definite programmer error. ArgumentNullException only happens when you pass an invalid argument and the caller is responsible for it, meaning there's either bad data or bad input validation somewhere in the call stack. Similarly, NotSupportedException is only raised when you misuse the client. That means you're hiding many potentially easy-to-fix bugs that might lead to even more serious consequences by catching all exceptions. No, despite what some magic animal slavery ring might dictate, you don't gotta catch 'em all. If we didn't have a return value, a simple argument error would cause files to be skipped, and we wouldn't even know if they were there. You should instead catch a specific exception that's probably not a programmer error, as listing 9.4 shows. We only catch WebException, which is, in fact, expected because you know a download can fail any time for any reason, so you want to make it part of your state. Catch an exception only when it's expected. We let other types of exceptions cause a crash because it means we were stupid and we deserve to live with its consequences before it causes a more serious problem.

Listing 9.4 Precise exception handling

```
private static bool downloadFile(Uri uri, string path) {
  using var client = new WebClient();
  try {
    client.DownloadFile(uri, path);
    return true;
  }
  catch (WebException) {          ◁─┐  You don't gotta
    return false;                   │  catch 'em all.
  }
}
```

That's why code analyzers suggest that you avoid using untyped catch blocks, because they are too broad, causing irrelevant exceptions to be caught. Catchall blocks should only be used when you really mean catching all the exceptions in the world, probably for a generic purpose like logging.

9.2.3 Exception resiliency

Your code should work correctly even without handling exceptions, even when it's crashed. You should design a flow that works fine even when you constantly get exceptions, and you shouldn't enter a dirty state. Your design should tolerate exceptions. The main reason is that exceptions are inevitable. You can put a catchall try/catch in your Main method, and your app would still be terminated unexpectedly when new updates cause a restart. You shouldn't let exceptions break your application's state.

When Visual Studio crashes, the file you were changing at that moment doesn't go missing. You get reminded about the missing file when you start the application again, and you're offered an option to recover the missing file. Visual Studio manages that by constantly keeping a copy of unsaved files at a temporary location and deleting one when the file is actually saved. At startup, it checks for the existence of those temporary files and asks if you want to recover them. You should design your code to anticipate similar problems.

In our self-updating app example, your process should allow exceptions to happen, and recover from them when the app's restarted. An exception-resilient design for our self-updater would look like figure 9.2, in which instead of downloading individual files, we download a single atomic package, which prevents us from getting an inconsistent set of files. Similarly, we back up original files before replacing them with new ones so we can recover in case something goes wrong.

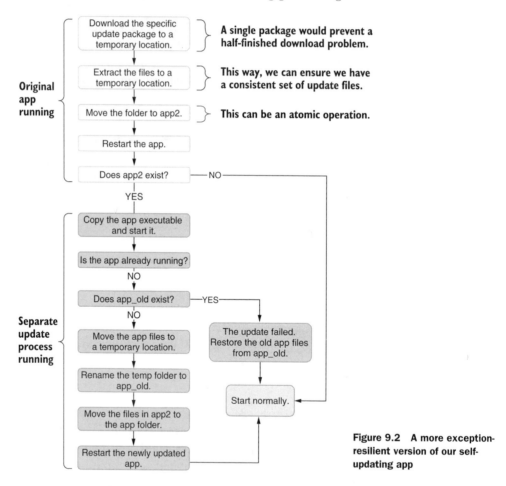

Figure 9.2   A more exception-resilient version of our self-updating app

How much time it takes to install updates on our devices hints that the software update is complicated, and I'm sure I've missed many cases where this design can fail. However, you can apply similar techniques to prevent a bad state in your app.

Achieving exception-resilient design starts with idempotency. A function, or a URL, is idempotent if it returns the same result regardless of how many times it's called. That might sound trivial for a pure function like Sum(), but it gets more complicated with functions that modify external state. An example is the checkout process of online shopping platforms. If you accidentally click the Submit Order button twice, does your credit card get charged twice? It shouldn't. I know that some websites try to fix this by putting up a warning like "Don't click the button twice!" but as you know, most cats walking on the keyboard are illiterate.

Idempotency is usually thought of in a simplified manner for web requests like "HTTP GET requests should be idempotent and anything non-idempotent should be a POST request." But GET requests may not be idempotent, say, for content with dynamically changing parts; or a POST request can be idempotent, like an upvote operation: multiple upvotes for the same content shouldn't change the number of times the users have upvoted for the same content.

How does this help us become exception resilient? When we design our function to have consistent side effects regardless of how many times it's called, we also gain some consistency benefits for when it gets interrupted unexpectedly. Our code becomes safely callable multiple times without causing any problems.

How do you achieve idempotency? In our example, you can have a unique order-processing number, and you can create a record on the DB as soon as you start processing the order and check its existence at the start of your processing function, as figure 9.3 shows. The code needs to be thread-safe, because some cats can walk really fast.

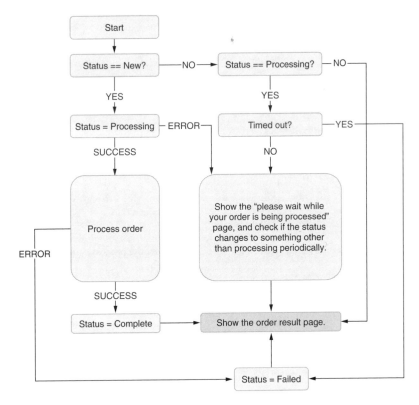

Figure 9.3 An idempotent example of order submission

DB transactions can help you avoid a bad state because they're rolled back if they somehow cut off because of an exception, but they may not be necessary for many scenarios.

In figure 9.3, we define an order status change operation, but how do we ensure that we do it atomically? What if somebody else changes it before we read the result? The secret is to use a conditional update operation for the database that makes sure the status is the same as the expected one. It might look like this:

```
UPDATE orders SET status=@NewState WHERE id=@OrderID status=@CurrentState
```

UPDATE returns the number of rows affected, so if the state changed during the UPDATE operation, the operation itself would fail and it would return 0 as the number of rows affected. If the state change is successful, it would return 1. You can use this to atomically update the record state changes, as shown in figure 9.3.

An implementation example would look like listing 9.5. We define every individual state the order can be in throughout order processing and enable our processing to handle the situation at different levels of processing. If it's already being processed, we just show the still-processing page and expire the order if it times out.

Listing 9.5   Idempotent order processing

```
public enum OrderStatus {
  New,
  Processing,
  Complete,
  Failed,
}

[HttpPost]
public IActionResult Submit(Guid orderId) {          Try
  Order order = db.GetOrder(orderId);                 changing
                                                      status
  if (!db.TryChangeOrderStatus(order, from: OrderStatus.New,  ◁── atomically.
    to: OrderStatus.Processing)) {
    if (order.Status != OrderStatus.Processing) {
      return redirectToResultPage(order);
    }                                                 Check the
    if (DateTimeOffset.Now - order.LastUpdate > orderTimeout) { ◁── timeout.
      db.ChangeOrderStatus(order, OrderStatus.Failed);
      return redirectToResultPage(order);
    }
    return orderStatusView(order);      ◁───── Show the processing page.
  }
  if (!processOrder(order)) {
    db.ChangeOrderStatus(order, OrderStatus.Failed);
  } else {
    db.TryChangeOrderStatus(order,
      from: OrderStatus.Processing,     If it fails, the result page will
      to: OrderStatus.Complete);        show the correct outcome.
  }
  return redirectToResultPage(order);
}
```

Despite that being an `HTTP POST` request, the order submission is perfectly okay to be called multiple times without causing any unwanted side effects, and therefore, it's idempotent. If your web app crashes and you restart your application, it can still recover from many invalid states, such as a processing state. Order processing can be more complicated than this, and it might require external periodic cleanup work for certain cases, but you can still have great resiliency against exceptions, even with no `catch` statements whatsoever.

9.2.4 *Resiliency without transactions*

Idempotency may not be enough for exception resiliency, but it provides a great foundation because it encourages us to think about how our function would behave at different states. In our example, the process-order step may cause exceptions and leave a dirty state around for a given order, preventing the same step from being called again. Normally, transactions protect against that because they roll back all the changes without leaving any dirty data behind. But not every storage has transaction support—file systems, for example.

You still have options even when transactions aren't available. Suppose you created an image-sharing app where people can upload albums and share them with their friends. Your content delivery network (CDN, a nifty name for file servers) could have a folder for each album with image files underneath, and you'd have album records in a database. It's quite impractical to wrap the operation of building these in a transaction because it spans multiple technologies.

The traditional approach to creating an album is to create the album record first, create the folder, and finally upload the images to the folder based on this information. But if an exception is raised anywhere in the process, you would get an album record with some of the pictures missing. This problem applies to pretty much all kinds of interdependent data.

You have multiple options to avoid this problem. In our album example, you can create the folder for images first at a temporary location, move the folder to a UUID created for the album, and finally create the album record as the last operation in the process. This way, users would never browse albums that are half complete.

Another option would be to create the album record first with a status value that specifies that the record is inactive and then add the rest of the data. You can finally change the status of the album record to *active* when the insertion operation is complete. This way, you wouldn't get duplicate album records when exceptions interrupt the upload process.

In both cases, you can have periodic cleanup routines that can sweep records that are abandoned and remove them from the DB. With a traditional approach, it's hard to know whether a resource is valid or a remnant from an interrupted operation.

9.2.5 *Exceptions vs. errors*

It can be argued that exceptions signify errors, and that may be true, but not all errors are qualified to be exceptions. Don't use exceptions for cases where you expect the caller to handle it most of the time. That's not an exceptional situation. A very familiar example is `Parse` versus `TryParse` in .NET, where the former throws an exception on invalid input, while the latter just returns `false`.

There was only `Parse` once. Then came `TryParse` in .NET Framework 2.0 because invalid input turned out to be common and expected in most scenarios. Exceptions are an overhead in those cases because they're slow. That's because they need to carry the stack trace with them, which requires walking the stack in the first place to gather stack trace information. That can be very expensive compared to simply returning a Boolean value. Exceptions are also harder to handle because you need all the `try/catch` ceremony, while a simple `result` value only needs to be checked with an `if`, as shown in the following listing. You can see that an implementation with `try/catch` involves more typing, it's harder to implement correctly because the developer can easily forget to keep its exception handler specific to `FormatException`, and the code is harder to follow.

Listing 9.6 A tale of two parses

```
public static int ParseDefault(string input,          ◁──┐  Implementation
    int defaultValue) {                                   │  with Parse
  try {
    return int.Parse(input);
  }
  catch (FormatException) {    ◁──   It's tempting to omit the
    return defaultValue;             exception type here.
  }
}

public static int ParseDefault(string input,          ◁──┐  Implementation
    int defaultValue) {                                   │  with TryParse
  if (!int.TryParse(input, out int result)) {
    return defaultValue;
  }
  return result;
}
```

`Parse` still has its place when you expect the input to always be correct. If you're sure that the input value is always correctly formatted, and any invalid value is actually a bug, you do want an exception to be thrown. It's a dare in a way, because then you're sure that an invalid input value is a bug. "Crash if you can!"

Regular error values are good enough to return responses most of the time. It's even okay not to return anything if you have no use for the return value. For example, if you expect an upvote operation to always be successful, don't have a return value. The function's return already signifies success.

You can have different types of error results based on how much you expect the caller needs the information. If the caller only cares about success or failure and not the details, returning a `bool` is perfectly fine, with `true` signifying success; `false`, on the other hand, is failure. If you have a third state or you're using `bool` already to specify something else, then you might need a different approach.

For example, Reddit has voting functionality, but only if the content's recent enough. You can't vote on comments or posts that are older than six months. You also can't vote on deleted posts. That means voting can fail in multiple ways, and that difference might need to be communicated to the user. You can't just say "voting failed: unknown error" because the user might think it's a temporary problem and keep trying. You have to say, "This post is too old" or "This post is deleted," so the user learns about that specific platform dynamic and stops trying to vote. A better user experience would be to hide the voting buttons so the user would immediately know they can't vote on that post, but Reddit insists on showing them.

In Reddit's case, you can simply use an `enum` to differentiate between different failure modes. A possible `enum` for a Reddit voting result could look like listing 9.7. That may not be comprehensive, but we don't need additional values for other possibilities because we don't have any plans for them. For example, if voting fails because of a DB error, that must be an exception, not a result value. It points to either an infrastructure failure or a bug. You want your call stack; you want it to be logged somewhere.

Listing 9.7 Voting result for Reddit

```
public enum VotingResult {
  Success,
  ContentTooOld,
  ContentDeleted,
}
```

The great thing about `enum`s is that the compiler can warn you about unhandled cases when you use switch expressions. You get a warning for cases you didn't handle because they're not exhaustive enough. The C# compiler can't do the same for `switch` statements, only for `switch` expressions because they're newly added to the language and can be designed for these scenarios. A sample exhaustive `enum` handling for an upvote operation might look like the following listing. You might still get a separate warning for the `switch` statement not being exhaustive enough because, in theory, you can assign invalid values to `enum`s due to initial design decisions made for the C# language.

Listing 9.8 Exhaustive enum handling

```
[HttpPost]
public IActionResult Upvote(Guid contentId) {
  var result = db.Upvote(contentId);
  return result switch {
```

```
    VotingResult.Success => success(),
    VotingResult.ContentTooOld
        => warning("Content is too old. It can't be voted"),
    VotingResult.ContentDeleted
        => warning("Content is deleted. It can't be voted"),
    };
}
```

9.3   Don't debug

Debugging is an ancient term; it even predates programming, before Grace Hopper made it popular in the 1940s by finding an actual moth in the relays of a Mark II computer. It was originally used in aeronautics for processes that identified aircraft faults. It is now being replaced by Silicon Valley's more advanced practice of firing the CEO whenever a problem is discovered after the fact.

The modern understanding of debugging mostly implies running the program under a debugger, putting breakpoints, tracing the code step by step, and examining the state of the program. Debuggers are very handy, but they're not always the best tools. It can be very time consuming to identify the root cause of a problem. It may not be even possible to debug a program in all circumstances. You may not even have access to the environment the code is running.

9.3.1   printf() debugging

Inserting console output lines inside your program to find a problem is an ancient practice. We developers have since gotten fancy debuggers with step-by-step debugging features, but they aren't always the most efficient tools for identifying the root cause of a problem. Sometimes, a more primitive approach can work better to identify an issue. `printf()` debugging gets its name from the `printf()` function in the C programming language. Its name stands for *print formatted*. It's quite similar to `Console.WriteLine()`, albeit with a different formatting syntax.

Checking the state of the application continuously is probably the oldest way to debug programs. It even predates computer monitors. Older computers were equipped with lights on their front panels that actually showed the bit states of the registers of the CPU, so programmers could understand why something didn't work. Luckily for me, computer monitors were invented before I was born.

`printf()` debugging is a similar way to show the state of the running program periodically, so the programmer can understand where the issue happens. It's usually frowned on as a newbie technique, but it can be superior to step-by-step debugging for several reasons. For example, the programmer can pick a better granularity for how frequently the state should be reported. With step-by-step debugging, you can only set breakpoints at certain places, but you can't really skip more than a single line. You either need a complicated breakpoint setup, or you just need to press the Step Over key tediously. It can get quite time consuming and boring.

More importantly, `printf()` or `Console.WriteLine()` writes the state to the console terminal that has history. That's significant since you can build a chain of reasoning between different states by looking at your terminal output, which is something you can't do with a step-by-step debugger.

Not all programs have visible console output, web applications, or services. .NET has alternatives for those environments, primarily `Debug.WriteLine()` and `Trace.WriteLine()`. `Debug.WriteLine()` writes the output to the debugger output console, which is shown in the debugger output window on Visual Studio instead of the application's own console output. The greatest benefit of `Debug.WriteLine` is that calls to it get stripped completely from optimized (release) binaries, so they don't affect the performance of the released code.

That, however, is a problem for debugging production code. Even if the debug output statements had been kept in the code, you'd have no practical way to read them. `Trace.WriteLine()` is a better tool in that sense because .NET tracing can have runtime configurable listeners apart from the usual output. You can have trace output written to a text file, an event log, an XML file, and anything you can imagine with the right component installed. You can even reconfigure tracing while the application is running, thanks to .NET's magic.

It's easy to set up tracing, so you can enable it while your code is running. Let's consider an example, a live, running web application where we might need to enable tracing while it's running to identify a problem.

9.3.2 Dump diving

Another alternative to step-by-step debugging is to examine crash dumps. While they're not necessarily created after a crash, crash dumps are files that contain the contents of the snapshot of the memory space of a program. They're also called *core dumps* on UNIX systems. You can manually create crash dumps with a right-click on a process name on

Windows Task Manager and then clicking on Create Dump File, as shown in figure 9.4. That's a non-invasive operation that would only pause the process until the operation is complete, but would keep the process running after.

You can perform the same kind of smooth core dumping on UNIX variants without killing the app, but it's slightly more involved. It requires you to have the `dotnet dump` tool installed:

```
dotnet tool install --global dotnet-dump
```

The tool's great for analyzing crash dumps, so it's a good idea to have it installed even on Windows. The installation command is the same for Windows.

There is a project on GitHub, under the examples for this chapter, called `InfiniteLoop` that consumes CPU continuously. That could be

Figure 9.4 Manually generate a crash dump on a running application.

our web application or our service running on a production server, and it's a good exercise to try to identify a problem on such a process. It's pretty much like honing your lock-picking skills on a dummy lock. You might not think you need lock-picking skills, but wait until you hear about a locksmith's fees. The whole code of the application is shown in listing 9.9. We basically run a multiplication operation in a `loop` continuously without any benefit to world peace. It probably still wastes way less energy than Bitcoin. We're using random values determined in the runtime to prevent the compiler from accidentally optimizing away our loop.

Listing 9.9 `InfiniteLoop` application with unreasonable CPU consumption

```
using System;

namespace InfiniteLoop {
  class Program {
    public static void Main(string[] args) {
      Console.WriteLine("This app runs in an infinite loop");
      Console.WriteLine("It consumes a lot of CPU too!");
      Console.WriteLine("Press Ctrl-C to quit");
      var rnd = new Random();
      infiniteLoopAggressive(rnd.NextDouble());
    }

    private static void infiniteLoopAggressive(double x) {
      while (true) {
        x *= 13;
      }
    }
  }
}
```

Compile the `InfiniteLoop` application and leave it running in a separate window. Let's assume this is our service in production and we need to find out where it's stuck or where it consumes so much CPU. Finding the call stack would help us a lot, and we can do that with crash dumps without crashing anything.

Every process has a process identifier (PID), a numeric value that is unique among other running processes. Find the PID of the process after you run the application. You can either use Task Manager on Windows or just run this command on a PowerShell prompt:

```
Get-Process InfiniteLoop | Select -ExpandProperty Id
```

Or, on a UNIX system, you can just type

```
pgrep InfiniteLoop
```

The PID of the process would be shown. You can create a dump file using that PID by writing out the `dotnet dump` command:

```
dotnet dump collect -p PID
```

If your PID is, say, 26190, type

```
dotnet dump collect -p 26190
```

The command would show where the crash dump is saved:

```
Writing full to C:\Users\ssg\Downloads\dump_20210613_223334.dmp
Complete
```

You can later analyze the command of `dotnet-dump` on that generated dump file:

```
dotnet dump analyze .\dump_20210613_223334.dmp
Loading core dump: .\dump_20210613_223334.dmp ...
Ready to process analysis commands. Type 'help' to list available commands or
    'help [command]' to get detailed help on a command.
Type 'quit' or 'exit' to exit the session.
> _
```

You'd use forward slashes for UNIX pathnames instead of the backslashes of Windows. This distinction has an interesting story that comes down to Microsoft adding directories to MS-DOS in its v2.0 instead of v1.0.

The `analyze` prompt accepts many commands that can be seen with help, but you only need to know a few of them to identify what the process is doing. One is the `threads` command that shows all the threads running under that process:

```
> threads
*0 0x2118 (8472)
 1 0x7348 (29512)
 2 0x5FF4 (24564)
 3 0x40F4 (16628)
 4 0x5DC4 (24004)
```

The current thread is marked with an asterisk, and you can change the current thread with the `setthread` command, like this:

```
> setthread 1
> threads
 0 0x2118 (8472)
*1 0x7348 (29512)
 2 0x5FF4 (24564)
 3 0x40F4 (16628)
 4 0x5DC4 (24004)
```

As you can see, the active thread changed. But the `dotnet dump` command can only analyze managed threads, not native threads. If you try to see the call stack of an unmanaged thread, you get an error:

```
> clrstack
OS Thread Id: 0x7348 (1)
Unable to walk the managed stack. The current thread is likely not a
```

```
managed thread. You can run !threads to get a list of managed threads in
the process
Failed to start stack walk: 80070057
```

You need a native debugger like WinDbg, LLDB, or GDB to do that kind of analysis, and they work similarly in principle to analyzing crash dumps. But we're not interested in the unmanaged stack currently, and usually, the thread 0 belongs to our app. You can switch back to thread 0 and run command `clrstack` again:

```
> setthread 0
> clrstack
OS Thread Id: 0x2118 (0)
        Child SP               IP Call Site
000000D850D7E678 00007FFB7E05B2EB
    InfiniteLoop.Program.infiniteLoopAggressive(Double)
    [C:\Users\ssg\src\book\CH09\InfiniteLoop\Program.cs @ 15]
000000D850D7E680 00007FFB7E055F49 InfiniteLoop.Program.Main(System.String[])
    [C:\Users\ssg\src\book\CH09\InfiniteLoop\Program.cs @ 10]
```

Apart from a couple of uncomfortably long memory addresses, the call stack makes complete sense. It shows what that thread has been doing when we got the dump down to the line number (the number after @) that it corresponds to, without even breaking the running process! It gets that information from debugging information files with the extension .pdb on .NET and matches memory addresses with symbols and line numbers. That's why it's important for you to deploy debugging symbols to the production server in case you need to pinpoint errors.

Debugging crash dumps is a deep subject and covers many other scenarios like identifying memory leaks and race conditions. The logic is pretty much universal among all operating systems, programming languages, and debugging tools. You have a memory snapshot in a file where you can examine the file's contents, the call stack, and the data. Consider this a starting point and an alternative to traditional step-by-step debugging.

9.3.3   *Advanced rubber-duck debugging*

As I discussed briefly at the beginning of the book, rubber duck debugging is a way to solve problems by telling them to a rubber duck sitting on your desk. The idea is that when you put your problem into words, you reframe it in a clearer way so you can magically find a solution to it.

I use Stack Overflow drafts for that. Instead of asking a question on Stack Overflow and wasting everybody's time with my perhaps silly question, I just write my question on the website without posting it. Why Stack Overflow, then? Because being aware of the peer pressure on the platform forces you to iterate over one aspect that's crucial when constructing your question: "What have you tried?"

Asking yourself that question has multiple benefits, but the most important one is that it helps you realize that you haven't tried all the possible solutions yet. Solely thinking about that question has helped me think of numerous other possibilities that I haven't considered.

Similarly, Stack Overflow mods ask you to be specific. Too-broad questions are considered off topic. That pushes you to narrow your problem down to a single specific issue, helping you deconstruct your problem in an analytical way. When you practice this on the website, you'll make this a habit, and you'll be able to do it mentally later.

Summary

- Prioritize bugs to avoid wasting your resources on fixing bugs that don't matter.
- Catch exceptions only when you have a planned, intentional action in place for that case. Otherwise, don't catch them.
- Write exception-resilient code that can withstand crashes first instead of trying to avoid crashes as an afterthought.
- Use result codes, or enums, instead of exceptions for cases where errors are common or highly expected.
- Use framework-provided tracing affordances to identify problems faster than clunky step-by-step debugging.
- Use crash dump analysis to identify problems on running code in production if other methods are unavailable.
- Use your drafts folder as a rubber duck debugging tool, and ask yourself what you've tried.

index